TEN
NEW ENGLAND
LEADERS

BY
WILLISTON WALKER

Wipf & Stock
PUBLISHERS
Eugene, Oregon

Wipf and Stock Publishers
199 West 8th Avenue, Suite 3
Eugene, Oregon 97401

Ten New England Leaders
By Walker, Williston
ISBN: 1-59244-488-1
Publication date 1/26/2004
Previously published by Silver, Burdett and Company, 1901

PREFATORY NOTE

THE lectures here presented were delivered on the "Southworth Foundation," in Andover Theological Seminary in 1898 and 1899. In the selection of the subjects of these biographical sketches the lecturer aimed to present as varied and as typical representatives of the religious thought of Congregational New England as the number of hours placed at his disposal would permit. Other names that will readily occur to the reader might fittingly have been added; but it is believed that each of the men whose portrait has here been attempted deserves the title of a leader of New England.

HARTFORD, CONN.,
April 15, 1901.

CONTENTS

	PAGE
I.—William Bradford	3
II.—John Cotton	49
III.—Richard Mather	97
IV.—John Eliot	137
V.—Increase Mather	175
VI.—Jonathan Edwards	217
VII.—Charles Chauncy	267
VIII.—Samuel Hopkins	313
IX.—Leonard Woods	361
X.—Leonard Bacon	409
Index	457

WILLIAM BRADFORD

I.

WILLIAM BRADFORD

IN undertaking the Southworth Lectures on Congregationalism, I am reminded that several themes of great importance have been treated, and in a sense made their permanent possession, by those who have stood at this desk before me. Our learned and beloved Dr. Henry Martyn Dexter, than whom none is more deserving of honored remembrance by all interested in Congregational history, here sketched out those marvellously patient studies on the beginnings of our religious story, afterward gathered into a stately volume under the title of *The Congregationalism of the last Three Hundred Years as Seen in its Literature*,— a volume which, though now eighteen years old, leaves to those who follow him but scanty gleanings of new facts to gather from his well-reaped field. Here, too, our honored Dr. A. Hastings Ross set forth, under the descriptive title of *The Church-Kingdom*, the most elaborate and, in some respects, the most suggestive presentation of our polity made in recent years. As incumbent of this lectureship, also, Dr. Amory H. Bradford has lately outlined the development of the churches of our order in England, and shown the spiritual and institutional kinship of the Congregational body on both sides of the Atlantic.

Barred thus from the selection of certain topics which master hands have wrought upon, the present lecturer has deemed it alike the part of modesty and of wisdom to choose a simpler theme. Instead of trying to unfold before you the development of a great religious movement as a whole, or attempting to outline the proper organization of the Body of Christ, he has thought it best to present to you a brief series of biographical sketches of men prominent in various epochs of Congregational history. In connection with these lives something of the story of Congregationalism as a whole will necessarily be glanced at; but the individual, human element will be kept as prominent as is consistent with a recollection that the prescribed theme of these lectures is " Congregationalism."

In selecting the subjects of our studies one is embarrassed by the number of those who have almost equal claim to a place in our consideration. Congregationalism has never produced a single leader of overshadowing influence, as has Lutheranism, or Methodism, or Moravianism. As befits a polity essentially democratic, it has enjoyed in all periods of its history many guides of strong individuality, forceful character, and high moral worth. And, therefore, as a selection is imperatively demanded by the limitations of a course of lectures, I shall present to you a series of men, all of them prominent in their times, but not the only, or exclusively the ablest, leaders of Congregationalism. I desire rather that they should be, as far as possible, typical not only of the periods in which they lived, but of a wide variety of Congregational life and thought. It is with this purpose in view that I have chosen William Bradford as the subject of this first lecture. Not a minister, not a holder, apparently, at any time of any churchly office, he was nevertheless so identified with the inception, the exile, and the transplanting of the Pilgrim Church that his experiences are an epitome of its history.

It is always difficult to picture to ourselves an era different from our own. We are, most of us, so much the creatures of the age in which we live that any appreciation of the thought, or even of the material surroundings, of a bygone generation is difficult; and even those of antiquarian tastes more often know a number of facts of interest regarding a past epoch than enter into its spirit. The past to us is like some strange country across the sea, from which explorers bring reports of customs and of interests which strike us as quaint or amusing because of their want of conformity to what we see about us; of heated excitement about questions which seem trivial because they do not happen to be the questions which concern us;— a land in which men move as in a haze, unreal, nebulous, not flesh and blood as men and women whom our morning newspaper brings to our acquaintance. It is, therefore, no easy task to transport ourselves in fancy back more than three hundred years to the little Yorkshire farming hamlet of Austerfield, where Bradford was baptized on March 19, 1590, probably very shortly after his birth. What life may have been in such a rural townlet for an orphaned boy, brought up by a grandfather's and then by an uncle's care, only vigorous imagination will enable us to conjecture from the few hints that have come down to us.

Though of a yeoman family, the best-to-do of any in the little community, Bradford's early life must have been outwardly the monotonous and laborious round of an agricultural toiler in that unpicturesque but fertile section of England, in days when farm machinery beyond the rudest implements was yet unthought of. To be sure, the great North Road from London to York ran, an unfenced horse-track, through the village of Bawtry, a mile away; yet Austerfield must have heard little of what went on in the world at large. Doubtless the defeat of the Spanish Armada, nearly two years before Bradford was born, brought rejoicing to Austerfield, but travellers of the yeoman class were few, and news from the great world outside filtered slowly among those who, as Bradford himself says, were " used to plaine countrie life."

Yet in that outer world it was a time of marked

events. The splendid reign of Elizabeth was drawing to its brilliant close. Relieved of fear of overthrow from without by the death of Mary, Queen of Scots, and the discomfiture of the avenging Spanish fleet, the English mind bloomed in a wealth and beauty of literature such as no other epoch of English story has displayed. The year of Bradford's birth witnessed the publication of Spenser's *Faerie Queene;* in 1593, when Bradford was perhaps learning his letters at his grandfather's knee, came that " first heir of [his] invention," the *Venus and Adonis* of Shakespeare. In 1597, the year after the orphaned Austerfield boy was transferred by the death of his grandfather to an uncle's care, Bacon's *Essays* first awoke the admiration of English readers. Of all these things of such vast moment in English letters little Austerfield knew nothing, and of any subsequent knowledge of them the boy who grew to youth while they were happening showed no trace.

But there was a concern which, more than any other, touched all men in England at that day, and that was religion. No feature of the great national drama which had been played before the eyes of two generations of Englishmen before Bradford's birth had so immediate and visible an interest to a young man of Austerfield, or of any other English village, as that which concerned the Church. The wars with Spain, the voyages of a Raleigh or of a Drake, were at best distant and shadowy compared with the changes tha had been witnessed in the hamlet place of worship, the gift of John de Builli to the Benedictines of Blyth more than four hundred years[1] before Bradford was brought to its font for baptism. Perhaps the first evidence of the royal revolt from Rome which Austerfield had seen had been in the youth of Bradford's grandfather, when, in 1536,[2] King Henry VIII., whom an obsequious Parliament had two years before declared to be " the only supreme Head in earth of the Church of England," had suppressed the monastery of Blyth, to which little Austerfield and the neighboring Bawtry looked for the appointment of their curates. The King ultimately transferred the monastic right of appointment at Blyth and consequently the determination of what spiritual oversight Austerfield should enjoy, to the newly founded Trinity College of Cambridge University. This suppression was itself only an incident in the general abolition of monasticism throughout England; but the stir occasioned in the minds of the Austerfield dwellers was doubtless very considerable, for the region had possessed a larger proportion of these monastic establishments than most parts of the realm. Cistercians, Carthusians, Gilbertines, Augustinians, Premonstratensians, and Benedic-

[1] See Raine, *History and Antiquities of the Parish of Blyth, passim.* Westminster, 1860.

[2] Raine, *ibid.*, 72, says 1535, but he is evidently confused between Old and New Style.

tines had all dwelt in the near vicinity.[1] The region had fiercely resented this royal invasion of ancient rights; Lincolnshire and Yorkshiremen, perhaps some from Austerfield itself, had risen in revolt in the interest of the older institutions in 1536, but the iron will of the sovereign had prevailed here as elsewhere.

Almost immediately after the dissolution of the monastery of Blyth, if the royal mandates were enforced, as there is every reason to believe that they were, a copy of the Bible in English was placed in Austerfield church, as in every other church in the kingdom.[2] Still the service continued almost entirely in Latin and substantially unaltered in doctrinal purport. Then, in 1549, Austerfield in all probability witnessed the introduction of the English Prayer Book, only to have a revised form substituted in 1552; to see this swept away in 1553 in favor of the ritual of the closing days of Henry VIII., and substantially restored in 1559. As late as 1569, after Bradford's father had grown to manhood, a great wave of insurrection directed against these changes rolled from the north almost to Austerfield; and so strongly had the old faith entrenched itself, that, even after Bradford's birth, several of the neighboring county families,[3] in-

---

[1] Joseph Hunter, *Collections concerning . . . the Founders of New Plymouth*, pp. 24, 25. London, 1854.

[2] J. A. Froude, *History of England*, iii., p. 80. Books were to be provided before August 1, 1537.

[3] Hunter, *Collections*, pp. 25, 108.

cluding that from which his uncle-guardian leased part of the acres that young Bradford tilled, were still its adherents.

There is no reason to suppose, however, that these changes of institutions and forms of worship were accompanied by any material alteration in the character of the Austerfield ministry, or any very strenuous insistance on vital religion. The curate of Bawtry, a mile away from Austerfield and, like it, a spiritual dependency of Blyth, is described in the visitation of 1548 as " unlerned."[1] What degree of ignorance this may have implied may be surmised perhaps from the contemporary statement of Bishop Hooper of Gloucester, that of the priests of that diocese under the Edwardine Reformation " one hundred and sixty-eight could not say the Ten Commandments."[2] Nor had matters grown much better twenty years later under Elizabeth, when, in 1569, a report from the diocese of Chichester,[3] a region in which the Reformation had made much more progress than in Yorkshire, affirmed that " in many churches they have no sermons, not one in seven years, and some not one in twelve years . . . few churches have their quarter sermons " [*i. e.*, the four yearly discourses, then the legal minimum of ministerial pulpit effort];

[1] Raine, *ibid.*, p. 177.
[2] William Clark, *The Anglican Reformation*, p. 181. 1897.
[3] Froude, *History of England*, ix., p. 512.

Cotton Mather affirms that the inhabitants of Austerfield in Bradford's boyhood were " a most ignorant and licentious people, and like unto their priest."[1] Happily there is reason to believe the description exaggerated. The curate of the little church, Henry Fletcher, certainly had the clerical merit, then by no means universal, of residing in the community of which he was the accredited spiritual leader; but the judgment of the antiquary, the Rev. Joseph Hunter, expressed more than forty years ago, is doubtless correct, that Bradford owed little to Fletcher's ministry;[2] and as to the widely prevalent unspirituality and ignorance of the ministry and people of England at the close of Elizabeth's reign there is abundant evidence.

That this state of affairs existed so generally was due to the peculiar character of the English Reformation. That movement, more than any corresponding development on the Continent, was checked and controlled by political considerations. National independence from foreign control was the one thought to which the English people, as a whole, readily responded; but, for many years after the papal authority had been rejected, nothing like a majority of the inhabitants of England could be counted as favorers of Protestant doctrine. A church essentially unchanged in organization and discipline, and largely Roman in ritual and belief, while English in language and gov-

[1] *Magnalia*, ed. 1853, i., p. 109. [2] *Collections*, pp. 112, 113.

ernment, was the preference not only of Elizabeth, but, certainly, till the defeat of the Armada, of a majority of Englishmen. Yet side by side with this conservative tendency ran the strong current of intense Protestant conviction, led especially by those who had come into contact with the Calvinistic divines of the Continent during the Marian persecutions,— a current sweeping into its control an ever increasing proportion of the people as Elizabeth's reign went on. These two antagonistic elements the great Queen kept from such civil conflict as France contemporaneously witnessed; but at the expense of a compromise policy that preserved the ancient ministry largely undisturbed by inquiry as to belief or fitness, and repressed severely the more strenuous desires of the Protestants. The latter sought the abandonment of such remaining Roman vestments and practices as they deemed superstitious; the maintenance of an educated, spiritually enlightened, earnest ministry, which should preach the intenser doctrines of Calvinistic Protestantism with soul-searching force; and the purification of each parish by the enforcement of rigorous discipline. To their thinking, the maintenance by the Queen of the half-reformed, unstrenuous, lax-disciplined, non-preaching clergy who so largely filled the land, was a deprivation of the people of the means of grace. In the view of the Queen, to have permitted the extremer Protestants, or, as they were usually nicknamed, the

" Puritans," to have their way would have been to throw the county into civil discord, to limit the royal supremacy, and to go counter to her own religious preferences, which were all anti-Protestant save on the question of her own supremacy. And so it came about that the Queen and the bishops whom she appointed everywhere repressed the Puritans, and insisted that they be held in conformity to the ritual prescribed by law; so it came about, also, that, while little Austerfield had a Bible, at least in its church, and enjoyed a ritual in the English tongue from which the more obnoxious features of Romanism had been purged away, its pulpit was silent, its minister ignorant and easy-going, and its discipline lax.

This repression by the constituted authorities induced Puritanism to take increasingly an intenser form. Before Elizabeth's reign had passed far into its second decade, some Puritans had raised the question whether a system of church government wherein the ecclesiastical authorities, particularly the bishops who were the immediate royal agents, had such powers to prevent the execution of what Puritans believed to be essential and Scriptural reforms, could be the right form of church organization. Under the lead of Thomas Cartwright, from 1569 onward, the more advanced Puritans, while clinging to the idea of a national Church of which all baptized inhabitants of England were members, denied the rightfulness of the

Anglican Establishment as tested by the Word of God, and began to agitate for its substantial alteration by governmental authority. To a small radical wing of the advanced Puritans even this seemed too slow a method of approximation to the standard which they thought was set up in the New Testament; and, beginning with Robert Browne in 1580, they taught that the true method of reform was the separation of Christian men and women from an Establishment which seemed to them so little answering to the apostolic congregations, and their organization by mutual covenant into churches designedly on the model of those of the Acts and the Pauline Epistles. If the Bible is the sole source of doctrine, as all Reformation divines held it to be, why is it not of polity also? was their argument; and, judged by the Biblical standard, was not the Establishment, which tolerated so much that was worldly and unspiritual and was ruled in a way so different from the churches of the first century, essentially un-Christian and therefore to be abandoned by those earnestly seeking the Kingdom of God? These were no mere speculative theories, but beliefs for which, within the fifteen years that preceded Bradford's fourth birthday, several hundred men and women from Norwich, Bury St. Edmunds, Gloucester, and London had suffered imprisonment and exile, and which no fewer than six men had sealed with a martyr's death.

But how was it that the youthful Bradford, in the remote country village of Austerfield, came to embrace the most strenuous type of Puritan faith? The explanation is to be found in the presence, in the near vicinity, of several sympathizers with advanced Puritan views. Of these the most influential were a clergyman and a layman, Rev. Richard Clyfton and Postmaster William Brewster. Both had been students at Cambridge University,[1] and had there come, if not before, under the dominant impress of Puritanism, then largely influential in that seat of learning. Both began their active work shortly before the time of Bradford's birth; Clyfton having become rector at Babworth,[2] nine or ten miles south of Austerfield, in July, 1586, at the age of thirty-three; and Brewster having begun to assist his invalid father as postmaster at the old archiepiscopal manor of Scrooby, less than three miles from Austerfield on the way to Babworth, early in 1589,[3] being then some ten years younger than Clyfton.[4] Clyfton's vigorous Puritan preaching and catechising[5] from his vantage as incumbent of the Babworth living, was ably seconded by Brewster's zeal in securing the services of other Puritan ministers for more temporary labors in the region. For this work

---

[1] Edward Arber, *Story of the Pilgrim Fathers*, pp. 51, 189. London, 1897. [2] *Ibid.*, p. 52. [3] *Ibid.*, pp. 71, 83.

[4] John Brown, *The Pilgrim Fathers*, p. 54. 1895. He was born in 1566-7.

[5] Bradford, *Dialogue*, in Young's *Chronicle of the Pilgrims*, p. 453.

Brewster's position as postmaster on the great North Road gave opportunity, and his own purse contributed more largely than that of anyone else to support the preaching that he desired.[1] The result, as described in Bradford's own words,[2] was that

"by the travell & diligence of some godly & zealous preachers, & Gods blessing on their labours, as in other places of ye land, so in ye North parts, many became inlightened by ye word of God, and had their ignorance & sins discovered unto them, and begane by his grace to reforme their lives."

One of those thus spiritually quickened was the youthful Bradford himself. Of a thoughtful turn of mind by reason of illness, he was led by his study of the Bible to desire some more awakening religious instruction than the ministrations, such as they may have been, of Henry Fletcher at Austerfield afforded. And so he began, as a boy of little more than twelve, to make his way, as opportunity offered, down the road and across the fields to Babworth; and, as he grew a little older, was introduced to that company of seekers for a warmer spiritual life who met under Brewster's roof at Scrooby. Such a course must have required no little resolution in the boy, for it had no countenance from his neighbors or his uncles;[3] and was sure to involve serious dangers of ecclesiastical

[1] Bradford, *History of Plimouth Plantation*, p. 490. Boston, 1898.
[2] *Ibid.*, pp. 11, 12.
[3] Mather, *Magnalia*, i., p. 110.

and governmental interference. Yet we may imagine that Bradford's boyish determination was greatly strengthened when, apparently in 1604, John Robinson,[1] fresh from Cambridge and Norwich, came to the region, not improbably as one of the preachers of Puritan earnestness obtained by Brewster, and speedily added his strong, wise, and generous leadership to the little company of seekers for a fuller reformation. To know Robinson was in itself an education. No nobler figure stands forth in the story of early Congregationalism than that of this .moderate, earnest, patient, learned, kindly man, who was for the next sixteen years to be Bradford's friend and guide. Nor shall we be far wrong, I take it, if we attribute to the influence of this one-time fellow of Corpus Christi College, aided perhaps in a less degree by that of Brewster and Clyfton, that love for learning, which in spite of a total lack of all the ordinary early advantages for an education, made Bradford proficient in Latin, Greek, and Hebrew, besides the considerable acquaintance with Dutch and French which his exile brought to him.[2] The coming of a very different, but equally earnest, man, the erratic, energetic, zealous John Smyth,[3] to the

[1] Dexter, *Congregationalism as Seen*, pp. 373-376.

[2] Mather, *Magnalia*, i., p. 113.

[3] The date, 1602, usually assigned for the beginning of Smyth's Gainsborough work has been subjected to recent criticism. Dr. Dexter, *True Story of John Smyth* (1881, p. 2), was inclined to accept it on the strength of Nathaniel Morton's *New Englands Memoriall* (ii.), though

important town of Gainsborough, some eight or nine miles east of Scrooby and Austerfield, probably late in 1605 or early in 1606, undoubtedly added to the general stir and ferment of the region.

It would not appear that Clyfton and Brewster, the spiritual guides of the youthful Bradford, desired or designed at first to separate from the Church of England. They earnestly wished the reform of the Establishment into something more nearly approaching what they deemed the Biblical model, they emphasized preaching, they sought a more strenuous moral discipline; but they were not as yet Separatists. Yet the opposition of the ecclesiastical authorities forced them ultimately to the Separatist position; and soon after the coming of Robinson and Smyth to the region, probably in 1606, two churches [1] were formed, designedly on the New Testament model. One of these churches was organ-

even he regarded it as "rather early." But Professor Arber, *Story of the Pilgrim Fathers* (1897, pp. 133, 134), shows pretty conclusively that Smyth was a "lecturer" in Lincoln as late as March, 1605, and therefore could not have begun his work at Gainsborough till after that time. On the other hand, Arber's identification of him with the John Smith who graduated M.A. at Cambridge in 1593 (*ibid.*, p. 132) rather than with the graduate who received that degree in 1579 (Dexter, etc.) seems less successful. Compare Thompson Cooper in *Dictionary of National Biography* (liii., p. 68). Since the organization of the Scrooby church, which crossed the Atlantic in the *Mayflower*, seems to have been occasioned by, or at least contemporary with (if not indeed originally in union with), the formation of Smyth's Separatist congregation at Gainsborough, the question of the date of the beginning of his ministry there is of importance in determining the age of the Mayflower church.

[1] Arber, *ibid.*, p. 54.

ized at Gainsborough, and though destined to encounter much distraction under the leadership of Smyth in the Netherlands, was to be the means of establishing the first Baptist church in England.[1] The other was gathered at Scrooby, and like that of Gainsborough speedily became an exile under Clyfton and Robinson in Holland, but was privileged to become the mother of the Congregational churches of New England.

The resolution thus to separate from the Church of their fathers was not quickly or rashly formed by these Christians. It was the outcome of their study of the Word of God under the illumination of the persecutions to which their reformatory efforts within the Establishment subjected them from its constituted authorities. Bradford himself points this out very clearly. Describing the steps which brought him and his associates to the organization of the Scrooby church, he says:[2]

"They [the reformers] were both scoffed and scorned by ye prophane multitude, and ye ministers urged with ye yoak of subscription, or els must be silenced; and ye poore people were so vexed with apparators, & pursuants, & ye comissarie courts, as truly their affliction was not smale; which, notwithstanding, they bore sundrie years with much patience, till they were occasioned (by ye continuance & encrease of these troubles, and other means which ye Lord raised up in those days) to see further into things by the light of ye word of God. How not only these base and beggerly ceremonies were unlawfull, but also that ye lordly

[1] A. H. Newman, *History of Anti-Pedobaptism*, p. 391. Philadelphia, 1897.   [2] Bradford, *Hist. Plim. Plant.*, pp. 12, 13.

& tiranous power of ye prelats ought not to be submitted unto; which thus, contrary to the freedome of the gospell, would load & burden mens consciences, and by their compulsive power make a prophane mixture of persons & things in ye worship of God. . . . So . . . they shooke of this yoake of antichristian bondage, and as ye Lords free people, joyned them selves (by a covenant of the Lord) into a church estate, in ye felowship of ye gospell, to walke in all his wayes, made known, or to be made known unto them, according to their best endeavours, whatsoever it should cost them, the Lord assisting them."

I have thus dwelt at considerable length on the origin and purpose of this Congregational church, of which Bradford, then entering on his seventeenth year, was one of the more youthful organizers; and I have done so, if for no other purpose, to show that it was no headstrong and hasty opposition to salutary authority that here found expression. The separation, when it came, was in this instance but the fruit of a deep conviction that the Church of England as then administered not only failed to be what a Scriptural church should be, but that it was irreformable by any efforts which these men and women of Scrooby, and Austerfield, and Babworth, and Gainsborough could make, and hence the only course open to them was to come out of it.

But to come out of it, as Bradford and those older than he speedily found, was to be subject to increased attack. They were now " hunted & persecuted on every side," [1] and, after some hesitation, took the momentous step of leaving home and country for the shelter and toleration of Holland. Yet, as Bradford records, " though they could not stay, yet were ye not suffered to goe," [2] and, attempting to escape in the autumn of 1607,[3] Bradford found himself in Boston prison. His youth, however, procured him speedy release; [4] and, in the spring of 1608, he, with his associates in exile, was in Amsterdam. Though released from persecution, life was full enough of difficulties for these poor farmers in their new city home. The strange sights of the new land were not without their impressiveness to the observant young Englishman; but, as he tells us, " though they saw faire & bewtifull cities, flowing with abundance of all sorts of welth & riches, yet it was not longe before they saw the grime & grisly face of povertie coming upon them like an armed man." [5]

To battle for his daily bread, Bradford learned the silkweaver's trade of some French refugee,[6] perhaps like himself an exile for conscience, though no easy taskmaster to the learner in the unaccustomed art. After the church of which Bradford was a member removed to Leyden in the spring of 1609, Bradford

[1] Bradford, *Hist. Plim. Plant.*, p. 14.
[2] *Ibid.*, p. 16.
[3] On date, see Arber, *Pilgrim Fathers*, p. 86.
[4] Mather, *Magnalia*, i., p. 111.
[5] Bradford, *Hist. Plim. Plant.*, p. 22.
[6] Mather, *ibid.*

pursued the same general means of livelihood, though now he wrought upon the stout cotton cloth then known as fustian. Indeed, it would seem that he invested the small sum that came to him from the sale of his inheritance at Austerfield, in 1611, in an independent business venture, but the enterprise brought him more experience than success, and Cotton Mather believed, probably truly, that he judged his loss " a correction bestowed by God upon him for certain decays of internal piety."[1] It was as by occupation a " fustian-maker " that he was entered in the public records[2] of Amsterdam, when, on November 30, 1613, at the age of twenty-three, he was married to the sixteen-year-old Dorothy May[3] of Wisbech in the home land, whose drowning seven years later, as the *Mayflower* swung at anchor in the harbor of Cape Cod, was to sadden Bradford's coming to the New World. His young wife was a granddaughter of John May, who had died as Bishop of Carlisle in 1598, and her elder sister had been for four years settled at Amsterdam as the wife of Jean de l'Ecluse, an elder in the Separatist church of which Ainsworth was the head. Certainly Bradford must have been prospered, in some small way at least, as he grew more acquainted with his new home and its business methods, for in April, 1619, he

[1] *Magnalia* i., p. 111.
[2] Arber, *Pilgrim Fathers*, p. 163 ; Dexter, *Cong. as Seen*, p. 381.
[3] On Dorothy May, see C. H. Townshend in *New England Historical and Genealogical Register*, l., p. 462.

sold a house in the city where he had then lived just a decade.[1]

Yet the chief value to Bradford of this severe experience in a foreign land was, doubtless, the preparation that it gave him for his greater work on this side of the Atlantic. Those formative years of labor and self-control, and especially of association with Robinson and Brewster in a company whose first desire was the service of God, ripened and broadened and deepened his natural qualities. The boy, who at fourteen or fifteen had been firm enough to resist his companions' jibes and his uncles' opposition, developed into no bitter and obstinate fanatic, but rather grew, under the hard discipline of his Leyden experience, into a wise and kindly manhood, so that when the emigration to New England came, in 1620, probably no other man of thirty could have been found better fitted to take prominent part in an enterprise demanding patience, courage, and forbearance.

Of the details of that emigration there is no occasion to speak here at length. We are, or ought to be, familiar with that heroic exodus story; with its beginnings in the desire of the exiles to live as Englishmen on English soil, to give better advantages spiritually and temporally to their children, and above all, as Bradford[2] himself wrote in noble phrase, in a

[1] Dexter, *True Story of John Smyth*, p. 77.
[2] Bradford, *Hist. Plim. Plant.*, p. 32.

"great hope & inward zeall . . . of laying some good foundation, or at least to make some way therurito, for ye propagating & advancing ye gospell of ye kingdom of Christ in those remote parts of ye world; yea, though they should be but even as stepping stones unto others for ye performing of so great a work."

Very interesting would it be, were not the facts so familiar, to follow the discussions of the Leyden church as timid souls raised difficulties of all magnitudes, from the expense and distance of the expedition and the barbarous cruelty of the natives, to the ability of the emigrants to substitute water for their accustomed beer.[1] Their negotiations with the English government, the unfortunate union with a company of speculative London merchants into which their poverty drove them, the difficulties of their long voyage, their arrival at the beginning of winter on another coast from that on which they had expected to make their landing, their December debarkation, and the rough winter experiences in home building in the wilderness, which cost them before the first springtime more of their number proportionately than have fallen from the ranks of an army in any great modern battle, are all worthy of filial remembrance. But it is with Bradford himself that we have more immediately to do.

There is no reason to suppose that the plan of emigration was especially his conception. Robinson, who

[1] Bradford, *Hist. Plim. Plant.*, pp. 32-35.

remained at Leyden, Ruling Elder William Brewster,[1] Robert Cushman, and John Carver were all more prominent in the negotiations leading to it than he. Yet we find him uniting with Fuller, Allerton, and Winslow in an independent protest against some of the agreements with the London merchant partners in the colonizing enterprise,[2] which shows that, before leaving Leyden, Bradford was one of the more important members of the Separatist community. But, by the time of the Pilgrims' arrival on the bleak New England coast, Bradford had shown himself a man of action, taking a conspicuous share in the search for a place of settlement;[3] so that when death removed the first Governor, John Carver, from the civil headship of the little commonwealth, in April, 1621, the community turned naturally and unanimously to Bradford [4] as his successor. That office, uniting as it did the duties of the executive, legislative, and judicial leadership, was thenceforward Bradford's by thirty-one [5] annual elections, and would have been his uninterruptedly throughout his life had he not insisted successfully at five of the thirty-six elections held in his lifetime on the desirability of rotation in office. He always served without salary.[6]

---

[1] Winslow (*Hypocrisie Unmasked*, pp. 88, 89) attributes its inception to Robinson and Brewster.

[2] Bradford, *Hist. Plim. Plant.*, pp. 61, 62.

[3] *Mourt's Relation*, in Young, *Chronicles of the Pilgrim Fathers*, pp. 126, 149.   [4] Mather, *Magnalia*, i., p. 111.

[5] J. A. Goodwin, *The Pilgrim Republic*, p. 456. 1888.   [6] *Ibid.*, p. 455.

So associated has the title, Governor, become in our minds with the headship of a great commonwealth that its application to Bradford is likely to deceive us with suggestions of a state and pomp of which his office showed no trace. Chosen the leader of the fifty-seven survivors of that first terrible winter, just after the *Mayflower* had left them in the spring of 1621, he saw the colony grow to about three hundred souls by 1630, while at his death in 1657 it may have numbered somewhat more than four thousand inhabitants.[1] Never an imposing station from a worldly point of view, the Plymouth governorship was a post, nevertheless, of great responsibility, for its successful occupancy in these formative years in which Bradford held it involved not merely the solution of the ordinary problems of pioneer settlement life, but the establishment of a democratic community and the maintenance of a democratic church polity under circumstances of constant peril. To tell with any fullness what Bradford did would be to give an outline of the early history of Plymouth. That is, of course, impossible in the space at our command. But we may glance briefly at four or five of the more important services that Bradford rendered to the colony of which he was Governor.

One conspicuous service, then, was the tiding of the colony over the trying period of its beginnings. As

[1] Compare Palfrey, *History of New England*, ii., p. 6; iii., p. 35.

for most of the *Mayflower* passengers, so for Bradford, the months after arrival in New England were a time of grief. His wife died in Provincetown harbor before the landing; and he was himself severely ill of the scurvy which cost half the company their lives within the first year. It was not till his marriage, in the summer of 1623, to Mrs. Alice Southworth, who as Alice Carpenter [1] had become the wife of one of his associates at Leyden the same year that he had married Dorothy May, that Bradford was able to have the comfort of a home. Yet under these discouragements he showed no want of courage or lack of faith in the success of the undertaking.[2] But perplexities of a public nature filled these years. Perhaps the most pressing was the crying need of food. With scarce other provisions from Europe than the scant supplies that were brought in the *Mayflower*, and unprovided with cattle till 1624, the colony for the first two or three years was reduced to the verge of starvation, except just after the autumn harvest. Bradford,[3] with a humor characteristic of him, after recording of the summer ot 1623 that

" all ther victails were spente, and they were only to rest on Gods providence; at night not many times knowing wher to have a bitt of any thing ye next day,"

adds that

[1] For her history, see Goodwin, *Pilgrim Republic*, pp. 247–249.
[2] Witness the confident tone of the, so-called, *Mourt's Relation*.
[3] *Hist. Plim. Plant.*, p. 164.

" as one well observed, [they] had need to pray that God would give them their dayly brade, above all people in ye world."

Of the same year he notes:[1]

" Many were ragged in aparell, & some litle beter then halfe naked. . . . But for food they were all alike, save some y^t had got a few pease of ye ship y^t was last hear. The best dish they could presente their friends with was a lobster, or a peece of fish, without bread or anything els but a cupp of fair spring water."

One readily credits his further statement [2] that

" ye long continuance of this diate, and their labours abroad, had something abated ye freshnes of their former complexion."

Yet this peril of famine was, perhaps, not the worst of the dangers of the early days. The Indians, whose reported barbarities had disquieted the Leyden church when the journey was under discussion, were a source of great anxiety. True, one of the most surprising and helpful events in the Pilgrim beginnings was the arrival in little Plymouth, on April 1, 1621, of Tisquantum, or Squanto. This sole survivor of the former Indian inhabitants of the township had gained acquaintance with the English speech and ways by reason of an enforced residence in England and in Newfoundland from 1614 to 1619, and he now became

[1] *Hist. Plim. Plant.*, p. 175.   [2] *Ibid.*

their instructor in planting the unfamiliar corn and their serviceable guide and interpreter.[1] But Massasoit, the leader of the Pokanokets, Corbitant, chief of the Pocassets, and Canonicus of the Narragansetts, to say nothing of Wituwamat and his more hostile associates of the Massachusetts tribe, had to be managed with great skill and firmness for the first three years of the colony's existence, if the struggling community was to maintain its life. Without detracting at all from the honor due to the high diplomatic and medical ability of Winslow, or the prompt executive force of Standish, no inconsiderable portion of the credit for the satisfactory relations with its Indian neighbors at which the settlement so speedily arrived belonged to the wisdom of Bradford.

But famine and Indian attack were not the only difficulties through which Bradford had to pilot the infant colony. Perils from his own countrymen were probably greater dangers than either. Thomas Weston, treasurer of the London partners in the Plymouth enterprise, and, more than any other man not a Pilgrim, responsible for the sending out of the *Mayflower*, had looked upon the Plymouth settlement simply as a money-making enterprise. The inevitable failure to pay prompt dividends turned him from a grasping and grudging supporter of the Pilgrims into

[1] Compare *Mourt's Relation* in Young, pp. 190, 191; Bradford, *Hist.*, pp. 114–155; Charles Francis Adams, *Three Episodes of Massachusetts History*, pp. 23–44.

an open enemy. In 1622 Weston sent out a trading expedition of his own, which, after testing the hospitality of Plymouth to the utmost, settled in unruly fashion at Wessagusset, on Boston Bay. Resolved not to burden his colony with wives and children, Weston gathered together a company of adventurers of no character, who, in spite of their boasts, were soon in such straits that they were only saved by the intervention of the Pilgrims, after having been the cause of frightful peril to Plymouth from the Indians whom their ill-treatment exasperated. No higher testimony could be had to the efficiency of the Pilgrim colony under Bradford's administration than its ability not only to defend itself but to rescue those who had at first claimed to have such superiority to it.[1]

Nor were this peril from Weston's adventurers, and that from Thomas Morton and his associates in riotous proceedings at Mount Wollaston in 1628,[2] the only dangers from their own countrymen which the colonists encountered. We often think of the population of Plymouth itself as homogeneous, devoted heart and soul to the advancement of the religious purpose which animated the Leyden emigrants. But such was by no means the case. The colony was founded by a joint partnership, that of London merchant speculators, who, moved by hope of profit, furnished most of

---

[1] Bradford, *Hist.*, pp. 137-160; Adams, *Three Episodes*, i., pp. 45-104.   [2] Bradford, *ibid.*, pp. 283-292; Adams, *ibid.*, pp. 162-208.

the money (in all some £7000),[1] and of the real Pilgrims. Both contributed men at the beginning and sent reinforcements during the first few years, but the quality of these respective contributions was very dissimilar, religion being the dominant motive with the Pilgrims proper, trade with their merchant partners. Hence the strange mixture of emigrants that Bradford notices,[2] for instance, in speaking of the arrival of the *Anne* in July, 1623, some of her passengers "being very usefull persons, and became good members of ye body . . . and some were so bad, as they were faine to be at charge to send them home againe ye next year." The consequence was that the dominance of Pilgrim principles, even in the colony itself, was maintained for a time with difficulty. This difficulty was much increased when the London merchants, in their desire to minimize those Separatist features of the colony which they fancied were interfering with its growth as a trading settlement, sent over John Lyford, a Puritan minister of the Church of England, with intent, as the event proved, to modify the religious institutions of Plymouth into something more satisfactory to the majority of Englishmen. Lyford at first appeared attached to the Congregational worship of the community and was consulted in public concerns, but he soon had the support of certain disaffected elements in

---

[1] Arber, *Pilgrim Fathers*, p. 320, from John Smith, *Gen. Hist. of Virginia*, vi., p. 247. [2] *Hist. Plim. Plant.*, p. 171.

the colony, notably of John Oldham and it was not long before he and his friends " set up a publick meeting aparte, on ye Lords day."[1] Here, then, was the introduction of a religious division which would transplant to the struggling colony the controversies of the mother country. It was a difficult situation that Bradford was called to face, complicated as it was by restiveness under civil control; but he met it with skill and courage, while Lyford's own want of character gave Bradford the decided advantage. Bradford's opening of Lyford's letters home to the disaffected merchant partners in London was undoubtedly highhanded, but his facing Oldham and Lyford in open town meeting was crowned with the success which his boldness deserved, and made the Leyden emigrants from this early summer of 1624 wholly masters of the internal affairs of Plymouth.[2]

The frustration by Bradford of this attempt to change the religious and political status of the Pilgrim colony led to the wellnigh complete alienation of the already disgruntled London partners in the enterprise, and became the occasion of yet another service rendered by him to the community of which he was the executive head. That partnership had never been satisfactory. The terms exacted of the Pilgrims were onerous, and the expectations of the merchants were

[1] *Hist. Plim. Plant.*, p. 209.
[2] Compare Goodwin, *Pilgrim Republic*, pp. 259–276.

wildly extravagant. There was never any complete community of goods at Plymouth, but at the beginning of the enterprise, by reason of the joint partnership of all in it—both of emigrants who labored and of merchants who furnished the supplies—the colonists drew food and tools and clothing from a common store, and turned into the same common treasury the results of their labor. In fact, it was an excellent example of the carrying into actual practice among a people, the majority of whom were God-fearing and conscientious in high degree, of the principles advocated by many of the more moderate of modern socialists. But it did not operate well. It caused friction at many points, and broke down, interestingly enough, as a system of efficient production. People worked under it. There were as few drones at Plymouth as in any community ever known. But, as the event proved, the colonists thus associated did not work enough to produce a result from their labors sufficient to meet the needs of the community. The first break came in 1623, at the height of the famine of which mention has already been made. The communitary methods of farming were not producing a sufficiency of food, and therefore Bradford, with the consent of his associates, reluctantly directed that in this one particular the communitary rule should be set aside and that each should plant, till, and possess corn as he saw fit. The result was so marked an increase in production that after that harvest Plymouth was never seriously threatened with extinction by starvation. Bradford[1] gives as the reason, that the plan of individual ownership

"made all hands very industrious, so as much more corne was planted then other waise would have bene by any means ye Govr or any other could use, and saved him a great deall of trouble, and gave farr better contente. The women now wente willingly into ye feild, and tooke their litle-ons with them to set corne, which before would aledg weaknes, and inabilitie; whom to have compelled would have bene thought great tiranie and oppression."

And Bradford[2] expressed the judgment of the communitary system in general, as experienced at Plymouth, that it

"was found to breed much confusion & discontent, and retard much imploymēt that would have been to their benefite and comforte. For ye yong-men that were most able and fitte for labour & service did repine that they should spend their time & streingth to worke for other mens wives and children, with out any recompence. The strong, or man of parts, had no more in devission of victails & cloaths, then he that was weake and not able to doe a quarter ye other could; this was thought injuestice. The aged and graver men to be ranked and equalised in labours, and victails, cloaths, &c., with ye meaner & yonger sorte, thought it some indignite & disrespect unto them. And for mens wives to be commanded to doe servise for other men, as dresing their meate, washing their cloaths, &c., they deemd

[1] *Hist. Plim. Plant.*, p. 162.   [2] *Ibid.*, p. 163.

it a kind of slaverie, neither could many husbands well brooke it."

The stage was small and the experience brief, I grant; but it was experience, and that, too, under favorable conditions; and a page of recorded experience is more truly illuminative than a library shelf of speculation, however picturesque or warm-hearted, as to the possible workings of systems of society of which we have no actual knowledge.

The once seemingly necessary yoking of the Leyden pilgrims with the London merchants, which had been the cause of this remarkable experiment, had proved thoroughly unsatisfactory to all concerned by the time of Lyford's downfall, and that collapse rapidly hastened the termination of the partnership. In 1626, the remaining London merchant partners sold out their interests to the Plymouth colonists for £1800, to be paid in nine annual installments. The colony thus obtained its independence; but, to make it possible, Bradford and seven of his associates bound themselves personally for its payment.[1]

Bradford's services to the religious system which he held dear were considerable. Till 1629 the Pilgrim church stood alone, sole representative of Congregationalism in the New World. But in 1628 the vanguard of the great Puritan immigration which was to possess most of New England reached Salem under

[1] *Hist. Plim. Plant.*, pp. 252–257.

the leadership of John Endicott. He and his associates, like the early New England Puritans generally, looked with disfavor on the Plymouth Separatists. Though the Puritans of the emigration rejected the hierarchy, the service, and the discipline of the Church of England, they had no intention of separating from that body, and they condemned those who did so. But neighborliness brought better knowledge. Dr. Samuel Fuller, the godly deacon and physician of Plymouth, ministered to the sick of Endicott's company, and talked polity with the well; and when Higginson and Skelton and a large body of settlers with them reached Salem in the early summer of 1629, they found Endicott and his associates not quite ready to approve Plymouth Separatism, but well pleased with Plymouth's faith and order. So it came about that when Bradford heard that the Salem people had organized a church of experimental believers in Christ, and had chosen part of its officers according to what Plymouth deemed the Scriptural appointment, and had fixed a day for further election and ordination,[1] he came in one of the little boats, in which the colonists then ventured along the coast, from Plymouth to Salem with a few companions, and, for the first time on this new continent, gave the " right hand of fellowship " to the new gathered congregation.[2] The head

---

[1] See Charles Gott's letter in Bradford, *Hist. Plim. Plant.*, pp. 316, 317.   [2] Morton, *New Englands Memoriall*, p. 99, ed. 1855.

of the older colony thus thought it well worth his while to welcome with Christian sympathy the Puritan newcomers to New England, and not a little of the ease and readiness with which emigrated Puritanism was led to organize its churches substantially on the Plymouth model was due to the welcome and example of Bradford and Fuller.

Time allows us no further glance at Bradford's manifold public activities for the good of the colony of which he was the civil head, nor at his relations to other settlers in New England, illustrated in his presidency, for some two years,[1] of the joint body of Commissioners which, from 1643 onward till after his death, represented the united interests of the four Congregational colonies. But one private and unofficial feature of his services to the colony of his residence cannot be passed by, and that is his writings. Were it not for Bradford's *Relation*, *History, and Letters*, little indeed would it be that we should know of Plymouth's beginnings. He not merely wisely directed his associates while they lived—he found time and inclination to preserve their memories and deeds for perpetual remembrance. His chief work is, of course, his *History*, begun about 1630, and continued till the close of 1646. That *History* has had a more picturesque fate than that of any other American manuscript. Kept for many years in the family of Bradford's son,

[1] 1648 and 1656.

William, and grandson, John, it was for some time in the hands of that sturdy Puritan, Judge Samuel Sewall. Hence, with the consent of its third American owner of the Bradford name, it passed, apparently in 1728, into the New England Library collected by that most gifted as well as most patient of early students of our beginnings, Thomas Prince, pastor of the Old South Church in Boston.[1] Deposited in the tower of the Old South Church, it was well known as late as 1767; but during the commotions incident to the Revolutionary struggle it disappeared, in what precise way seems impossible to discover, to be mourned as hopelessly lost. The happy identification in 1855, by a comparatively minor Massachusetts historian, of certain quotations from manuscript sources in an English book already nine years in its second edition,[2] at length revealed to American investigators the fact,—not very much to the credit of their breadth of reading be it confessed, since the fact had been published in yet another English book seven years before,[3]—that the desired volume was in the library of the Bishop of London at Fulham. Printed in 1856, it became at once, as it had been to Morton, Hubbard, Mather, Prince, and Hutchinson, the prime source on the beginnings of Plymouth colony; and so permanent is the interest it excites that a reproduction in photographic facsimile was issued as recently as

[1] See Preface to the 1856 edition of Bradford, *Hist. Plim. Plant.*, x., xi.   [2] *Ibid.*, iv.

[3] Dexter, Bibliography, in *Cong. as Seen*, under No. 5791.

1896. Of the honors of its home-coming on May 26, 1897, brought by an ambassador of the United States who had in a peculiar measure won the good-will of the English people, and welcomed by the Governor and the senior Senator of Massachusetts in the presence of the Legislature of the commonwealth, it is only needful to remind you. The newspaper descriptions of that scene, though too often misnaming the recovered manuscript the " Log of the *Mayflower*," must be distinct in all our memories.

Besides his *History*, Bradford's busy pen produced other work of value. The graphic account of the inception of the Plymouth settlement, published at London, in 1622, and generally known as *Mourt's Relation*, was largely his work, though with the assistance of his colleague in the leadership of Plymouth affairs, Edward Winslow.[1] In more advanced life, about the year 1648, Bradford put into the form of a brief dialogue his information and his recollections concerning the beginnings of Congregationalism and its leaders in England and Holland. Regarding many of these personages and events we know much more than he, thanks to the labors of Dr. Dexter and other students of Congregational beginnings. It may be, as has been charged, that his judgment of men was occasionally over kindly.[2] But with all its brevity and

[1] Young, *Chronicles of the Pilgrims*, p. 115.
[2] *E. g.*, by Arber, *Pilgrim Fathers, passim*.

limitations, the *Dialogue* gives us many hints and pictures of value. The volume in which Bradford copied his more important letters was discovered about a hundred years ago, in grievously mutilated condition, in a baker's shop in Halifax.[1] Besides these more important writings, and some Hebrew exercises, which have come down in more or less perfect form to our time, Bradford left, and Prince certainly handled, several smaller treatises and records, the character of one of which, as described in Bradford's will, throws an amusing light on a trait markedly characteristic of the early settlers of New England, the disposition to write what they believed to be poetry. Bradford valued his compositions in rhyme, for he said to his executors, " I commend to you a little book with a black cover, wherein there is a word to Plymouth, a word to Boston, and a word to New England, with sundry useful verses."[2] There is nothing in such rhymes as have survived to give the impression of any loss to New England letters by the perishing of these compositions, and in his deficiency in real poetic gift this author was no exception among the divines, magistrates, and founders of colonies, who so generally attempted poetic expression.

Bradford's prose style is simple, direct, dignified. Often there is a kind of eloquence in his straightforwardness and force. Oftener there is a touch of

[1] Goodwin, *Pilgrim Republic*, xiv.   [2] *Ibid.*, p. 457.

almost unconscious pathos;[1] as of one who had endured and suffered much. Sometimes, though rarely, there appears a flash of grim humor, that makes you feel him to have been not without appreciation of the incongruous and the absurd.[2] To a modern historian his paucity of definite dates, and his occasional substitution of indefinite generalities for the concrete facts we desire is a source of regret;[3] but his meaning is rarely doubtful. His writings are marked throughout by courage and cheer. They give us the best picture of the man himself; the modest, kindly, grateful, generous, honorable leader in a great enterprise. Shrewd and sober of judgment, profoundly religious with a religion that masters his actions rather than seeks expression in words, self-forgetful, without cant, and with far less superstition than many of his associates, it is a sweet, strong, noble character that has unconsciously written itself in the pages of his *History*. You feel that the man whose native generosity of spirit prompted him to give a passing Jesuit a dinner of fish of a Friday,[4] who took on himself a great share of the debt which weighed on the whole community, who refused to profit by a charter which, if strictly enforced, would have given large pecuniary gain to him and to his family, and would even have legally allowed him

---

[1] *Hist. Plim. Plant.*, *e. g.*, pp. 13, 131. [2] *Ibid.*, *e. g.*, 134, 135, 164.
[3] *E. g.*, his account of the beginnings of the Pilgrim church.
[4] Gabriel Druillettes in 1650; Palfrey, *History of New England*, ii., p. 308,

to treat his fellow colonists as his tenants,[1] was one who not merely deserved the respect but the love of his associates, and you can appreciate their unflagging desire that he should be their Governor.

Bradford's last years were not without their trials. Plymouth was at best a hard place in which to obtain a livelihood; its scanty soil, its limited pasturage, its remoteness from the rivers which were the main avenues of access to trade with the Indians, and its disadvantages as a commercial port, all led to a scattering of its early settlers, as soon as the prohibition of removal was raised, in 1632; indeed the dispersion had begun even before. Plymouth, though remaining the capital, steadily waned, and Bradford had the sorrow of membership in what must be termed, I think, a decaying church. The strength of the old *Mayflower* congregation was largely drawn elsewhere in the colony. Nor could the ministry of Ralph Smith, who laid down in 1636, as Bradford says, " partly by his own willingness . . . and partly at the desire, and by ye perswasion, of others,"[2] the pastoral office which he had assumed in 1629, or of the much abler John Reynor, whose ministry continued nearly to Bradford's death, compare in spiritual edification with that of Robinson, the pastor of Bradford's young manhood, or even of Brewster, the ruling elder who was essentially the pastor

---

[1] Mather, *Magnalia*, i., p. 113; Goodwin, *Pilgrim Republic*, pp. 337, 338.   [2] *Hist. Plim. Plant.*, p. 418.

of the first nine years of the colony. Bradford made the spiritual good of the little commonwealth his first concern, and his last days were distressed by what he deemed the neglect of the people over whom he was Governor to provide the pecuniary means for securing a more able ministry than the scattered towns of the colony enjoyed. He would have had them raise the salaries of their ministers by a tax, as in the other Congregational colonies, instead of depending on the precarious device of voluntary contributions.[1] But, while he worried about many matters, nothing could disturb the essential serenity of his life, or his trust in God. Though his physical frame gradually weakened throughout his last winter, his confidence in the divine mercy toward him remained unshaken, and found expression in a triumphant declaration to his friends the day before his death, " that the good Spirit of God had given him a pledge of his happiness in another world, and the first fruits of his eternal glory."[2] He died May 9, 1657.

They bore him to his rest up the steep hillside to the wind-swept top, whence the eye glances over the little town below, and on to the distant slope where Bradford's helpful comrade, Standish, made his later home ; or looks out seaward, past the Gurnet, guarding the harbor, over the waves once plowed by the *Mayflower;* till it rests, in clear weather, on Cape Cod,

[1] Goodwin, *Pilgrim Republic*, p. 458.   [2] Mather, *Magnalia*, i., p. 114.

where Bradford first stepped upon American soil. From that place of thronging memories you can compass the scenes of most of his life in that raw, new wilderness. There below you he planted his garden; there at the foot of the steep southward slope runs the town brook as it did when, in the springtime of Bradford's first election, Squanto taught the Pilgrims the value of its then abundant fish;[1] up the steep hill-path toward you, to the structure at once fort and meeting-house that then crowned its top, Bradford used to come to Sunday worship, in his long robe, with Brewster and Standish walking in state on either hand.[2] And here, somewhere beneath your feet, they laid him, without a word of prayer or a verse of comfort from God's Word, for such was to be the unbroken custom of New England till a generation after his burial;[3] yet as Morton[4] says:

"with the greatest solemnities that the jurisdiction to which he belonged was in a capacity to perform, many deep sighs, as well as loud volleys of shot declaring that the people were no less sensible of their own loss, who were surviving, than mindful of the worth and honor of him that was deceased."

Bradford's own pen has recorded, in halting verse, his sense of the divine guidance in his life:[5]

[1] *Hist. Plim. Plant.*, p. 121.
[2] Letter of De Rasières, in Palfrey, i., p. 227.
[3] Till 1685. Even seventy-five years after Bradford's death prayer at funerals was by no means universal.
[4] *New Englands Memoriall*, p. 176, 1855.   [5] *Ibid.*, p. 171.

> From my years young in days of youth,
> God did make known to me his truth,
> And call'd me from my native place
> For to enjoy the means of grace.
> In wilderness he did me guide,
> And in strange lands for me provide.
> In fears and wants, through weal and woe,
> A Pilgrim passed I to and fro."

It was this deep and abiding trust in God and willingness to follow God's truth as he understood it that made Bradford what he was. His talents were undoubtedly great, his administrative ability conspicuous, his patience wellnigh unfailing; he was a man whom other men trusted and revered; — but the power which led him through the vicissitudes of his changeful life was that of an unreserved consecration to the service of God. The covenant of the Congregational church of which he was a member from its organization at Scrooby, through its Amsterdam and Leyden exile, and in its Plymouth transplantation till his death, had pledged him and his associates [1]

" to walke in all his [God's] wayes, made known, or to be made known unto them, according to their best endeavours, whatsoever it should cost them."

He kept this pledge, and, in so doing, he became a noble example of a Christian layman of the early days of Congregationalism, and one whose name Congregationalists delight to honor.

[1] *Hist. Plim. Plant.*, p. 13.

JOHN COTTON

II.

JOHN COTTON

THERE was occasion to point out, in the first lecture of this course, the steps which gradually led such a company as that accustomed to gather in Brewster's home in the Scrooby manor-house to separation from the Church of England. It was seen that Clyfton and Brewster labored long within the Establishment to secure for their district of England an earnest, educated, preaching ministry, and such a degree of instruction and discipline as would give a new spiritual tone to the inhabitants of its parishes. It was noted, furthermore, that John Robinson probably came to the region of Scrooby and Austerfield as a preacher in the employ of those still, nominally at least, within the Church of England, and that it was not till a year or two after Robinson's Lincolnshire ministry began that the little company to which Bradford belonged, and of which Robinson had become a conspicuous leader, withdrew from the Establishment under the stimulus of ecclesiastical interference with their attempt to introduce reforms, being further led to this withdrawal, as they believed, by truer views of the Biblical teaching as to what a church should be. But this extreme measure, which Bradford described as a shaking off of the " yoake of antichristian bondage,"[1] seemed far too radical to all save a few of the people of England. To most of those who sought a further reformation, the Separatists who denied the churchly character of the Establishment were as objectionable as the bishops who prevented reform. Yet as the Puritans read their Bibles, under the light that came from Geneva, they drew much the same conclusions that the Separatists did as to the lack of warrant for existing diocesan episcopacy; the desirability that a congregation should have a voice in the selection of its minister; the bondage, and as they deemed it, the perversion of the ceremonies and worship of the Church; and the wrongfulness of a system which allowed persons of unworthy life practically unrestrained access to sacraments administered too often by an ignorant and unspiritual clergy.

To effect the amendment of these ills the Puritans looked to governmental action. Hence, no sooner had Elizabeth passed away than they besought her successor, King James I., to introduce some of the changes that they desired, only to find in him a determined supporter of a system so consonant with his own lofty ideas of the royal prerogative. But other forces than royal disfavor opposed Puritanism. The

[1] *Hist. Plim. Plant.*, p. 13.

old Anglicanism of the Elizabethan period, conspicuously represented in that vigorous opponent of Puritanism, Archbishop Whitgift, which looked upon existing ecclesiastical institutions as finding their chief warrant in their establishment by governmental authority, gave way to a new school, largely raised up by the fierceness of the Puritan attack. From the time when, in 1589, the later Archbishop Bancroft advanced the theory at Paul's Cross, till it rose in William Laud full-panoplied to contend for the mastery of England, this new party asserted with growing positiveness that episcopacy and apostolic succession were essential to the existence of a true Church. Arminian speculations, too, entered England, as the great anti-Calvinistic controversy in Holland ran its public course from 1604 onward, and commended themselves to many of the High Church party by reason of the very vigor of the Calvinism of the Puritans. So that, through the first three decades of the seventeenth century, while Puritanism was constantly growing in the number of its adherents and in the intensity of its convictions, the High Church party grew, also; and, aided by the royal authority, its hand fell with unabating severity on Puritan offenders of English ecclesiastical laws—a severity that was markedly augmented when Laud became Bishop of London in 1628. Neither Puritans nor Anglicans were seekers for religious liberty in any modern sense of the phrase; but the Puritan laid primary insistence on right belief and strenuous moral practice as judged by his interpretation of the Word of God, while the Anglican emphasized conformity to the ceremonies, ritual, and hierarchy established by law.

If Puritanism found no favor from the King, it gained increasing approval from the English Parliament as the reign of James went on, not only by reason of the general growth of the Puritan party in the land, but because two Puritan principles taught the lesson of constitutional government to an age whose more open minds were ready to receive it. The Puritan contention that a minister should be chosen with the consent of his people, to whom he was thus in a measure responsible, could not but raise in some minds the query whether the sovereign himself was in reality the irresponsible ruler by divine right that the Stuart kings asserted. The Puritan belief that no law of man constrained any obedience should it run counter to the will of God revealed in the Scriptures, similarly encouraged resistance to arbitrary enactments by suggesting that all statutes must approve themselves by some other test than mere imposition by royal authority. But Parliament could offer no efficient resistance to the Stuart absolutism as yet; and, in 1629, Charles I. dispensed with it altogether, thenceforth calling no session of the representatives of the English people till on the eve of the great catastrophe of the civil war eleven years later.

Baffled and harassed by the growing tyranny of the crown and the increasing oppression by the ecclesiastical authorities that the crown supported, many Puritans of the opening years of the reign of Charles I. despaired of the accomplishment of their reforms in the home land. Led, in part, by the success of the Pilgrims at Plymouth, they began to look across the Atlantic. There, in the wilderness, they might plant a new England where the Gospel might have sway in a purity of teaching and administration denied it, they believed, in the land of their birth. And so the great emigration began, in 1628, with the departure of Endicott and his associates for Salem; and the stream flowed stronger in 1629, when Higginson and Skelton and their fellow-colonists followed him under the protection of a Company now provided with an ample royal charter and enlisting widely the sympathies of English Puritanism; till, in 1630, the tide ran full, carrying Winthrop, Johnson, Saltonstall, Dudley, Wilson, Phillips, Ludlow, Warham, and Maverick, with about a thousand beside, across the sea, and leading to the immediate settlement of Dorchester, Charlestown, Boston, and Watertown. Thenceforward the emigration was at its flood till the great political changes, foreshadowed by the summons of Parliament once more in 1640, brought it to a sudden end. By that time more than twenty thousand people had transferred their homes to New England, while Connecticut, New

Haven, and Rhode Island colonies had been added to Massachusetts and its predecessor, Plymouth.

With this immigration had come the establishment of churches on this new soil, substantially like to that of Plymouth in organization and forms of worship, the first being that of Salem in 1629, and their number reaching at least thirty-four by 1640. " God sifted a whole nation that He might send choice Grain over into this Wilderness," said William Stoughton in 1668 in an oft-quoted phrase describing the character of these founders. They were, indeed, a picked body of men. No meaner motive and no less noble cause could have gathered together such a representation of what was best in the well-to-do, sober, intelligent, God-fearing middle-class population of England, or of their leaders in spiritual things. But I think we shall best comprehend the character of the movement, at the general story of which we have just glanced, if we look at it through the biography of one of its most conspicuous ministerial leaders, John Cotton.

Bradford was a country lad and of farmer parents; Cotton was town-born and the son of a member of one of the learned professions. Bradford's opportunities for education were fortuitous; Cotton enjoyed as good training as contemporary England afforded. Born in the enterprising market-town of Derby, on December 4, 1585,[1] the son of Roland Cotton, a lawyer of stren-

[1] *Magnalia*, i., p. 253. 1853-5. For his early life, see also the

uous religious life, and of a devotedly Christian mother, his gifts were rapidly developed under the tuition of a schoolmaster whom his grandson, Cotton Mather, designated as " one Mr. Johnson," [1] so that, " in the beginning of [his] 13th year," [2] he entered the University of Cambridge as a member of Trinity College [3] — that great educational foundation whose remote spiritual dependence we have already seen Austerfield to be. What the youthful collegian there found of teaching or of customs has been described by no one more graphically than by the late Dr. Dexter, picturing from this desk the similar experiences of John Robinson.[4] One of the very youngest of perhaps twenty-five hundred students, Cotton doubtless shared with three associates a chamber in the college of which he was a member, and was compelled to occupy the trundle-bed by means of which sleeping accommodations were provided for two of the occupants of the crowded room.[5] At six, he breakfasted on bread and beer; at eleven, he dined on a bit of beef, mutton, or fish; and at seven he supped on an omelette. His course of study was spent chiefly on logic and philosophy, and in the acquisition of Latin, Greek, and He-

more valuable sketch of Cotton by his friend, Rev. Samuel Whiting, from which Mather freely drew, printed in Young, *Chronicles of Massachusetts*, pp. 419–430.

[1] *Magnalia*, i., p. 254.
[2] Cotton, *Way of the Congregational Churches Cleared*, p. 33. 1648.
[3] Whiting, in Young, p. 420.
[4] Dexter, *Cong. as Seen*, pp. 365–370. [5] *Ibid.*, p. 367.

brew—in which languages there is abundant evidence that the young student became remarkably proficient.[1] What we should call the Freshman year was apportioned to Rhetoric in the broad, Roman sense of the word; Sophomore and Junior years were called years of Logic, and Senior year that of Philosophy. Following, thus, the round of student life, Cotton graduated Bachelor of Arts in 1602–3, and then went on till he received his Master of Arts degree at Trinity in 1606[2]—just as the Scrooby church of which Bradford was a member was being organized. This second degree implied not merely further study along the lines already four years pursued, but some acquaintance with Astronomy, Perspective, and Divinity as well.

Comfortably supplied with money from the earnings of his father's successful practice, Cotton vigorously followed his native scholarly bent. His own college being unable to choose him to a fellowship by reason of a temporary embarrassment of its funds, he obtained that coveted position at Emmanuel College, by the successful passage of an examination in which the crucial test was as to his proficiency in Hebrew.[3] The institution with which he now became connected had been founded by that zealous Puritan courtier of Queen Elizabeth, Sir Walter Mildmay, shortly before Cotton's

[1] Whiting, in Young, pp. 421, 422.
[2] Records of Trinity College, for the M.A. cited in Ellis, *History of the First Church in Boston*, p. 27. 1881.
[3] Whiting, *ibid.*

birth, and was at this time the most Puritanly inclined of the colleges of the then prevailingly Puritan University of Cambridge. Thomas Hooker, Samuel Stone, Thomas Shepard, and John Harvard, to mention no other names honored in the history of early New England, were also of its sons. But it is curiously illustrative of the mutability of institutions in this changing world that Archbishop Sancroft and the non-juror William Law,[1] to whom Wesley was greatly indebted, looked to Emmanuel as their *alma mater*, and were as representative of its later position, at least in their High Churchism, as Cotton was of its earlier Puritanism. The head of Emmanuel, during Cotton's residence, was Laurence Chaderton, who, as one of the leaders of the Puritan party in the country at large, had appeared before King James at Hampton Court in 1604, while Cotton was studying for his second degree, and vainly urged the sovereign to grant the reforms which the Puritans desired. And under Chaderton's leadership, spite of the statutes of uniformity, public worship at Emmanuel had taken on an almost Genevan simplicity.[2]

Into this atmosphere, strongly charged with Puritan thought, the youthful Cotton came; and here at Emmanuel he experienced a real spiritual awakening. Its

[1] Hort, *The Christian Ecclesia*, p. 296. 1897.

[2] See a report to Laud, of date September 23, 1633, in Cooper, *Annals of Cambridge*, iii., p. 283. The state of affairs was doubtless much the same twenty-five years earlier.

first public manifestation may be described in the words of Cotton's parishioner in old Boston, and ministerial neighbor in New England, Samuel Whiting, first pastor of Lynn, Mass., who entered Emmanuel just as Cotton left it:[1]

"The first time that he became famous throughout the whole University, was from a funeral oration which he made in Latin [in 1608] for Dr. Some, who was Master of Peter House; which was so elegantly and oratoriously performed, that he was much admired for it by the greatest wits in the University. After that, being called to preach at the University Church, called St. Mary's, he was yet more famous for that sermon, and very much applauded by all the gallant scholars for it. After that, being called to preach there again, God helped him not to flaunt, as before, but to make a plain, honest sermon, which was blessed of God to famous Dr. Preston's soul's eternal good."

To have been the human means of the religious awakening of this "most celebrated of the Puritans,"[2] the future head of Emmanuel itself, was in itself no small contribution to the Puritan cause. Cotton's own spiritual quickening, which thus found public expression, is said to have been due to a similar discourse by the eminent Puritan fellow of St. John's College, Richard Sibbes.[3] All Cotton's work was faithfully

[1] Young, *Chron. of Mass.*, pp. 421, 422.

[2] Echard, quoted by Young, *ibid.*, p. 506.

[3] Mather, *Magnalia*, i., p. 255. Mather rewrote Whiting's simple sketch with characteristic verbosity and pedantry, but with occasional additions of fact.

JOHN COTTON

done. At Emmanuel he became, during the six years of his residence, as Whiting records, " head-lecturer, and dean, and catechist," and " a diligent tutor to many pupils." [1]

Such a man naturally attracted attention; and, on June 24, 1612, when about half-way through his twenty-seventh year, he was chosen vicar of the magnificent parish church of St. Botolphs, in the busy Lincolnshire seaport of Boston.[2] Unlike most English livings, the patronage of Boston was not in the hands of an individual, but of the city government. Cotton Mather states, what was not improbably the fact, though it is otherwise unattested, that the City Council was a tie on Cotton's election, and that the Mayor, who was his opponent, twice gave, by accident, the casting vote in his favor.[3] The young vicar-elect seems to have been acceptable to the Puritanly inclined people of Boston in general, but Whiting strongly intimates that Bishop Barlow of Lincoln was only brought to acquiesce in the appointment by the employment of something very like bribery with one of his chief agents by some of Cotton's Boston supporters—a transaction in which there is no evidence that Cotton himself had any part.[4]

Here, at Boston, Cotton settled happily, and here, next year, he brought his young wife, Elizabeth

[1] Whiting, in Young, p. 421.
[2] Thompson, *History and Antiquities of Boston*, pp. 17, 412.
[3] *Magnalia*, i., p. 257.   [4] Young, pp. 422, 423.

Horrocks, who died childless, and greatly lamented by the parish for her Christian helpfulness, after eighteen years of wedded life;[1] and here, in 1632, he married his parishioner, Sarah Hankridge, the widow of William Story, who accompanied him to America, and, surviving him in the new home across the Atlantic, became, in 1656, the wife of Rev. Richard Mather, of the New England Dorchester.[2]

There can be no question that Cotton's ministry of nearly twenty-one years greatly endeared him to the people of the English Boston. The cold pages of the records of the Corporation bear repeated testimony to this esteem. Thus, on May 28, 1613, that body paid him £20, " as a gratuity," he " being . . . a man of very great desertes." In 1616 a similar gift of £10 was accompanied by an expression of gratitude for " his pains in preaching very great "; and in 1619, £10 more were voted him " in consideration of his pains in preaching and catechising." [3]

Samuel Whiting, who knew him well at this period, gives an extended account of his laborious activities.[4]

---

[1] The date of the wedding was July 3, 1613, and the place, Balsham, county of Cambridge. She "was living as late as Oct. 2, 1630." Cotton Mather says the marriage was at the advice of "his dear friend, holy Mr. Bayns." See *Magnalia*, i., pp. 258, 262 ; Young, *Chron. of Mass.*, p. 433 ; Ellis, *Hist. First Church in Boston*, p. 29.

[2] Ellis, *ibid*. The wedding was April 25, 1632. She survived her third husband, dying May 27, 1676.

[3] See Thompson, *History and Antiquities of Boston, passim*.

[4] Many of the details of this paragraph are from Whiting, in Young, pp. 424–426.

Sunday mornings, as was the Puritan custom, his preaching was prevailingly experiential and pastoral; and during his ministry in England " he preached over the first six chapters of the Gospel by John, the whole Book of Ecclesiastes, the Prophecy of Zephaniah, and many other Scriptures"; Sunday afternoons, during those twenty years, he " went over thrice the whole body of divinity in a catechistical way," and at his Thursday lectures " he preached through the whole 1st and 2d Epistles of John, the whole book of Solomon's Song, [and] the Parables of our Saviour." Beside these more formal services, he preached Wednesday and Friday mornings, and Saturday afternoons; " and read to sundry young scholars that were in his house, and some that came out of Germany, and had his house full of auditors." Many of these themes were repeated in Cotton's new home across the ocean, and several of these expositions, notably of Canticles and Ecclesiastes, were ultimately printed [1] and were greatly valued by the Puritans on both sides of the Atlantic. In this manifold effort, Cotton had the assistance, during the latter part of his Lincolnshire ministry, of Anthony Tuckney, who was to be his successor at the English Boston, and even more famous for his labors on the two catechisms put forth by the Westminster Assembly. Nor was this all of Cotton's service to the region. As Whiting notes, " he an-

[1] *Canticles*, first in 1642; *Ecclesiastes*, 1654.

swered many letters that were sent far and near; wherein were handled many difficult cases of conscience, and many doubts by him cleared to the greatest satisfaction."

One monument of this form of conscientious, time-consuming effort remains, and may be cited as an illustration, doubtless, of many others. The most considerable controversy of Cotton's opening ministry was a defense of the characteristic doctrines of Calvinism against the then novel Arminian speculations introduced into his parish by a prominent physician of his congregation, Dr. Peter Baron. Victor in this discussion, and deemed especially successful in clearing " the Doctrine of Reprobation against . . . exceptions,"[1] he was appealed to, about 1618, by a neighboring minister to settle some doubts in regard to this much debated point of divinity. Cotton replied at once, and his answer was still in circulation in manuscript thirty years later, and so influential that Dr. William Twisse, the famous supralapsarian moderator of the Westminster Assembly, felt constrained, as late as 1646, to print a criticism of its, to his thinking, deficient Calvinism.[2]

---

[1] The story is told at length by Cotton, *Way of the Cong. Churches Cleared*, pp. 32-35, London, 1648; and by Twisse in the Preface to his *Treatise of Mr. Cotton's clearing certaine Doubts concerning Predestination*. London, 1646.

[2] Twisse's argument, not his Preface, was apparently written as early as 1630.

Such a life of activity as this shows what a gulf there was between the Puritan thought of the ministry, and that easy-going, spiritually unstrenuous conception, satisfied with a perfunctory repetition of the service, and fulfilling at most the minimum requisition of the law as to preaching, which prevailed very largely outside of Puritan ranks. It shows, also, why it was that those who had once felt the power of such a ministry often preferred exile to its discontinuance. One readily credits the statement of his friend Samuel Whiting, that " he was exceedingly beloved of the best, and admired and reverenced of the worst of his hearers." [1] Not the least evidence of this affection is the desire of the people of this parish, repeatedly expressed to the then long-absent former pastor in New England, that he should return and take up again the work which the tyranny of Laud compelled him to lay down; but for which the downfall of episcopacy, in 1642, seemed again to open the door. Absent, he was never forgotten, and some remembrance of his past services, probably of a pecuniary character, was sent to him by his former congregation annually as long as he lived.[2]

In glancing at Cotton's English ministry, we notice as its most dramatic feature his rejection of conformity to those usages of English ceremonial which the Puri-

[1] Young, p. 426.
[2] See Cotton's grateful Preface to his *Holinesse of Church-Members*. London, 1650.

tans opposed. He was always a Puritan in inclination; but at his settlement he followed the rubrics of the Prayer Book without serious scruple. A change came in his feeling about 1615;[1] brought about, as he records, through two considerations:[2]

" 1. The significancy and efficacy put upon them [the ceremonies] in the Preface to the Book of Common Prayer, [and] the second was the limitation of Church-power . . . to the observation of the Commandements of Christ, which made it appear to me utterly unlawfull, for any Church-power to enjoyn the observation of indifferent Ceremonies which Christ had not commanded."

Under the stress of this conviction, that forms of worship must have express warrant from the Word of God, he modified the services of the church of his charge from the ritual prescribed by law. Just how far this modification went it is difficult to say. Cotton, writing thirty-two years later, in 1647, declared that he " forbore all the Ceremonies alike at once ";[3] but a letter to his bishop in January, 1624, shows that though he had abandoned the surplice, the sign of the cross in baptism, and kneeling at communion, he still retained the ring in marriage and the usage of standing during the repetition of the Creed.[4] The liturgy of

[1] Whiting, in Young, p. 423.
[2] *Way of the Cong. Churches Cleared*, pp. 18, 19.
[3] *Ibid.*, p. 18.
[4] See the letter of January 31, 1624, to Bishop Williams in *N. E. Historical and Genealogical Register*, xxviii., pp. 137-139.

the Prayer Book was still employed in public worship as late as 1624, and possibly was not abandoned by Cotton so long as he remained in England.[1] The discrepancy in these two statements is not great,—in any case the abandonment involved the principal ceremonies attacked by the Puritans;—and from this position of rejection Cotton was to be moved neither by threats nor by offers of preferment.[2] His congregation loyally supported him, and, thus encouraged, he went further, after a time, in the direction of Congregationalism. As he himself records:[3]

"There were some scores of godly persons in *Boston* in *Lincoln-shire* . . . who can witnesse, that we entered into a Covenant with the Lord, and one with another to follow after the Lord in the purity of his Worship."

That is to say, that within the general congregation a special circle of seekers for a truer spiritual life was formed which, had it further developed, might have become a church on the New England plan. Indeed, Cotton states that he and his associates had so far advanced toward the doctrine of the independence of the local congregation that they very largely disregarded the episcopal courts.[4]

[1] *N. E. Historical and Genealogical Register*, xxviii., pp. 137–139. Cotton Mather (*Magnalia*, i., p. 261) asserts that it was set aside. Cotton, in his letter to the bishop, does not say that *he* used it, yet the implication would seem to be that he did. At all events, it was in regular use in his church either by himself or by his assistant.

[2] *Way of the Cong. Churches Cleared*, p. 19.
[3] *Ibid.*, p. 20. [4] *Ibid.*

5

Naturally, these things from time to time attracted the attention of the ecclesiastical authorities; but, thanks to the hearty support of his congregation, the friendship of the earls of Lincoln and Dorset, and the good-will of John Williams, later Archbishop of York, who, from 1621 onward as long as Cotton remained at old Boston, was Bishop of the Lincoln diocese to which Boston ecclesiastically belonged, Cotton was for many years unhindered to a degree very unusual among the Puritan ministry.

But, though more secure of his own position for a time than most of his party, by reason of the degree of influence that he could command, Cotton seems to have sympathized with the Puritan movement for the colonization of New England from its beginning, and to have looked upon it as one in which he might have a personal share. It must have been through his influence that the English Boston was conspicuously represented in the negotiations of 1629, which resulted in the great emigration of that year and of 1630.[1] Nor can it have been without his countenance that his Lincolnshire friends and sympathizers, Thomas Dudley, and William Coddington, came to the new land with Winthrop and his company in the year last named. Cotton himself preached a sermon to the departing emigrants at Southampton, whither he had accompanied them to show his good-will toward their

[1] *Records of . . . Massachusetts*, i., p. 28.

undertaking.¹ This discourse was the first of his writings to appear in print.

But Cotton's own security could not much longer continue unassailed now that Laud was daily increasing in power. In 1632 process was begun against him in the High Commission Court — to appear before which tribunal meant for him, as his earliest biographer expressed it, "scorns and prison."² Like Thomas Hooker under similar circumstances, and with the approval of the chief members of his congregation,³ he sought safety and concealment in flight. In disguise he reached London and was there concealed by John Davenport, whose growing non-conformity was greatly strengthened by Cotton's arguments. Thence, on October 3, 1632, he wrote⁴ to his "dear wife, and comfortable yoke-fellow":

"If our heavenly Father be pleased to make our yoke more heavy than we did so soon expect, remember (I pray thee) what we have heard, that our heavenly husband, the Lord Jesus, when he first called us to fellowship with himself, called us unto this condition, to deny ourselves and take up our cross daily to follow him. . . . Where I am for the present, I am fitly and welcomely accommodated, I thank God; so, as I see, here I might rest, (desired enough,) till my friends at home shall direct further."

¹ Young, *Chron. of Mass.*, p. 126. The sermon was printed as *God's Promise to His Plantation*. London, 1630.
² Young, p. 428.
³ *Ibid.*, p. 440; Cotton, *Holinesse of Church-Members*, Preface.
⁴ Letter in Young, p. 432.

Such a life of concealment could not long be maintained; and consequently, moved partly by the entreaties of his friends who had gone to the New World, Cotton resigned his vicarate, on May 7, 1633, in a noble letter to the Bishop of Lincoln,[1] and prepared to go to New England. The watch set upon the ports to catch him made his escape difficult,[2] but he and his wife slipped secretly onto the *Griffin* as she lay anchored at the Downs early in the following July, and got safely away. In the same ship, beside Thomas Hooker, Samuel Stone, and John Haynes, all destined to be instrumental in founding Connecticut, were Thomas and John Leverett, Atherton Hough, Edmund Quincy, William Pierce, and probably others of his English parishioners; and the vessel thus freighted with three prominent Puritan ministers, and their faithful adherents, had a Puritan feast of preaching all the voyage through, each minister ordinarily discoursing daily to the ship's company—" Mr. Cotton in the morning, Mr. Hooker in the afternoon, Mr. Stone after supper."[3] Yet perhaps the most significant incident of the voyage was one which showed Cotton's own advance toward the full theory of early Congregationalism. His first child, a son named Seaborn, in remembrance of the momentous voyage, was

[1] In Young, pp. 434–437.
[2] Winthrop, *Journal*, i., p. 130, 1853.
[3] Mather, *Magnalia*, i., p. 265.

born on shipboard, but Cotton refused to baptize him then, as he afterwards explained to the church in the New England Boston, "not for want of fresh water, for he held, sea water would have served; [but] 1, because they had no settled congregation there; [and] 2, because a minister hath no power to give the seals but in his own congregation."[1] Viewed as a departure from current English practices this was radical enough.

They landed at Boston on September 4th, and, four days later, Cotton and his wife were admitted on confession of faith to the Boston church.[2] But the new arrival was a man of such fame and abilities that, as Winthrop records: " he was desired to divers places," and to determine where his lot should be cast " the governor and council met at Boston, and called the ministers and elders of all the churches," less than two weeks after his landing. The decision was for Boston, already provided with one minister in the person of John Wilson, and, accordingly, on October 10th, after his parishioner in old England, Thomas Leverett, had been ordained a ruling elder of the American Boston church, Cotton himself was elected teacher of that congregation; and, to quote from Winthrop, who was an eye-witness,[3]

"Then the pastor [Wilson] and the two elders laid their

[1] Winthrop, *Journal*, i., p. 131.
[2] *Ibid.*, i., pp. 128, 131, 132.   [3] *Ibid.*, i., p. 136.

hands upon his head, and the pastor prayed, and then, taking off their hands, laid them on again, and, speaking to him by his name, they did thereby design him to the said office, in the name of the Holy Ghost, and did give him the charge of the congregation, and did thereby (as by a sign from God) indue him with the gifts fit for his office, and lastly did bless him."

He had not renounced the separate congregations that made up the Church of England as false churches, — that he never did, — but he had renounced the government and ceremonies of that Church; and in accepting office in his new congregation was ordained to its particular charge as, in his judgment, the only rightful ordination that a minister could have. And so he entered on his New England ministry.

Here his ministry had much the same quality as in the home land. The same indefatigable labor in preaching and in the exposition of Scripture, the same affectionate reverence from his congregation, the same capacity to mold strong men to his way of thinking, that had marked his career in old Boston, were his in added degree. We can almost picture him to our imagination as he stood on Sundays and Thursdays in the pulpit of the rude New England meeting-house, soon after his arrival, short of stature [1] and rather inclined to stoutness, ruddy faced, his long hair already showing traces of that snowy whiteness that it ultimately attained; his sermon simple, plain, direct,

[1] These details are from the *Magnalia*, i., pp. 275, 280.

levelled in language to the capacities of the humblest
of his hearers; his delivery dignified, never florid, or
oratorical, always forceful, and emphasized by occasional gestures of his right hand. Not so remarkable
in the pulpit, perhaps, as Thomas Hooker or Thomas
Shepard, men always heard him gladly. It is difficult to
give an illustration of his pulpit style within our scanty
limits; but at the risk of injustice, which the presentation of a fragment always involves, I select the following brief passage from his volume of sermons entitled
God's Way, not as peculiar but as typical of his style.
He is speaking of the spirit of prayer:[1]

"These ever go together, where there is a spirit of Grace,
there is a spirit of Prayer. On the contrary, if you cannot
pray, if you neither know what to pray, nor how to pray, if
you goe to Prayer unwillingly, not any work so wearisome,
or straining to you as Prayer is; if for any businesse that
comes to you, you can be content to avoid Prayer; if any
idle company come to your house, all must be set aside to
mind them; not but that a man's businesse may sometimes be such as may hinder him for a time: but if a man
be glad of any such occasion, and he comes to Prayer as a
Beare to a stake, then be not deceived, you may think you
are gracious, but the truth is, unlesse you find some measure
of ability, and liberty, and necessity to pray, you yet want
a spirit of Grace. You would scarce think a child were
living, if it did not cry as soone as it is borne; if still-borne,
you take it for dead-borne. If thou beest a still-borne
Christian, thou art dead-borne; if thou hast no wants to

[1] London, 1641. pp. 9, 10.

tell God of, if yet unlisty to pray, and would be glad of any occasion to shut out Prayer, be not deceived, where there wants Prayer there wants Grace; no Prayer, no Grace; little Prayer, little Grace; frequencie of Prayer, argues power of Grace."

It was this power to make great themes readily comprehensible with familiar illustration in simple language, that made his effectiveness as a preacher;—and it is a power as demonstrative of his learning and talents as is his knowledge of Hebrew, Greek, and Latin in which he had probably no contemporary equal in the New World.[1]

At home Cotton's habits were severely studious. His grandson, Cotton Mather, says that he was accustomed to call twelve hours " a scholar's day."[2] His reading in the fathers and the schoolmen was wide, but Calvin was his delight, and, as he said in old age, he loved " to sweeten [his] mouth with a piece of Calvin before [he went] to sleep." With his household he worshipped morning and evening, but " was very short in all, accounting . . . that it was a thing inconvenient many ways to be tedious in family duties." Yet he found time for an abundant, though simple hospitality; and there must have been a kind of grim humor in his make-up, of which the anecdote recorded by Flavel and by Mather is an illustration.

[1] *Magnalia*, i., p. 273.
[2] For the facts in this paragraph, see *ibid.*, i., pp 274-277.

One of a party of half-drunken roisterers, so the story goes, declared to his companions, as he saw the aged Boston minister coming, " ' I 'll go and put a trick on old Cotton.' Down he goes, and . . . whispers these words into his ear: ' Cotton,' said he, ' thou art an old fool.' Mr. Cotton replied, ' I confess I am so: the Lord make both me and thee wiser than we are.' "

Cotton Mather affirms of his grandfather that he " had a great aversion from engaging in any civil " affairs.[1] The statement is true only in the narrowest sense of unwillingness to hold office or undertake quasi-judicial duties. No minister in New England history was ever more broadly influential or more consulted in political or legislative concerns. His pulpit, especially at the Thursday lecture, was the place of frequent declaration of his opinion on current discussion, as, for example, in 1639, when he made a legal process against a Boston merchant who had been accused of charging unduly high prices the occasion for a discussion of the principles of trade;[2] or, in 1641, reproved those members of the legislature who proposed to drop from office "two of their ancientest magistrates because they were grown poor ";[3] or when, even more conspicuously, in 1634, preaching at the request of the General Court, he successfully defended the veto power of the magistrates—the later upper house of the legislature—against the opposition of the representatives of

[1] *Magnalia*, p. 277.   [2] Winthrop, i., p. 381.   [3] *Ibid*, ii., p. 67.

the Massachusetts towns.[1] In these matters Cotton was not in advance of his age. As there will be later occasion to notice, he held it to be the duty of a ruler to suppress error in matters of belief. He heartily approved the limitation of the suffrage to church-members,[2] introduced, indeed, in 1631, two years before his coming, and to escape from which was probably a strong inducing cause of the settlement of Connecticut by Cotton's fellow voyagers in the *Griffin*, and his early associates in Massachusetts, Hooker, Stone, and Haynes. He entertained much higher views than Hooker, for instance, as to the authority of rulers. Though he asserted it to be " the people's duty and right to maintain their true liberties,"[3] he affirmed in a famous phrase:[4]

"Democracy, I do not conceyve that ever God did ordeyne as a fitt government eyther for church or commonwealth. . . . As for monarchy and aristocracy, they are both of them clearely approoved, and directed in Scripture yet so as [God] referreth the soveraigntie to himselfe, and setteth up Theocracy in both, as the best form of government."

Occasionally, indeed, his recommendations were not approved. The Massachusetts legislature, in 1641, adopted the code of laws which Rev. Nathaniel Ward of

[1] Winthrop, i., p. 168.
[2] *Magnalia*, i., p. 266.
[3] Winthrop, i., p. 169.
[4] Letter, of 1636, to Lord Saye and Sele, quoted in *N. E. Hist. and Gen. Register*, x., p. 12.

Ipswich had drawn up, aided in his task by his early training as a lawyer, rather than the strongly Mosaic outline of suggested judicial enactment prepared by Cotton in 1639, and printed in 1641.[1] But, on the whole, there is as much truth as exaggeration in the affirmation of the historian Hubbard regarding Cotton, that " whatever he delivered in the pulpit was soon put into an Order of Court, if of a civil, or set up as a practice in the church, if of an ecclesiastical concernment."[2]

There are, however, three special features of Cotton's American life that cannot be neglected in any treatment of him, though the hour at our disposal gives scanty opportunity for more than a mention of them. First, in the commotion which it excited in its own day, and in the difficulty of defining Cotton's relation to it, is the so-called Antinomian controversy. That most turmoiling of early New England religious disturbances began in the criticisms passed on the preaching of most of the ministers in the vicinity of Boston by a warm admirer of Cotton, Mrs. Anne Hutchinson,[3] who, with her husband, had followed him from Lincolnshire in 1634 to enjoy his ministry in the New

[1] Winthrop, i., p. 388 ; ii., p. 66 ; Palfrey, *Hist. of N. E.*, ii., pp. 22-30. For the rare work, *An Abstract or the Lawes of New England*, see Hutchinson's *Collection of Papers*, or 1 *Coll. Mass. Hist. Soc.*, v., pp. 173-187. [2] *General Hist. of N. E.*, p. 182.

[3] The best modern treatment of this controversy is that by Charles Francis Adams in his *Three Episodes of Massachusetts History*, and *Antinomianism in the Colony of Massachusetts Bay*.

World. Mrs. Hutchinson's views were essentially those now known as of the "higher life"; but they were presented in the form of an extreme assertion of the personal indwelling of the Holy Spirit in the believer, that divine Person becoming so one with him as to render all other proof of sanctification than a consciousness of this indwelling not merely unnecessary but vain. He who sought evidence of Christian character in growing enjoyment of the worship of God, or improvement of conduct, was still under a " covenant of works "; while only he who based the proof of his acceptance with God on a sense of personal union with the divine Spirit was under the " covenant of grace."

These views Mrs. Hutchinson taught to many in the Boston church, who were drawn to her by her skill and self-sacrifice in nursing; and being a woman of keen mind, warm heart, and a ready tongue, she soon became the leader of well-attended meetings in Boston, at which her peculiar views were set forth, and criticisms freely passed upon the Sunday sermons. At these meetings Mrs. Hutchinson declared that Cotton and her husband's brother-in-law, John Wheelwright, were preachers of the " covenant of grace," while all the rest of the ministers, Thomas Shepard possibly excepted, were under the " covenant of works," and their labors therefore of very dubious spiritual value. To these opinions she drew a majority of the people of

Boston, and among them, Henry Vane, who became
Governor of Massachusetts in 1636; while a minority of
the Boston church, led by its pastor, John Wilson, and
John Winthrop, opposed her, and had the sympathy
in this opposition of most of the inhabitants of other
towns of the colony. The Boston church was turmoiled; a ministerial meeting tried in vain, in October,
1636, to heal the breach. In December, Mrs. Hutchinson and the colonial ministers generally discussed
the case in the presence of the magistrates. The same
month Mrs. Hutchinson's supporters tried to discipline
Pastor Wilson. The gubernatorial election of 1637
turned on the issue, the choice of Winthrop being distinctly an anti-Hutchinsonian victory; but at Boston
the halberd-bearers refused to do honor to the Governor, and most of the Boston quota for the Pequot
campaign of that summer refused to serve because
Wilson was chaplain and was under the " covenant of
works." Then followed the opening, on August 30,
1637, of the first synod or General Council of Congregational history, — ministers and delegates of the
churches meeting and condemning some eighty-two
erroneous opinions alleged to be held in New England,
to be followed in turn in November by the banishment
by the General Court of Wheelwright and Mrs. Hutchinson and the disarming of their followers; the painful
story of fanaticism and persecution closing with the
excommunication of Mrs. Hutchinson in March, 1638.

Now, what was the relation of Cotton to this melancholy controversy? As has already been pointed out, Mrs. Hutchinson had come to New England as his admirer, and had held him up to praise as one of the two New England ministers who taught a " covenant of grace." Cotton did, indeed, at first give large support to her and her followers. As Cotton himself later explained:[1]

" being naturally (I thank God) not suspicious, hearing no more of their Tenents from them, then what seemed to mee Orthodoxall, I beleeved, they had been far off from such grosse errors, as were bruited of them."

More than this, he regarded her religious labors as valuable means by which[2]

" many of the women (and by them their husbands) were convinced, that they had gone on in a Covenant of Works, and were much shaken and humbled thereby, and brought to enquire more seriously after the Lord Jesus Christ."

Cotton, who was something of a mystic, held to " the indwelling not onely of the Gifts of the Holy Ghost, but of his Person also in the Regenerate," as " an holy Truth of God;"[3] a view which a much more subtle theologian than Mrs. Hutchinson might have found difficulty in discriminating from the theory to which she converted Vane, that the believer is in " personal union with the Holy Ghost."[4] Acting in

[1] *Way of the Cong. Churches Cleared*, p. 39.
[2] *Ibid.*, p. 51. [3] *Ibid.*, pp. 36, 37. [4] Winthrop, i., p. 246.

sympathy with the Hutchinsonian party, at first, Cotton was asked by his fellow ministers twice during the autumn and winter of 1636-7 to answer in writing their questions on the disputed points; and did so, not wholly to their satisfaction.[1] On the last day of 1636, he publicly rebuked his colleague, John Wilson, the pastor of the Boston church of which he was teacher, for his attitude of opposition to the Hutchinsonian movement. When the anti-Hutchinsonian party, restored to power by the political overturn which placed Winthrop in the governor's chair in May, 1637, made an ungracious use of its victory by enacting a law which rendered further immigration of sympathizers with Mrs. Hutchinson wellnigh impossible,[2] Cotton, supported by some sixty of his congregation, planned to transfer themselves to the place then known as "Quinipyatk," but destined to be settled by John Davenport and his associates a year later and to bear the name that they gave it, New Haven.[3]

Yet, as the controversy went on, the views advanced by the Hutchinsonian party were less and less pleasing to Cotton. Many in his own church had come, by January, 1637, to believe "that the letter of the Scripture holds forth nothing but a covenant of works,"

[1] Winthrop, pp. 249-253. The second of these series of questions and Cotton's answers thereto were published as *Sixteene Questions of Serious and Necessary Consequence.* London, 1644.

[2] *Records of . . . Massachusetts,* i., p. 196.

[3] Cotton, *Way of the Cong. Churches Cleared*, pp. 52-54.

and to entertain an almost Quaker confidence in "assurance by immediate revelation."[1] To Cotton, as to the New England ministry generally, the doctrine of " immediate Revelations without the Word, and these as infallible as the Scripture itself" was " vile Montanism."[2] To attack the plainness, authority, or absolute finality and completeness of the Divine Word, was to undermine the very citadel of Christianity. So it may well have been that Cotton came seriously to doubt the character of the Hutchinsonian movement as he came to know it better. The defeat of the Hutchinsonian party politically, and the entreaties and arguments of his ministerial brethren in the synod of August and September, 1637, undoubtedly also had weight with him; and, by the conclusion of the synod, he had completely gone over to the opponents of the Hutchinsonian movement. Yet he retained sufficient regard for Mrs. Hutchinson herself to do what he could for her at the trial before the General Court which led to her banishment in November, 1637.[3] But the tide ran strong; and Cotton was soon declaring that " he had been abused and made their stalking-horse "[4] by the Hutchinsonian party and turned almost savagely upon it. In the merciless church trial of the unfortunate woman he admonished her two sons because they

[1] Winthrop, i., p. 252.
[2] Cotton, *Way of Cong. Churches Cleared*, p. 36.
[3] Compare Adams, *Three Episodes*, pp. 492–508.
[4] Winthrop, i., p. 304.

stood by their mother, and he now attacked Mrs. Hutchinson with a vehemence almost equal to that of Wilson himself.[1] Though much may be said in excuse of Cotton's conduct, it is not a page that is pleasant to look upon. A few years later, when Cotton had come to be regarded as the great expounder of Congregationalism by the supporters of that polity in the Westminster Assembly, this episode was turned against him by Presbyterian champions like Robert Baillie,[2] the Scotch commissioner to that famous body, and he was charged with "Montanism," "Antinomianisme and Familism," and various other ill-titled heresies on its account; but it never diminished his commanding influence in New England, or seriously affected the regard in which he was held in the land of his birth.

A second controversy in which Cotton was involved, less important indeed than that which has just been outlined, was a two-fold debate with Roger Williams, that much employed his pen in the decade following the Antinomian struggle. As we all doubtless remember, Roger Williams was banished from Massachusetts by its legislature—an event which occurred on October 9, 1635. It would be an aid to historic accuracy were it as generally remembered that Williams was not at this time a Baptist, and that views of baptism

---

[1] Winthrop, i., pp. 306, 307; Adams, *Antinomianism*, pp. 332, 333.
[2] See Baillie, *Dissuasive from the Errours of the Time*. London, 1645.

had nothing to do with his sentence; and that "soul-liberty," also, though undoubtedly one of its causes, was not its only occasion. Williams himself has recorded with approval the summary of the grounds of his banishment formulated by Governor Haynes in pronouncing the verdict, as involving:[1]

"*First*, That we have not our Land by Pattent from the King, but that the Natives are the true owners of it, and that we ought to repent of such a receiving of it by Pattent.

"*Secondly*, That it is not lawfull to call a wicked person to Sweare, to Pray, as being actions of God's worship.

"*Thirdly*, That it is not lawfull to heare any of the Ministers of the Parish Assemblies in England.

"*Fourthly*, That the Civil Magistrates power extends only to the Bodies and Goods, and outward State of men."

It was about the views expressed in the third and fourth of these articles that the controversy with Cotton turned. The human mind is often a strange compound; and Roger Williams illustrated this fact by combining, like Robert Browne half a century earlier, an almost modern liberality of view as to the wrongfulness of persecution for matters of religious faith, with the most strenuous and illiberal attitude of critical hostility to the Church of England. The same spirit which led him to restrict all religious observances to the companionship of the really regenerate, so that a man might not rightfully pray or say grace over the

[1] Williams, *Mr. Cottons Letter lately Printed, Examined and Answered*, pp. 4, 5. London, 1644.

common meal if an unregenerate member of his family were present,[1] induced him to hold that men must repent of ever having been associated in the mixed congregations of the Church of England, and, if providentially in that land, should hear the sermons of none of its ministers. Williams himself, probably in 1631, had refused the very office of teacher held by Cotton in the Boston church, " because I [he] durst not officiate to an unseparated people "[2]—that is, to a people who still looked upon the Church of England as a Christian body, for the Boston church was fully Congregational in organization and government.

It was these views that induced Cotton soon after Williams's banishment, perhaps in 1637,[3] to send a letter to Williams, which, as printed in 1643, contains an epitome of its purpose in its title, to show " that those ought to be received into the Church who are Godly, though they doe not see, nor expressly bewaile all the polutions in Church-fellowship, Ministry, Worship, Government."[4] In this letter Cotton incidentally remarked of Williams's banishment, " I dare not deny the sentence passed to be righteous in the eyes of God."[5] Roger Williams was in London when

[1] Winthrop, i., pp. 193, 194 ; Cotton, *Reply to Mr. Williams*, p. 9. London, 1647.

[2] Williams's Letter, in *Proc. Mass. Hist. Soc.*, March, 1858, p. 316.

[3] Cotton, *Reply to Mr. Williams*, p. 1.

[4] London, 1643. Reprinted in *Publications of the Narragansett Club*, i. [5] *Ibid.*, p. 1.

this already six-years-old letter got into print, apparently without the knowledge of Cotton or himself, and he naturally answered with an account of his banishment, but even more with a defense of his position regarding the proper penitential attitude of those who came out of the Church of England. To this answer of 1644,[1] Cotton replied at much length in 1647, beating over the already well-threshed straw of discussion, without indicating any change of view on his own part, or apparently effecting any on that of Williams.[2]

Contemporary with this discussion, wherein Cotton defended the more kindly view of the Church of England against Williams, ran a second debate between these two champions, which showed Cotton in a much less pleasing light from the view-point of our own age, though one in which he undoubtedly had the approval of most of his associates in the New England of his day. Here, too, the discussion began by an interchange of written papers, long before it came into print.[3] When Williams reached England on his visit

[1] *Mr. Cottons Letter lately Printed, Examined and Answered.* Reprinted in *Pub. Narr. Club,* i.

[2] This *Reply to Mr. Williams his Examination* was printed as an appendix to Cotton's *Bloudy Tenent Washed.* It forms the principal content of *Pub. Narr. Club,* ii.

[3] Williams's and Cotton's recollections disagreed about the circumstances of the beginning of the debate. Cotton, writing in 1647, thought that, about 1635, Williams had sent him a letter in favor of toleration written by an English Baptist prisoner, and that he had replied to it speedily in an essentially private letter. According to Williams's memory, the interchange of papers was between Cotton and

of 1643, the question of religious toleration had been brought to the front as never before, the Westminster Assembly was beginning, the religious constitution of the land was to be remade, and Williams determined to put his views before the public. Therefore, making Cotton's brief letter of 1635 the text, he put forth an elaborate dialogue in 1644, entitled *The Bloudy Tenent, of Persecution, for cause of Conscience, discussed, in a Conference betweene Truth and Peace*.[1] To this Cotton replied at much length in 1647, under the title of *The Bloudy Tenent, Washed, And made white in the bloud of the Lamb;* and in 1652 Williams made an extensive rejoinder: *The Bloudy Tenent Yet More Bloudy by Mr. Cottons Endeavour to wash it White in the Bloud of the Lamb*.[2] Cotton did not live to give further answer, had he so desired. But his own view probably never altered from that which he expressed in 1647:[3]

"It is a carnall and worldly, and indeed, even ungodly imagination, to confine the Magistrates charge to the bodies, and goods of the Subject, and to exclude them from the care of their Soules."

How far this "care of soules" might go, Cotton plainly indicates:[4]

"Better a dead soule be dead in body, as well as in

John Hall of Roxbury, and that from the latter the papers came into Williams's hands. See *Pub. Narr. Club*, iii., pp. iv., v.

[1] *Pub. Narr. Club*, iii. [3] *Bloudy Tenent, Washed*, pp. 67, 68.
[2] *Ibid.*, iv. [4] *Ibid.*, p. 83.

Spirit, then to live, and be lively in the flesh, to murder many precious soules by the Magistrates Indulgence."

Certainly in this argument Williams, rather than Cotton, has been justified by time.

It must be evident, from what has been said, that Cotton held a ready pen. We have been able to glance at only a few of his writings. His controversies already considered were undoubtedly the most dramatic events in his New England life, but they were less valuable or permanently fruitful than the series of treatises, published chiefly between 1640 and 1650, which did more than the work of any other single laborer to fix the views and consolidate the polity of our churches. Cotton was not alone in this work. Thomas Hooker and Richard Mather did a very similar service. Probably Hooker was a greater preacher and a more efficient and far-sighted organizer. Certainly Mather was singularly gifted in explaining and formulating Congregational polity. But while others excelled him in one point or another, in the full circle of his talents and services, and in the degree in which he was viewed as the characteristic New England religious pioneer both here and in England he was foremost.

Besides the unwearied pulpit activity already noted, many fruits of which were published, Cotton's special treatises did much to direct New England thought. Thus, in an *Answer to Mr. Balls Discourse of set formes of Prayer*,[1] published in London just as the King and Parliament were beginning the great war in 1642, Cotton laid down the principle that these prescribed petitions were a " sinne against the true meaning of the second Commandement."[2] Extravagant as the thought is, it undoubtedly represented and strengthened the then prevailing New England view. Four years later came Cotton's *Milk for Babes*, the most widely used formula for youthful instruction in New England, till the Westminster Shorter Catechism, prepared largely by Cotton's assistant and successor in his English parish, Anthony Tuckney, gradually displaced it. The next year, 1647, saw the publication of two argumentative treatises, beside the *Bloudy Tenent, Washed*, already referred to. One was entitled *Singing of Psalmes a Gospel-Ordinance*, in which Cotton argued against all who believed that printed songs were under the same condemnation that he laid on printed prayers. But it was no general use of hymns or organs that Cotton urged.[3]

" We hold and beleeve, that not onely the *Psalmes* of *David*, but any other spirituall Songs recorded in Scripture, may lawfully be sung in Christian Churches," and

[1] John Ball was an excellent, and moderate, Puritan minister at Whitmore, Staffordshire. In the year of his death, 1640, he published an admirably written little volume, entitled : *A Friendly Triall of the Grounds tending to Separation ; In a plain and modest Dispute touching the Lawfulnesse of a stinted Liturgie and set form of Prayer*. To this Cotton replied.

[2] *Answer to Mr. Ball*, p. 19. [3] *Singing of Psalmes*, p. 15.

"wee grant also, that any private Christian, who hath a gift to frame a spirituall Song, may both frame it, and sing it privately, for his own private comfort. . . . Nor doe we forbid the private use of an Instrument of Musick therewithall."

This rejection of the public use of all uninspired hymns and of all music but that of the human voice remained characteristic of New England for a century after Cotton wrote.

The other tract of 1647 was a plain, simple argument in favor of infant baptism,[1] its one hundred and ninety-six pages having been written originally with no thought of publication, but for the instruction of a son of members of Cotton's church in old England, who, coming to America, had embraced Baptist beliefs. It well illustrates Cotton's laborious pastoral faithfulness in that which was little as well as in that which was greater in the public view. The same long continuing pastoral affection induced him, in 1650, to dedicate to the people of his former charge at the Lincolnshire Boston his essay on *The Holinesse of Church-Members*, in which he set forth, against the objections of the Scotch Presbyterian champions, Samuel Rutherford and Robert Baillie, the New England view that only persons of recognized Christian character should be admitted to the full privileges of church membership.

[1] *The Grovnds and Ends of the Baptisme of the Children of the Faithfull.* London, 1647.

JOHN COTTON

But the tracts of greatest repute penned by Cotton were those in which he exhibited the distinctive traits of Congregational polity. It was a theme on which he began to write early in his New England ministry. In 1642, there was published at London a brief sketch of his composition,[1] begun as early as January, 1635,[2] in which, in the course of thirteen pages, the nature, membership, officers, worship, sacraments, and discipline of a Congregational church were set forth with abundant proof-texts and much plainness of definition. The time when this tract was issued was one of the epochal years in English history—in August the great civil war broke out, in October the first bill for an Assembly to revise English religious beliefs and institutions passed Parliament, in December the bill for the abolition of Episcopacy was introduced into the House of Commons. In such a period of discussion and examination of the religious foundations of the land, Cotton's tract naturally aroused the attention of those Puritans who were satisfied neither with Episcopacy nor Presbyterianism. It passed through two editions in 1642, and a third in 1643. But this sketch was slight and elementary, compared with one written a few years later by Cotton,[3] and sent to England in

[1] *The Doctrine of the Church*, etc.

[2] Another draft of this tract, printed as *Questions and Answers upon Church Government*, in *A Treatise of Faith*, etc., probably of 1713, in the Library of Yale University, reads, "begun 25. 11 m. 1634."

[3] See *Way of the Churches*, "Epistle to the Reader."

manuscript, probably in 1643. This *Way of the Churches of Christ in New England* was a full and elaborate account of the theory, methods, and usages of the New England congregations, and is one of the sources of prime importance for any picture of their nature, organization, and worship, during their first quarter century on New England soil. But it is curiously illustrative of the slow publication of books in those days, especially of books that had to cross the ocean, that this volume had so considerable a circulation in manuscript that it was answered in Prof. Samuel Rutherford's *Due right of Presbyteries* in 1644, yet did not get into print till 1645, and then from so imperfect a transcript of the original manuscript as to cause the author considerable annoyance.[1]

A year before this belated appearance of the *Way of the Churches*, Cotton's greatest formative treatise on Congregational polity was published under a title characteristic of the technicalities of seventeenth-century theologic discussion: *The Keyes of the Kingdom of Heaven*. It had been sent to England a year later than the *Way*, and its composition was evidently subsequent to that work. It is a careful, clear, and exceedingly able presentation of the Congregational theory of the Church, as it lay in the decidedly un-

---

[1] Cotton, *Way of the Cong. Churches Cleared*, part ii., p. 2 ; Increase Mather, *Attestation to Cotton Mather's Ratio Disciplinæ*, ii. ; *Magnalia*, i., p. 281.

democratic minds of the founders of Massachusetts. In size it is about one half that of the *Way of the Churches;* and, lacking the descriptive qualities of that work, it is less interesting; but to the painstaking student it demonstrates its value as sharing with Hooker's *Survey* and the *Cambridge Platform* the honor of being the most conspicuous explanation of early Congregationalism. But something more than the argumentative force therein displayed gave distinction to the *Keyes;* it had a peculiar timeliness in its appearance that gave it a special value and use. The Westminster Assembly had opened its sessions on July 1, 1643. Cotton himself, as well as his New England associates, Thomas Hooker and John Davenport, had been asked by influential members of the English Parliament to allow their names to be included in the list summoned to its sessions, and had it not been for Hooker, who foresaw the hopeless minority in which the Congregationalists would find themselves in that body, he would have done so.[1] Yet, though no New Englanders were of that body, there were five prominent Congregationalists,[2] and perhaps as many more less pronounced supporters of the Congregational polity in the Assembly. On a count of votes they made small show against the Presbyterian majority; but they were treated with great respect by

[1] Winthrop, ii., pp. 91, 92.
[2] They were Thomas Goodwin, Philip Nye, Sidrach Simpson, Jeremiah Burroughs, and William Bridge.

that majority, because of the growing sympathy for their views, especially in the army.

The Congregationalists in the Westminster Assembly attacked and delayed the Presbyterians, but their own support in the country at large was made up of so many elements that it was much easier to depend upon it for aid in an attack on a polity which promised to be rigid and oppressive than in the formulation of any constructive principles. Desirous of advocating a definite Congregational system, and yet hesitant about putting their names to any exposition of it of which they should appear to be the authors, these Congregationalists in the Assembly now welcomed, published, and circulated Cotton's *Keyes*, declaring it to be the " Middle-way between that which is called Brownisme, and the Presbyteriall-government";[1] that is, the golden mean in church polity. Thus supported, it had an influence even greater in England than in America, and was looked upon on both sides of the Atlantic as the most authoritative exposition of Congregationalism set forth by an individual writer. That position of repute it cannot be said to have lost[2] even now, though it is no longer consulted save by those of antiquarian tastes.

These two works, the *Way of the Churches* and the *Keyes*, aroused opponents for themselves and their

[1] *Keyes*, " To the Reader," by Goodwin and Nye.
[2] Dexter, *Cong. as Seen*, pp. 433, 434.

author, notably Prof. Samuel Rutherford, whose *Due right of Presbyteries*[1] has already been mentioned; an anonymous pamphlet entitled *Vindiciæ Clavium: or a Vindication of the Keyes of the Kingdome of Heaven, into the hands of the right owners;*[2] and a savage personal attack from that ardent Presbyterian champion, Prof. Robert Baillie, of the Westminster Assembly, in his general collection and refutation of supposed heresies, *A Dissuasive from the Errours of the Time.*[3] To all of these Cotton replied in 1648, in a volume full of biographical details of value, the *Way of the Congregational Churches Cleared.* Already recognized as the foremost controversial defender of the New England polity, Cotton was naturally chosen, in 1646, by the Cambridge Synod, one of three ministers to prepare a " model of church government "[4] for submission to the body. In the *Cambridge Platform*, actually adopted in 1648, preference was given to the draft formulated by Richard Mather, but considerable use was made of the work of Cotton, and it was his pen that wrote the Preface to the *Platform* as it went forth to the churches.

Cotton's life was one of activity almost to the end. A severe cold, caught when returning from a sermon to the students of Harvard College in the autumn of 1652, developed into more extensive complications of

[1] London, 1644.
[2] *Ibid*, 1645.
[3] *Ibid.*
[4] *Magnalia*, ii., p. 211.

the respiratory organs. On November 21st, he preached for the last time, and he died on December 23d, in the fullness of the Christian hope.[1]

It must have been with a sense of peculiar bereavement that the people of New England met the loss of such a religious leader. His death was the passing from this stage of human affairs of one who had been among the foremost in a great movement in old England and in the new; and there were none of the second generation fully able to take his place. He belonged to a world of great activities, he had borne his part in a struggle of national proportions, he had been a leader in planting a new continent. The generation that succeeded was, of necessity, provincial; narrowed by poverty, struggle with the wilderness, and isolation from the current of great affairs. With the going of Cotton and Hooker, and the other leaders of the hopeful and heroic age of the beginnings, those that followed felt that a glory and a strength had departed from the land; and the feeling was true. But, to us, Cotton stands preëminently as a typical Puritan minister, illustrative alike, in his virtues and his defects, in his studiousness, learning, zeal, moral earnestness, spirituality, breadth of interest in State and Church, yet narrowness of sympathy and intolerance, of the strength and the failings of the remarkable race of men that founded New England.

[1] *Magnalia*, i., pp. 271–273.

RICHARD MATHER

III.

RICHARD MATHER

IT was remarked, in speaking of Cotton, that he was widely and justly viewed by his contemporaries as the typical representative of New England religious thought. Yet New England has never had any exclusively commanding expounder of its characteristic ecclesiastical polity. Others beside Cotton wrought on the fabric. Others, perhaps even more than he, found delight in the solution of the problems which it involved and in tracing out the minuter ramifications of its principles. It is to one who bore large part in all that concerned the development or the exposition of the Congregational system in his day that I shall call your attention in this lecture — that is, to Richard Mather of Dorchester. Not so profound a scholar as Cotton, his kindly spirit and shrewd common sense, no less than his unfeigned enjoyment of conventions and debates, made him in no opprobrious sense an ecclesiastical politician. His wisdom, his skill, and his native leadership give him rank, if not as the first, yet among the first four or five in eminence of the ministerial founders of New England.

Richard Mather was of Lancashire origin, the son of Thomas Mather and of Margaret Abrams, his wife.[1] His place of birth was the village of Lowton, just out of what is now the great seaport of Liverpool, but was then an insignificant harbor, with less than one hundred and fifty families dwelling about it. The household in which he saw light, some time in 1596, was, so Increase Mather declared,[2] in reduced circumstances by reason of " unhappy mortgages "; and the few glimpses that we get of his early home indicate that it was one in which expenditure had to be a matter of careful calculation. Of the circumstances of his childhood we know nothing, and the motives which induced his father to send him to school seem to have been something of a mystery to Richard himself.[3] The school which he entered was typical of the smaller preparatory educational institutions scattered at that day over England. That land then had no national

[1] The prime source regarding Richard Mather's life is his son Increase's *Life and Death of that Reverend Man of God, Mr. Richard Mather*. Cambridge, 1670. This sketch Cotton Mather incorporated, with slight changes, in the *Magnalia*. Horace E. Mather, *Lineage of Rev. Richard Mather*, Hartford, 1890, has some facts of value ; and J. P. Rylands has thrown some light on the Mathers of Lancashire in the *N. E. Hist. and Geneal. Register*, xlvii., pp. 38, 177, 330. Richard Mather himself kept a journal—to his thirty-ninth year, says Increase Mather. The part relating to his voyage to America has been frequently published, *e. g.*, Young, *Chronicles of Massachusetts*, pp. 447–480. The remainder is lost. Regarding his mother, see *N. E. Hist. and Geneal. Register*, liv., 349.

[2] Increase Mather, *Life and Death of . . . Richard Mather*, p. 43, ed. of 1850.   [3] *Ibid.*, p. 43.

RICHARD MATHER

system of elementary public instruction,—indeed, it was to have none till 1871,—but private beneficence, or royal favor, had founded many "grammar schools" where preparation for Cambridge or Oxford could be obtained. These were the schools which our ancestors sought to introduce when, in 1647, Massachusetts enacted the celebrated statute, ordering that [1]

" where any towne shall increase to ye numb^r of 100 families or househould^{rs}, they shall set up a grañer schoole, ye m^t thereof being able to instruct youth so farr as they may be fited for ye university."

They were in a true sense the ancestors of our great academies; though they gave as little prophecy of the growth and fruitage exhibited, for instance, in the foundation which has made Andover famous, as the Harvard of 1642 revealed of the generous university of to-day.

The particular " grammar school " to which Richard Mather was sent was at Winwick, four miles from Lowton. The institution had been founded not far from seventy years before Mather became its pupil, and endowed with a rent of £10 annually.[2] The gift seems small enough, but the impulse thus imparted has proved sufficient to carry the Winwick Grammar School to our own day; though its modest quarters, not larger than a good-sized dwelling-house, show

[1] *Records of* . . . *Massachusetts*, ii., p. 203.
[2] H. E. Mather, *Lineage of Richard Mather*, p. 31.

that it has never been one of the more famous seats of preparatory education. Here Richard's parents boarded the boy in winter; but in summer household poverty impelled him to walk the eight miles that measured the distance from his home to school and back daily.

The boy's school life was not without its trials. Neither home nor school discipline was then unwilling to employ the rod for the correction of almost all offenses, trifling or grave. But Mather's master was notorious for his harshness, so that the boy begged his father again and again to be allowed to abandon the scholar's life. Yet, though Mather when grown to manhood never quite forgave the brutality of his teacher,[1] he was honest enough to recognize that to that teacher's discernment he owed his scholarly career. For, by the entreaties and remonstrances of his severe instructor his father was persuaded to put aside an attractive offer of an apprentice's position in the neighboring town of Warrington,[2] which impressed both father and son as too good a business opportunity to be let slip.

How long Richard Mather studied at Winwick is uncertain, but at fifteen he was ready for the university and would gladly have gone thither. Such a preparation did not imply the precocity which enabled his grandson, Cotton Mather, to graduate from Harvard

[1] See his remarks in I. Mather, *Life and Death of . . . Richard Mather*, p. 44. [2] *Ibid.*, p. 45.

at the same age, sixty-six years later; but it certainly shows much confidence in the stability and thoroughness of the boy that, on the invitation of the people of Toxteth Park, now within the limits of Liverpool, he at this early age became first master of their new-founded grammar school. The duties of such a position were, indeed, not what now fall to the share of the head of a preparatory school. The original conditions to be fulfilled for entrance at Harvard doubtless represent with substantial accuracy the nature of the instruction which Mather was expected to instill into his pupils. It was true then, as in New England in 1642, that [1]

"When any Schollar is able to understand *Tully*, or such like classicall Latine Author *ex tempore*, and make and speake true Latine in Verse and Prose, *suo ut aiunt Marte;* And decline perfectly the Paradigim's of *Nounes* and *Verbes* in the *Greek* tongue: Let him then and not before be capable of admission into the Colledge."

But the work was well done by the youthful teacher; and the six years between 1612 [2] and 1618, which were spent by Mather in instruction at Toxteth Park, were formative in many respects. Chief in the experiences which came to him in his foundation years was his conversion. We know little of the religious influences of his home, but, judged by the fact that Richard's

[1] Sibley, *Harvard Graduates*, i., p. 11.
[2] Anthony Wood, *Athenæ Oxienses*, ii., p. 427, gives the date of his going to Toxteth Park as 1612.

father had no scruples in consenting to apprentice him to a Roman Catholic,[1] they cannot have been of a strongly Puritan character. The sermons of Rev. Mr. Palin of Leigh had already impressed him; but the immediate occasion of his spiritual awakening was the Christian example of the family of Edwin Aspinwall, of Toxteth Park,[2] of which family the young schoolmaster was a member. It was an intense spiritual struggle through which Mather passed. Touched by a sermon preached in his hearing by Rev. John Harrison, the non-conforming Puritan vicar of Histon; alarmed by the searching tract of the powerful Cambridge preacher, William Perkins, on the extent to which a man may go forward in an apparently religious life and yet be one of the reprobate ; impressed by the Christian character of the household in which he lived, Mather passed through despairing agonies of soul, till, some time in 1614,[3] he attained peace and comfort in the conscious acceptance of the Gospel. We shall have occasion to see, later, that this struggle was natural to Mather's temperament; but more than temperament lay behind it. The intense, introspective, self-examinatory, exacting conceptions which the Puritans entertained of the process of conversion, of the dangers of self-deception connected with it, and of the contrast in feeling and life which should distinguish him who

[1] Increase Mather's *Life and Death of . . . Richard Mather*, p. 45.
[2] *Ibid.*, p. 48.   [3] Wood, *Athenæ Oxienses*, p. 427.

was a Christian from him who was not, made these struggling spiritual births seem the normal method of entrance into the Kingdom of God. Mather's experiences brought him out a Puritan.

It would not appear that Mather's conversion was followed by an immediate determination to enter the ministry. For four years more he remained the head of the school at Toxteth Park, till desire for a further education drove him to Oxford. May 9, 1618,[1] saw his entrance into the student body of Brasenose College. But his university experiences were brief. Already a man of much learning and decided maturity of mind, and about twenty-two years of age, the people of Toxteth Park gave the most conspicuous testimony possible to the character and repute of their former schoolmaster by inviting him to become their minister. Mather accepted the call, and on November 30, 1618, entered on his labors, his first sermon, as is not uncommon with those of young ministers who have anything to say, being marked by an attempt to present matter sufficient, so his son, Increase, declared, for six ordinary discourses.[2] Like the early Puritans generally, Mather preached without notes; and one is reminded of Judge Samuel Sewall's youthful experiences in the pulpit, when, nervous with excitement, he dared not watch the hour glass, and, fearful lest he

[1] Wood, *Athenæ Oxienses*, p. 427.
[2] Increase Mather, *ibid.*, p. 50.

defraud the congregation of some portion of their dues, he held forth," ignorantly and unwillingly," he records, for " two hours and a half." [1]

But whatever may have been the infelicities of his first discourse, the people of Toxteth Park liked the young preacher, with his " loud and big " voice, his " deliberate vehemency " of utterance, and his " awful and very taking majesty " of pulpit manner.[2] They renewed their request that he become their pastor, and accordingly Mather procured ordination at the hands of Thomas Morton, Bishop of Chester.[3] It shows clearly the intensity of the feeling of opposition to the episcopal system which the fathers of New England entertained that Mather came later to experience, as his son records,[4] " no small grief of heart " at the recollection of this conformity; and, years later, when the same son, rummaging in boyish fashion in his father's study in the raw New England town, discovered a torn parchment, he was told by the then middle-aged Mather that the document was a memorial of this ordination at Bishop Morton's hand; but, to quote Mather's own words to the youthful questioner,[5] " I tore it because I took no pleasure in keeping a monument of my sin and folly in submitting to that superstition, the very remembrance whereof is grievous to me."

[1] Sewall's *Diary*, i., p. 9. 1878.   [3] Increase Mather, *Life*, p. 50.
[2] Cotton Mather, *Magnalia*, i., p. 452.   [4] *Ibid*.   [5] *Ibid*.

Mather's change of attitude toward his ordination illustrates the fact that Puritan opposition to the ceremonies and government of the Church of England was a development. From the beginning of his ministry he was Puritan in sentiment. He never wore the surplice.[1] Yet he habitually preached on the holy days; though for the characteristic Puritan reason that[2] " there was then an opportunity to cast the net of the Gospel among much fish in great assemblies, which then were convened, and would otherwise have been worse employed," rather than by reason of any special sanctity in the days themselves. In his ideals of preaching Mather undoubtedly represented the typical, painstaking Puritan conception. Like Cotton and Hooker, he preached over large portions of Scripture in his English ministry, setting forth sections of Proverbs, the Psalms, Isaiah, Luke, Romans, Timothy, John, and Jude.[3] To his own people at Toxteth Park he preached twice every Sunday,[4] and, not content with his home ministration, he maintained a " Tuesday Lecture " every other week at Prescot, some six or seven miles from his home, and preached frequently in other towns in Lancashire.[5]

Some six years after his ministry began, on September 29, 1624, he married Katherine Holt, a daughter of a resident of position in Bury, about twenty

---

[1] I. Mather, *Life*, p. 56.
[2] C. Mather, *Magnalia*, i., p. 447.
[3] I. Mather, *Life*, p. 54.
[4] *Ibid.*, p. 52.   [5] *Ibid.*

miles from Toxteth Park. The courtship was protracted; the reason of the delay being, as Increase Mather records,[1] "her Father's not being affected towards Nonconformable Puritan ministers." Marriage was followed by the purchase of a house at Much-Woolton, three miles from Toxteth Park,[2] and the establishment of the young minister and his bride in very comfortable surroundings, with every prospect of a peaceful, honored, and successful ministry.

But, as we have already seen, the years following Mather's settlement at Toxteth Park were years of increasing religious and political confusion in England. James I. closed his troubled career of resistance to the growing demands of the Commons and of opposition to the Puritan wing of the Church six months after the marriage of the young Toxteth clergyman. The year 1628 saw the elevation of that opponent of all that Puritanism represented, William Laud, to the head of the great, Puritanly inclined bishopric of London; it witnessed also the beginnings of the Puritan colonization of Massachusetts in the settlement of Endicott and his associates at Salem. The year 1629 beheld the dismissal of Parliament, not to meet again till eleven years had passed and the country stood on the eve of the great civil war. In 1633, Laud himself was raised to the primacy of the English Church through his elevation to the see of Canterbury, and

[1] I. Mather, *Life*, p. 51.   [2] *Ibid.*, p. 52.

the powers of Church and State, united in his own person as Primate and Prime-Minister, were directed, as never before in England since Protestantism obtained firm footing with the accession of Elizabeth, to the enforcement of ceremonial and liturgical uniformity in ecclesiastical affairs. Mather's parish was aside from the main currents of English life, and these events for a long time seem to have occasioned him little disturbance, nor does he appear to have busied himself, as did Davenport, Cotton, and Hooker, for instance, with the beginnings of the Puritan settlement of Massachusetts. Doubtless his people at Toxteth Park largely sympathized with him. It was at Prescot, where he conducted a Tuesday lectureship, rather than in his home parish, that his Puritanism attracted unfavorable notice. But the growing strictness which Laud infused into the administration of the Church of England would allow no man of prominence long to escape scrutiny; and, in August, 1633, Mather found himself suspended from his ministry for non-conformity:—the offense charged being, apparently, omission of the disputed ceremonies. Influential friends in Lancashire procured his restoration in November of the same year, but it was only a brief respite, and a few months later, visitors representing Archbishop Richard Neile of York inhibited his ministry permanently.[1]

[1] I. Mather, *Life*, pp. 54, 55.

The growing difficulties of his pastorate, thus culminating in its abrupt termination, set Mather anew to studying the foundation principles of church government; and the investigation not merely confirmed his previous Puritanism, but left him a radical of the Puritan party. He now determined to go to New England — a decision which he argued out, pen in hand, in a curious series of reasons that has come down to our own time;[1] and the determination was strengthened by a letter from Thomas Hooker, and possibly one also from John Cotton, both of whom were already in the new land.[2] And so, in April, 1635, Mather, his wife, his four children, and a considerable number of his friends and associates made the journey to the West of England seaport of Bristol, where they were to take their ship.[3] Their voyage, of which Mather has preserved a most graphic account in his journal,[4] was illustrative of the delays of navigation in those days — delays due as much to the inefficiency of the

[1] I. Mather, *Life*, pp. 57–68.

[2] An extract from that of Hooker is given, *ibid.*, p. 69. It has been suggested with some plausibility that the letter of Cotton, dated December 3, 1634, in Young, *Chronicles of . . . Mass.*, pp. 438–444, was to Mather.

[3] Cotton Mather (*Magnalia*, i., p. 449), following his father, Increase, states that Richard Mather was compelled to make his way to Bristol in disguise. Such testimony is probably accurate; yet Mather's journal plainly shows that his journey was rather a leisurely one, and that he encountered no such difficulties in getting out of the reach of the ecclesiastical authorities as Cotton and Hooker experienced in 1633.

[4] Young, *Chronicles of . . . Mass.*, pp. 447–480.

human agents as to the uncertainties of the winds and waves. After waiting a month at Bristol for the ship to make ready, they embarked on May 23d; but did not sail till June 4th, and then, till June 22d, they lay in harbors or tried in vain to get clear of the land. Once fairly at sea, an easy and prosperous voyage carried them almost to their journey's end, till, on August 15th, when anchored off the Isles of Shoals, a West Indian hurricane, famous as the great storm of early New England history, caught them in its giant grasp, and nearly caused their destruction; but, at last, on August 17, 1635, they landed safely at Boston. Here Mather settled temporarily, till he could look about for a more permanent home; and here he and his wife joined the church of which Wilson and Cotton were pastor and teacher, on confession of their faith, October 25, 1635.[1]

Such a man could not long remain without a parish; and Mather was soon invited to settle over the Mayflower church at Plymouth, the congregation at Roxbury, and that at Dorchester. The advice of Cotton and Hooker determined him to accept the latter call. The situation at Dorchester was curiously illustrative of the migratory character of the first settlers of New England. A church, organized at Plymouth, England, in March, 1630, under the joint pastorate of John Warham and John Maverick, had settled there and

[1] Savage, *Notes to Winthrop*, i., p. 218. 1853.

founded the town in the early summer of 1630. But, by the autumn of 1635, its numbers were largely emigrating to what was soon named Windsor, Conn., and in the summer of 1636, if not earlier,—the same season that Thomas Hooker and his Cambridge congregation removed to Hartford,— its surviving minister, Warham, followed his flock to Connecticut and completed the transfer of its organization to the new location. So completely did the church of 1630 abandon its Dorchester home that it was felt necessary that a new church should be gathered, and of this new congregation, Richard Mather was asked to become the "teacher."[1]

The organization of the new Dorchester church was, however, beset with difficulties that cast an illuminating light upon the thoroughness of that examination of candidates for church membership which early New England demanded. Under the impulse of the controversies aroused by Roger Williams, the Massachusetts legislature, in March, 1636, had passed a law forbidding the formation of any further churches without first informing and obtaining the approval of "the magistrates & the elders of the great^r p'te of the

[1] The editors of the *Records of the First Church at Dorchester*, vii.-xxiii., try to show that the churches of Windsor, Conn., and of Dorchester, are equally entitled to date back to that organized in 1630; but there can be no question that what Mather was called to preside over as teacher was a newly organized church, even if it contained some who were members of the church of 1630, who did not care to remove from Dorchester to Windsor.

churches"[1] in the colony. This statute, more than anything else, caused the gathering of a council at the organization of a church to become a regular part of Congregational procedure. It was under this enactment, then not a month old, that Mather and his associates in the new Dorchester enterprise made application for the prescribed civil and ecclesiastical approval. The magistrates and ministers gathered on April 1st, and Winthrop, who was undoubtedly present, records their experiences.[2] The examination was thorough. The confession of faith presented by the associates in the would-be church was satisfactory; but when the council examined into the spiritual life of each of the proposed members, they found only Mather and one other of the candidates worthy of approval, since "most of them had builded their comfort of salvation on unsound grounds"[3]—so Winthrop and the rest of the assembled magistrates and ministers thought:

"viz., some upon dreams and ravishes of spirit by fits; others upon the reformation of their lives; others upon duties and performances, wherein they discovered three special errors; 1. That they had not come to hate sin, because it was filthy, but only left it, because it was hurtful. 2. That, by reason of this, they had never truly closed with Christ (or rather Christ with them). . . . 3. They expected to believe by some power of their own, and not only and wholly from Christ."

[1] *Records of . . . Mass.*, i., p. 168.
[2] *Journal*, i., pp. 218, 219. 1853.
[3] *Ibid.*, p. 219.

Just how they satisfied these conscientious critics of their spiritual estate we do not know; but nearly five months later, on August 23, 1636,[1] the church was at last organized, by Mather and six associates, " with the approbation of the magistrates and elders."[2] To them many others were speedily added. Of this church Mather remained the " teacher " till his death, nearly thirty-three years later. Several colleagues were, indeed, briefly associated with him, of whom the first was Rev. Jonathan Burr, once rector at Rickingshall in Suffolk, whose short pastoral relation to the Dorchester church, begun in 1640, was ended by his untimely demise in August, 1641.[3] His settlement gave rise to one of the earlier of New England advisory councils, for Mather suspected him, apparently with some show of justification, of those " higher life " views then branded as " Familism." The matter being laid before the Dorchester church, Burr wrote a long statement of his opinions, from which Mather culled a series of alleged " errors," and reported them to the church without first exhibiting his unsavory list to Burr. The latter was naturally incensed; and, as Winthrop records, " it grew to some heat and alienation." But it also led to a desire for a mutual council, and on February 2, 1640, some ten of the neighboring pastors, with Gov. Thomas Dudley and John Win-

---

[1] *Records of the First Church at Dorchester*, pp. 1, 2.
[2] Winthrop, i., p. 231.   [3] See *Magnalia*, i., pp. 368–375.

throp to represent the lay membership, met at Dorchester, and after four days' patient hearing of the case came to the sensible conclusion that " both sides had cause to be humbled for their failings," [1] and that they be " advised to set a day apart for reconciliation." The advice was happily successful, for the suspected young minister fully renounced his supposed errors, and, as Winthrop records:

" Mr. Mather and Mr. Burr took the blame of their failings upon themselves, and freely submitted to the judgment and advice given, to which the rest of the church yielded a silent assent."

Mather's second colleague was Rev. John Wilson, of the first class that graduated from Harvard College, but the relationship lasted only from 1649 to 1651, when Wilson entered on a pastorate of forty years' duration at Medfield.[2] William Stoughton, Mather's parishioner, afterward Lieutenant-Governor of Massachusetts, often preached for him, and, it is said, six or eight times declined a colleague settlement.[3] But, for the greater part of his life in America Mather was the sole minister of the Dorchester church, and the pastorate was a time of internal peace and growth for the congregation. Yet, as I have already intimated, it was not always a time of spiritual calm for the pastor himself. The early ministers of New England were as

[1] For this council and its doings, see Winthrop, ii., pp. 26-28.
[2] Sibley, *Graduates of Harvard*, i., p. 65.   [3] *Ibid.*, i., pp. 195, 196.

strenuous in their own self-examination as in that of others. John Warham, who removed with his church from Dorchester to Windsor, Conn., just before Mather came thither, would sit unparticipating at the Lord's table where he broke the bread and poured the wine for others, feeling his own unworthiness to partake.[1] William Tompson, Mather's ministerial neighbor alike in old England and the new, was even more grievously a prey to melancholy thoughts of his spiritual state.[2] And Mather's spiritual course, for several years after coming to Dorchester, was one of doubt and struggle, or, as his grandson phrases it, of "internal desertions and uncertainties about his everlasting happiness;"[3] doubts which he did not impart to his people, but which long made his ministry a period of distress to him; till, partly by the clearing of his own spiritual vision, and partly through the spiritual comforting of John Norton of Ipswich and Boston, he came at length into inward peace; so that the latter part of his American pastorate was as much a satisfaction to himself as a source of strength to others.

Our present interest is, however, in Mather's relations to the development of Congregationalism, rather than in his somewhat uneventful experiences in his New England pastorate. Though by no means so voluminous a writer as his son, Increase, or his grandson, Cotton, Richard Mather held a ready pen, and

[1] *Magnalia*, i., p. 442.   [2] *Ibid.*, i., p. 439.   [3] *Ibid.*, i., p. 451.

though Rev. John Cotton's first brief sketch of ecclesiastical polity[1] was written several years earlier than any treatise by Mather, the latter's *Church-Government and Church Covenant Discussed* was the first elaborate defense and exposition of the New England theory of the Church and its administration to be put forth in print. Mather's volume was drawn out by a series of thirty-two questions covering the whole range of church practice in the new land. These inquiries were sent over to him by some of his former ministerial associates in Lancashire or Cheshire[2] in 1638 or early in 1639; and Mather's answer was written and despatched to England in the latter year, though it was not put into print till 1643, and then with a title which made no mention of Mather's name, but ascribed its authorship collectively to " the Elders of the severall Churches in New England "— a title deserved indeed by the merit of its exposition, but not warranted by the facts.[3] In this tract Mather informed his English querists that in Massachusetts more heads of families were church members than were not, and " likewise sundry children and servants."[4] He described the New England churches as neither " meerly Demo-

[1] *Doctrine of the Church*, etc. London, 1642, begun in January, 1635.
[2] Cotton, *Way of the Churches Cleared*, p. 70.
[3] On its authorship, see Cotton, *Reply to Mr. Williams, his Examination*, in *Pub. Narragansett Club*, ii., p. 103 ; Nathanael Mather, Preface to *Disputation Concerning Church-Members*, p. 7, London, 1659 ; Increase Mather, *Order of the Gospel*, p. 73, Boston, 1700.
[4] *Church-Government and Church Covenant Discussed*, pp. 7, 8.

craticall or meerly Aristocraticall"; [1] he affirmed the full power of a company of Christian men and women, even as few as four or five if need be, to form a church, self-governing in every respect, and choosing and ordaining its own officers; he denied to women the right to vote in church affairs; he defined the duties of pastors and teachers, answered questions as to the churchly character of English parish assemblies, and the status of those who came from them to New England. In fact, Mather gave his readers a treatise which was not only the most careful explication of the "New England way" that had yet appeared, and an effective contribution to the great debate regarding polity which renewed its strength in England with the opening of the Westminster Assembly, but one which presents our best picture of how Congregational polity actually shaped itself in the minds of its creators within ten years of the establishment of the first Puritan church on this side of the Atlantic.

It illustrates the care with which these early Puritans worked out the problems of ecclesiastical polity which were to them of such vital importance, that, in the same year in which Mather's answers to the Thirty-two Questions were prepared, he drafted an extensive essay on that basal compact of a Congregational church — the covenant. This essay, so Richard Mather's son Nathanael records, "he wrote for his

[1] *Church-Government and Church-Covenant Discussed*, p. 57.

private use in his own Study, never intending, nor indeed consenting to its publication ";[1] but, three thousand miles from convenient printing, it was not easy for New England ministers to control their manuscripts, and four years after this private investigation was written, it appeared in England, printed probably from a copy lent to his ministerial neighbor, John Cotton,[2] with a title-page which declares it to be " an answer to Master Bernard "—that is, to Rev. Richard Bernard of Batcombe, an earnest Puritan, but a no less earnest opponent of the Congregationalism which, years before, under the influence of John Robinson, he had been almost persuaded to embrace. And, as if to make the title still more erroneous, the work, as published, bore on its face, *An Apologie of the Churches in New England for Church-Covenant.* It is a close-knit argument, written in popular style, to prove " that a company [of Christians] becomes a Church, by joyning in Covenant."[3] But this leads ultimately to the question: " Doth not this doctrine blot out all those Congregations [of England] out of the Catalogue of Churches "?[4] to which Mather replies, as nearly all early New England divines did, by denying the existence of a National Church in the home land, but at the same time affirming that the parishes of England, by their union for various acts of worship, their baptismal vows,

---

[1] Preface to the *Disputation Concerning Church-Members*, p. 7.
[2] *Ibid.*   [3] *Apologie*, p. 5.   [4] *Ibid.*, p. 36.

and other similar agreements, were congregations actually bound together by a real, though implicit and imperfect covenant, and hence were true, though imperfect, churches.[1] And, finally, he replies to the possible objection that a covenant was not taught by the founders of New England before their emigration from their native land by asserting that " some of us when we were in England, through the mercie of God, did see the necessitie of Church-Covenant; and did also preach it to the people amongst whom we ministred, though neither so soone nor so fully as were meete "[2] — a statement which we have already seen was true regarding Cotton in his Lincolnshire parish.[3]

Mather bore his personal part also on other occasions in the great debate regarding the constitution of the Church into which the civil war threw England. The New England Congregationalists felt that the battle was their own as truly as that of their Puritan brethren who remained in the home land; and they felt an added interest in defending and championing their own system against the Presbyterian critics who were dominant in the Westminster Assembly, and were there formulating the creed, ritual, and organization of the English Church, as men fondly believed, for all time. As a contribution to the questions at issue, and impelled by a meeting of the ministers of

[1] *Apologie*, pp. 36–41.
[2] *Ibid.*, p. 44. [3] *Way of the Congregational Churches Cleared*, p. 20.

New England held at Cambridge, Mass., under the moderatorship of John Cotton and Thomas Hooker in September, 1643, where some incipient signs of Presbyterianism in the New England colonies were frowned upon,[1] Richard Mather united with his friend William Tompson of Braintree in what was entitled *A Modest and Brotherly Answer to Mr. Charles Herle, his Book against the Independency of Churches*.[2] This was a brief and vigorous reply to a tract with the descriptive title, *The Independency on Scriptures of the Independency of Churches*, then recently published [3] by Charles Herle, who was at the time of this interchange of pamphlets the rector of that Winwick where Mather went to school as a boy, and was soon to be also the Prolocutor of the Westminster Assembly itself. Samuel Rutherford's important critique of Congregationalism, *The Due right of Presbyteries*, which appeared the same year that Mather's reply to Herle was printed, drew forth from Mather an answer published in 1647, to be followed by the even more elaborate refutations by Thomas Hooker and John Cotton printed the next year. Mather's own method of conducting debate was extremely courteous for that age, when religious controversy was too often an interchange of opprobrious epithets:[4]

"As for bitternesse of spirit and tartnesse of contests," said

[1] Winthrop, ii., p. 165 ; Walker, *Creeds and Platforms*, pp. 137-139.
[2] London, 1644.   [3] London, 1643.
[4] *A Reply to Mr. Rutherford*, " Epistle Dedicatory," p. v.

he, "I never thought that to be Gods way of promoting truth amongst brethren. . . . For those that give apparent Testimonies that they are the Lord's, and so that they must live together in heavens, I know not why they should not love one another on earth, what ever differences of apprehensions may for the present be found amongst them in some things."

The services to the cause of New England Congregationalism just considered were personal and self-initiated, however fully representative the books described may have been of the general beliefs and practices of New England. But the labors at which we shall now glance were of a more public and delegated nature. First in point of time to attract our attention is Mather's conspicuous share in the production of what is usually known as the *Bay Psalm Book*. That translation grew directly out of the general Puritan conviction, shared and intensified by the fathers of New England, that nothing should find place in the public service of song but the lyrics of the Scriptures. The version of the Psalms in general use in England at the time that the Puritans came to New England was that prepared by Thomas Sternhold, John Hopkins, and others, then generally bound with the Prayer Book. It had seemed too inexact a rendering to the scholarly "teacher" of the London Congregational church, Henry Ainsworth, in his exile in Amsterdam; and, in 1612, he had published a version that the Pilgrim Fathers brought with them across

RICHARD MATHER

the Atlantic, which was in use at Plymouth for seventy years, and was also employed at Salem and elsewhere. But even this careful paraphrase did not seem to the founders of New England a sufficiently literal and uninterpolated version of the inspired words. Anxious to secure the most faithful rendering possibly consistent with such remaining concessions to English meter as usableness in song absolutely required, a number of Massachusetts ministers undertook, in 1639, a new translation.[1] Chief among them were Richard Mather, Thomas Welde, and John Eliot, the missionary to the Indians. The result was the publication from the newly established press at Cambridge in 1640 of the *Whole Booke of Psalmes*—a volume which enjoys the distinction of being the first book printed in the English colonies. Mather's share in it was conspicuous. Besides his contributions to its versions, he prepared the Preface, and therein announced the object of the work to be: "Rather a plain translation then to smooth our verses with the sweetness of any paraphrase." Probably the resulting compositions were as melodious as essentially unpoetic men could be expected to produce under the severe limitations of a faithful translation; yet the result was far enough removed from what modern taste would approve. The rendering of the twenty-third Psalm shows the work at fully its average height of merit:

[1] See Mather, *Magnalia*, i., p. 407.

" The Lord to mee a shepheard is,
    want therefore shall not I
He in the folds of tender grasse,
    doth cause me downe to lie :

" To waters calme mee gently leads
    Restore my soule doth hee :
he doth in paths of righteousnes
    for his names sake leade mee ; "

while selections like the following from the fifty-first Psalm reveal the more laboring side of the attempt to be at once literal and singable:[1]

" Create in mee cleane heart *at* last
    God : a right spirit in mee new make.
Nor from thy presence quite me cast,
    thy holy spright not from me take.

" Mee thy salvations joy restore,
    and stay me with thy spirit free.
I will transgressors teach thy lore
    and sinners shall be turned to thee."

But the standards of our own age are not those of another, and if successive editions of a volume are any test of merit, this laborious translation possesses ample claims to regard, for it was in popular use in New England for more than a century, and even obtained a considerable foothold in Scotland and England; while its editions number at least seventy.

Already so identified with the exposition and the furtherance of Congregationalism in New England, it was but natural that, when the Congregational churches

[1] Compare Tyler, *History of American Literature*, i., p. 276.

undertook to formulate their polity in a united declaration, Mather should have a large share in the work. That time came with the gathering of the Cambridge Synod in 1646. New England men had, from the first, been ready to give a reason for their practices, but the meeting of the Westminster Assembly made a united presentation of principles more than ever desirable.[1] That body, it was well known, was preparing a confession of faith, an order of worship, and a pattern of church government, which, if approved by Parliament, would be the legal standard of England and Ireland; and might readily be extended to the American colonies. The majority in the Assembly were well known to be *jure divino* Presbyterians. And, besides this danger of forcible interference with New England institutions by Parliamentary action from without, there were not a few critics of Congregationalism in New England itself, some opposing its limitation of access to the Lord's Supper to professed disciples of Christ; others finding cause of complaint in its restriction of baptism to the children of church members; still others dissenting from any baptism of children at all; or opposing its reference of church acts ultimately to the votes of the membership. These critics made no secret of their readiness to appeal to the now Presbyterianly inclined

[1] The Cambridge Synod is discussed with a good deal of fullness in Walker, *Creeds and Platforms*, pp. 157-237.

Parliament of England, if necessary, for forcible interference with the exclusive supremacy of the "New England way." It was high time that the polity, and, if necessary, the creed of New England should be clearly defined; and, therefore, on May 15, 1646, the Massachusetts legislature called on all the churches in the various Congregational colonies to meet, on September 1st, at Cambridge for a synod. Into the details of the doings of that body there is no need for us here to enter. The essential point for our notice is that it decided to define the polity of New England, and appointed Richard Mather of Dorchester, John Cotton of Boston, and Ralph Partridge of Duxbury each to prepare tentative drafts of Platforms for submission to the synod's consideration. It was not till its third session, in August, 1646, that the synod came to a full discussion of these suggested outlines of polity; but at that time, Mather's draft was preferred, and though largely amended, and reduced to half its original size, by the synod, the *Cambridge Platform* is his work. Mather did not, indeed, write all sections anew. In its composition he made large use of what he and Cotton had already written on Congregational government. Perhaps Cotton wrote, or revised, some sections of the *Platform* as finally adopted; but the work was essentially Mather's.

It was the natural consequence of this authorship that the Massachusetts ministers, in 1651, appointed

Mather to answer the criticisms of the *Platform*, which had been referred to them by the Legislature. Of the *Platform* itself time will scarcely permit us to speak. Interest in it is, indeed, now historic rather than practical, but it remains the most valuable monument of Congregationalism as it lay in the minds of the first generation after nearly twenty years of experience on New England soil. Its basal principle, that " the partes of Church-Government are all of them exactly described in the word of God;" and " that it is not left in the power of men, officers, Churches, or any state in the world to add, or diminish, or alter any thing in the least measure,"[1] we few of us hold ; but had not the men of that age believed it with all intensity of conviction there would have been no New England. We may read with curious eyes its chapters on the duties of pastors, teachers, and ruling elders, on the maintenance of church officers, on the power of magistrates in ecclesiastical matters; but though here and there the *Platform* is as archaic in practice as it is everywhere in expression, one leaves it with the conviction that it sets forth with the utmost plainness the abiding features of Congregationalism.

In Mather's original draft of the *Cambridge Platform*, but omitted by the synod because of the strenuous opposition of a few, was a paragraph declaring that [2]

---

[1] Chapter i., sec. 3.
[2] Walker, *Creeds and Platforms*, p. 224.

"such as are borne in ye ch: as members, though yet they be not found fitt for ye Lords Supper, yet if they be not culpable of such scandalls in Conversation as do justly deserve ch: Censures, it seemeth to vs, w^n they are marryed & have children, those their children may be recd to Baptisme."

The quotation gives us a glimpse into the most serious controversy which disturbed the first century of New England religious life — that over the Half-Way Covenant.[1] It was one in which Mather bore a conspicuous share, and to the decision of which in the way it was settled by the first and second generation on New England soil he powerfully contributed. The question involved in the Half-Way Covenant debate has often, but wholly erroneously, been declared to be political. None but church members, it is said, were allowed to vote — a statement true of Massachusetts till 1664, and in a modified degree till 1684, and of New Haven colony till 1665, but never of Plymouth or Connecticut. It was to increase the voting list — it has been affirmed — that an easier method of entrance into church fellowship was sought. But the controversy raged as hotly in Connecticut and Plymouth as in Massachusetts, and naturally so, for the question was in fact purely religious, and Half-Way Covenant membership brought with it no political privileges, and its ecclesiastical privileges did not include

[1] The controversy is described with considerable fullness in Walker, *Creeds and Platforms*, pp. 238-339.

a vote in churchly concerns. It was a perplexing and embarrassing problem; but its essential point was not, how shall the State enter the Church, but how shall the Church retain control of its wandering sons and daughters.

The early New England theory of the Church made the rise of the Half-Way Covenant discussion inevitable. That theory held that only evident Christians, of well-tested intellectual faith and spiritual experiences, conscious of the transforming power of God in their own lives, could enter into the covenant which constituted the local Church. But this covenant, like that with Abraham of old, was made, so early Congregationalism held, not with the believer alone, but with his children. Hence there were two ways of entering a church; by profession of personal faith and repentance, and by birth. But how about the member by birth who when grown to manhood could not honestly claim any consciousness of a work of God's Spirit in his own soul, yet was faithful in prayer and worship and in parental government ? Was he a member still ? And, if he was, could he not bring his own children to baptism ? And, if he was not a member, when, or by what act on his part, did he cease to be one ? When had the Church ceased to owe him watch and discipline ?

To the solution of this difficult question Mather early directed his attention. In his first considerable treatise on Congregational polity, the answer to the Thirty-Two Questions,[1] written, it will be remembered, in 1639, Mather, indeed, took the ground that

" Such Children whose Father and Mother were neither of them Believers, and sanctified, are counted by the Apostle (as it seemes to us) not fæderally holy, but uncleane, whatever their other Ancestors have been, (1 *Cor.* 7. 14). And therefore we Baptise them not."

But by 1645, when Mather wrote an elaborate, but unfortunately never published, exposition of Congregational polity,[2] he had advanced to the position thus expressed by question and answer:[3]

" When those that were baptized in Infancy by the Covenant of their Parents being come to Age, are not yet found fit to be received to the Lords Table, although they be married and have Children, whether are those their Children to be baptized or no."—" I propound to Consideration this Reason for the *Affirmative, viz.* That the Children of such Parents ought to be baptized: the Reason is, the Parents as they were born in the Covenant, so they still continue therein, being neither cast out, nor deserving

[1] *Church-Government and Church Covenant Discussed,* p. 22.

[2] Increase Mather says (*Life and Death of* . . . *Richard Mather,* p. 84) that Richard Mather " prepared for the Press an Elaborate Discourse Entituled, *A Plea for the Churches of New England,* divided into two Parts : *The former being an Answer to Mr.* Rathbands *Narration of Church-Courses in* New-England ; *The other containing Positive Grounds from Scripture and Reason, for the Justification of the Way of the Churches in New England.*"

[3] This bit, the only portion in print, as far as I am aware, of the treatise described in the above note, is given in Increase Mather, *First Principles,* pp. 10, 11 ; see also Walker, *Creeds and Platforms,* p. 252.

so to be, and if so, why should not their Children be baptized, for if the Parents be in Covenant, are not the Children so likewise?"

In the view indicated by this quotation Mather remained all the rest of his life; and he had with him an ever-growing proportion of the New England ministry, for to him, and to others, it seemed that to abandon this hold upon the young people, and recognize no church membership in those " born in the covenant " who were yet not conscious disciples of Christ was to surrender them to heathenism. Passed by at the Cambridge Synod, where, if pushed to a vote, it would undoubtedly have received the support of a majority, it aroused increasing discussion, and was apparently first put in practice at Ipswich in 1656. But, by that time, Connecticut was so aroused on the subject that, as a result of legislative action in May of that year, a list of twenty-one questions was sent by Connecticut to the Massachusetts legislature, which promptly called a Ministerial Convention, to meet at Boston on June 4, 1657, and invited all the colonies to be represented;—an invitation willingly accepted by Connecticut, ignored by Plymouth, and vigorously declined by New Haven as likely to lead to the approval of the new and looser method. Mather's name is the first in the list of the thirteen ministerial representatives appointed by Massachusetts,[1] and his hand drafted the

[1] *Records of* . . . *Mass.*, iv., part i., p. 280.

conclusions in which the Convention summed up the results of the fifteen days of discussion.[1] The tract is a dialectically acute, clear, and often forcible document,[2] setting forth with the utmost distinctness the position that those who were of the Church by reason of their parents' covenant were so far members, even in the absence of any conscious work of grace in their own hearts; that they could, in turn, present their children for baptism, provided they themselves gave an intellectual assent to the faith of the Church and seriously assumed its covenant obligations, as far as they were able in their unconverted estate. It also made equally evident the view of the Convention that such half-way members, so long as they remained without personal religious experience, should not be admitted to the Lord's Supper or to a vote in church affairs.

Here was a radical departure from the early New England theory in the direction of the " parish way " of old England. It was a departure which ultimately worked great harm; but it was entered on by good men in all earnestness of pastoral solicitude. The Ministerial Convention did not, however, abate the discussion in Massachusetts or Connecticut, and so

[1] Dexter, *Cong. as Seen*, Bibliography, p. 287. The original is in the library of the American Antiquarian Society at Worcester.

[2] It was printed at London in 1659, under the title of *A Disputation concerning Church-Members and their Children in Answer to XXI Questions;* large extracts are given in Walker, *Creeds and Platforms*, pp. 291–300.

energetically was it carried on, that in December, 1661, the Massachusetts Legislature ordered a Synod of all the churches of that colony to meet at Boston on March 11, 1662,[1] to " consider of such questions . . . for the setling of peace and trueth in these churches." To this peremptory call some seventy ministers and delegates responded. The Dorchester church was represented by its pastor, Richard Mather, and his gifted youngest son, Increase.[2] It was a stormy and strenuously contested session; but when the battle was over, the views which we have seen Richard Mather championing in the Convention of 1657 were reaffirmed by a vote of seven to one; yet that minority contained the able president of Harvard, and two of Mather's own sons, Eleazer and Increase. Richard Mather did not this time draft the result of the Synod; but it was not in a Mather to withhold his pen, and in the controversies that followed he was as active in defense of the decision as his sons were in opposing it. Yet I am not aware that this division of view made any separation between the Mathers, however unseemly such contrariety in public debate may appear; and within a few years, even before his father's death, Increase Mather so altered his opinions that he was speedily the foremost defender of the principles which he attacked at the synod.

[1] *Records of . . . Mass.* iv., part ii., p. 38.
[2] *Records First Church, Dorchester*, p. 39.

This division of sentiment suggests the fact that, though Richard Mather could be a leader of conventions and synods, he could no more control the action of his own church on this point than regulate the views of his own family. As early as March, 1655, Mather's church had begun to debate the matter; but it had then " seemed strange and unsaffe unto Divers ";[1] and the debate had dragged on.[2] Mather acquainted the church with the doings of the Synod, and made plain his own wishes, but a New England church was then no more the unthinking servant of its minister than it now is, and it was not till January 29, 1677, more than seven years after Mather's death, that his church voted to practice what he had advocated.[3]

Mather's church was not divided on this issue. He seems to have been too good a pastor to force his views, however strongly held, on what was after all a minor and not vitally essential feature of ecclesiastical practice, to the point of open quarrel in his flock. But not all the churches of New England were as fortunate as his. The First Church in Boston, for example, was rent on the issue. Its majority was strenuously opposed to the larger baptism, and called that eminent champion of the older ways and opponent of the late Synod's conclusions, Rev. John Davenport of New Haven, to its vacant pastorate in 1668. Its minority,

[1] *Records First Church, Dorchester*, p. 164.
[2] *Ibid.*, pp. 34-36, 40, 55, 168.   [3] *Ibid.*, pp. 69-75.

favoring the larger practice, and not approving some of the methods and circumstances of Davenport's call, withdrew, after a bitter struggle on the part of the majority to retain them, and repeated advice from councils, to form the Third, or Old South, Church in Boston.[1] In these councils, and in the attempts to find an honorable and peaceable solution of the disagreement, Mather bore his full share. It was at the second of these advisory councils, where he was serving as Moderator, on April 16, 1669, that Mather was seized with the distressing malady which six days later ended his earthly pilgrimage.[2] His brief illness, though of much suffering, was of much patience; and the one burden on his heart was a pastoral lament strikingly consonant with his long advocacy of the Half-Way Covenant, and curiously illumined by what we have seen as to the refusal of his church to adopt it. To his son, Increase, who asked a last message, the dying man said:[3]

" A special thing which I would commend to you is, care concerning the rising generation in this country, that they be brought under the government of Christ in his church, and that when grown up, and qualified, they have baptism for their children. I must confess I have been defective as

---

[1] For this controversy see H. A. Hill, *History of the Old South Church, Boston*, i., pp. 13-112 ; *Records First Church, Dorchester*, pp. 54, 58.

[2] The stone, with total stoppage. See Increase Mather, *Life and Death of . . . Richard Mather*, pp. 78-80. He died April 22, 1669.

[3] *Ibid.*, pp. 79, 80.

to practice; yet I have publickly declared my judgment and manifested my desires to practice that which I think ought to be attended; but the dissenting of some in our church discouraged me. I have thought that persons might have right to baptism, and yet not to the Lords Supper: and I see no cause to alter my judgment, as to that particular."

We may believe the remedy which he commended for the laxity of the young people of his time a bad one; but we cannot doubt the absolute sincerity of conviction with which he approved it.

So passed away, at the ripe age of seventy-three, one of the most useful ministers of early New England. Not so brilliant as Cotton or Hooker, he was a strong, learned, simple, practical, impressive man, a good companion, a helpful associate, and above all a lover of Congregationalism, because he believed it the way of the Scriptures. He died rich in the possession of five sons, four of them eminent in the ministry; rich also in the grateful recollection of many services well done not only for his day and generation, but for the development of the branch of the Kingdom of God whose interests he made his first care.

JOHN ELIOT

IV.

JOHN ELIOT

ANYONE who glances over a general catalogue, such as is issued by Andover Seminary, must be struck first of all by the number of names of those who, while faithful servants of God in their generation, have left little record among men. Few of us can expect even a line in the biographical cyclopædias of a century hence. It is to that truer and more perfect record of those whose names are written in heaven that we, most of us, must look for whatever memorial is to abide of the fact that we have lived and labored for the advancement of the Kingdom of God. But, among the comparatively limited number of names which arouse recollection as of historic moment as one turns the pages of such a catalogue as I have mentioned, a few seem to exhale a peculiar fragrance that inclines the reader to linger on them with special regard. As one glances through the list of those connected with Andover in the first three years of its existence, what pictures of consecration, of sacrifice, and of endeavor the names of Adoniram Judson, Samuel Newell, Gordon Hall, and Samuel J. Mills conjure up before the mental vision! The Church proves that it has never lost the consciousness of that primal apostolic commission in this, if in no other, way, that it feels a special thrill of satisfaction as it contemplates the lives of its missionaries. Its Pauls, its Columbas, its Xaviers, its Careys, its Pattesons stand forth to grateful recollection radiant with a peculiar charm which attaches to none of its dogmaticians, teachers, or administrators. So among the founders of New England, the name of John Eliot, known since 1660 as the " apostle,"[1] draws forth remembrances of the most winsome aspects of Puritan character, and shines with a luster distinctly its own among the leaders of early Congregationalism.

John Eliot was the son of a yeoman, or middle-class farmer, Bennett Eliot, a man of considerable property, whose home was at Nazing, county of Essex — some sixteen miles almost directly north of London.[2] But though Nazing was John's boyhood home, the fact that he was baptized at Widford, some ten or twelve miles yet farther northward of London, on August 5, 1604, in the church of St. John Baptist, commemorated in Charles Lamb's well-known poem, *The Grandame*, makes it probable that Widford was his birthplace, since our modern fashion of delayed baptisms did not

[1] So first named by Thomas Thorowgood, see Dr. Ellsworth Eliot in Appleton's *Cyclopædia of American Biography*, ii., p. 321.

[2] See *N. E. Hist. and Geneal. Register*, xxviii., pp.140-145.

obtain in the England of that day. Widford, moreover, was the place of the marriage of his parents, October 30, 1598.[1] Of his boyhood and early education we know little. Cotton Mather has preserved a single remark of Eliot's that shows his thankfulness in old age for the memories of a religious home;[2] but whatever its degree of religious vigor, the spiritual life of his parents' home would not appear to have inclined to Puritanism, for, in March, 1619, he entered Jesus College at Cambridge instead of the warmly Puritan Emmanuel College of that University. While a student here his father died, and left him £8 a year for the prosecution of his education.[3] And here Eliot graduated a Bachelor of Arts in 1622. What next employed his thoughts we do not know; but it would appear probable that he was ordained a minister of the Church of England. Our first definite glimpse of him after his graduation, however, is seven years later, at the close of 1629, or the beginning of 1630, when we find him assisting Rev. Thomas Hooker, afterward eminent among the founders of Connecticut, in teaching a school kept by Hooker for a few months at Little Baddow,[4] a country village about thirty miles northeast of London.

[1] See *N. E. Hist. and Geneal. Register*, xlviii., p. 80.

[2] *Magnalia*, i., p. 529.

[3] Buried November 21, 1621; will, November 5, 1621; *N. E. Hist. and Geneal. Register*, xxviii., p. 145; Dr. Ellsworth Eliot, as cited.

[4] *Magnalia*, i., p. 335.

The circumstances which had compelled Hooker[1] to establish this school were typically illustrative of the religious state of England. Thomas Hooker had graduated at Emmanuel in 1608, and after further study and service as catechist and lecturer at his *alma mater*, had exercised a ministry of some years at Esher, a hamlet of Surrey, till, in 1626, his fame as a preacher led to his appointment as Puritan lecturer at Chelmsford. These lectureships were a favorite device of the more earnest Protestants of the opening years of the seventeenth century to secure a preaching ministry in parishes where the legal incumbent was unable or unwilling to give sermons to his people. Supplementary services were conducted, occasionally with the full approval of the legal rector, by ministers of sermonic ability, supported by the gifts of sympathetic hearers. And from his Chelmsford pulpit Hooker preached a deep, searching, spiritual, intensely Calvinistic and powerfully awakening series of discourses that won him the support of the more earnest element of the region round about. But Laud viewed the lectureship system as one of the chief bulwarks of Puritanism, to the extirpation of which he had set himself. In spite of the favorable petition of a large portion of his beneficed clerical neighbors, Hooker was silenced in 1629; and, as a means of earning his livelihood, took scholars into his family in the quiet retreat of Little Baddow. Even this

[1] See G. L. Walker, *Thomas Hooker*, pp. 18-51.

JOHN ELIOT

occupation could not shield Hooker from Laud, and in order to escape imprisonment, or worse, he had to flee the country, finding refuge in Holland before the close of 1630.

Eliot's experiences as Hooker's " usher," or assistant, in the Little Baddow school were therefore brief; but short as the time of this association was it was permanently influential in his religious life. As Eliot himself later said of his sojourn in Hooker's household:[1]

" To this place I was called, through the infinite riches of God's mercy in Christ Jesus to my poor soul: for here the Lord said unto my dead soul, *live ;* and through the grace of Christ, I do live, and I shall live forever! When I came into this blessed family I then saw, and never before, the power of godliness in its lively vigour and efficacy."

Eliot's conversion evidently made him fully a Puritan, if he had not been so before; and he seems to have entered into an agreement with friends,[2] some of whom were from his home village of Nazing, to be a pastor to them if possible in the New World. He doubtless felt that the opposition which drove his friend and spiritual father, Thomas Hooker, into exile would make it impossible for him to exercise an efficient ministry in England. Accordingly, leaving his " intended wife " to follow him,[3] he sailed in the *Lyon*,

[1] *Magnalia*, i., p. 336.

[2] See his own statement in *Roxbury Church Records*, in *Report of the Record Commissioners*, City of Boston, *Document 114*, p. 76. [3] *Ibid.*

and, after a voyage of ten weeks' duration, landed at Boston, November 4, 1631.[1]

The time of Eliot's arrival in Boston was opportune. The teacher of the Boston church, John Wilson, had sailed for a temporary sojourn in England in April previous, and the Boston congregation gladly welcomed Eliot's services. Eliot himself became one of its members, and on Wilson's return, in 1632, the Boston church urged upon Eliot with insistence the position of association in its pastorate which was a year later bestowed on John Cotton.[2] Eliot felt himself bound to his English friends, some of whom had settled at Roxbury, where a church had been formed in July, 1632, of which Rev. Thomas Welde had been made pastor. On the call of this church in the November following its organization, just a twelvemonth after his arrival in Boston, Eliot entered on the office of "teacher" at Roxbury, which he was to occupy for more than fifty-seven years.[3] He had already gone to Roxbury to live some months before his settlement, for the first marriage recorded in that place is that of Eliot, on September 4, 1632, to Hanna Mumford, the betrothed bride who had followed him from England, —a woman of remarkable abilities and consecration of spirit, a true helper to him in his life work, of whom

[1] Winthrop, i., pp. 76, 77, 80.
[2] *Ibid.*, i., p. 111. He was offered the teachership.
[3] *Ibid.*; *Roxbury Church Records*, p. 76.

he could say, as she lay in her coffin after fifty-five years of companionship, that she was a " dear, faithful, pious, prudent, prayerful wife."[1] Indeed, it was to her careful management of his worldly affairs that Eliot owed whatever measure of outward comfort — a very moderate measure be it said — that he attained. Like Jonathan Edwards or Nathanael Emmons after him, he believed business cares incompatible with the ministerial office, and so absurdly divorced himself from all concerns in his own property, that he did not even know his own cattle as they stood before his study window.[2] Fortunately for him his wife was competent to supply his deficiencies in household economics.

But, however indifferent to his own pecuniary welfare, as a pastor Eliot gave himself unsparingly to his people. His long ministry was not unaided. From his settlement in 1632 to 1641, Thomas Welde was his associate, and indeed his superior in public repute, as was natural for one older in years and in ministerial experience. From 1649, till death removed him in 1674, Samuel Danforth was Eliot's younger colleague; and in 1688, near the close of Eliot's long life, Nehemiah Walter was installed by his side; but the enumeration of these bare names and dates shows how large a portion of pastoral labor came to Eliot's constant share. Whatever honor is his as a missionary, it should not

[1] *Magnalia*, i., p. 529. [2] *Ibid.*, i., p. 538.

be forgotten that he was always a pastor, and that the great toils which his missionary service brought him were in addition to the strenuous duties of a parish. No man could have endured such labors had he not been blessed, as was Eliot, with good health, and that basis of good health, a cheerful disposition.[1] The expressions of this temperament which have been recorded sound a good deal like cant to our time, when direct religious allusions fall so seldom from our reluctant lips; but they did not sound so then, nor did they so impress the men of early New England. On the contrary, they admired his " singular skill of raising some *holy observation* out of whatever matter of discourse lay before him."[2] Thus, as he climbed wearily up the hill to his meeting-house, Cotton Mather records that he said to the man on whose arm he leaned:[3] " This is very like the way to heaven, 't is uphill," and glancing at a bush by the wayside, he instantly added, " and truly there are thorns and briars in the way, too." The same capacity to draw a lesson from every-day occupations is shown in his remark to a man of business whose account books he saw on the table, while the religious books were in a case against the wall:[4] " Sir, here is earth on the table, and heaven on the shelf; let not earth by any means thrust heaven out of your mind." But perhaps Eliot's constant sweetness and kindliness of temper, as well as his transparent

[1] *Magnalia*, i., p. 532. [2] *Ibid.* [3] *Ibid.*, i., p. 533. [4] *Ibid.*, i., p. 534.

fidelity to fact, most appears in his elaborately kept church records, from which I quote but a single entry, illustrative of the spirit of many others. Eliot is noting the death of a member of his Roxbury parish:[1]

"William Chandler he came to N. E. aboute the yeare 1637 . . . he lived a very religious & Godly life among us, & fell into a consumption, to w^h he had bene long inclined, he lay neare a yeare sick, in all w^h time, his faith, patiens, & Godlynesse & contentation so shined, y^t Christ was much gloryfied in him, he was a man of weak p^{ts}, but excellent fath & holyness, he was a very thankfull man, & much magnified Gods goodnesse, he was pore, but God so opened the hearts of his naybe to him, y^t he never wanted y^t w^h was (at least in his esteeme) very plentifull & comfortable to him; he dyed . . . in the yeare 1641, & left a sweet memory & savor behind him."

The man who penned such records as these cannot have been other than a good pastor, nor can anyone doubt what interests he placed first.

Eliot's charity to the poorer members of his flock was unfailing, and far out of proportion to his means as charity is ordinarily bestowed even by the generous. The story is told that one of the officers of the Roxbury church, knowing Eliot's freedom in gifts, on one occasion tied up the portion of his salary paid to him firmly in a handkerchief lest the pastor should part with any of it before reaching home. On his homeward way Eliot visited a family in distress, and as the

[1] *Roxbury Church Records*, p. 83.

pastoral call lengthened his eagerness to aid increased, till, fumbling in vain at the knots that he could not loosen, he at last handed the handkerchief and all its contents to the mother of the household with the exclamation: " There, there, take it all. The Lord evidently meant it all for you."[1]

Eliot's public prayers had a directness almost as marked as those of President Finney. When Captain William Foster of Charlestown and his son Isaac, later pastor of the First Church in Hartford, were captured by the Mohammedans on a voyage in 1671, and it became known to their friends that the ruler of the territory where the Fosters were slaves — probably some part of Algiers — had declared that he would never let his captives go, Eliot prayed:[2]

" Heavenly Father, work for the redemption of thy poor servant Foster; and if the prince which detains him will not, as they say, dismiss him as long as himself lives, Lord, we pray thee to kill that cruel prince; kill him, and glorify thy self upon him."

And this prayer his congregation believed they saw answered in the speedy death of the piratical ruler and the release of the captives. So, too, Eliot spoke out freely in prayer that love of schools which made Roxbury eminent, under his care, for its excellent instruction. At the Reforming Synod of 1679, he uttered the petition:

[1] 1 *Coll. Mass. Hist. Soc.*, x., p. 186.
[2] For these illustrations, see *Magnalia*, i., pp. 544, 551.

"Lord, for schools everywhere among us! That our schools may flourish! That every member of this assembly may go home, and procure a good school to be encouraged in the town where he lives! That before we die, we may be so happy as to see a good school encouraged in every plantation of the country."

No picture of Eliot would be true that did not recognize another trait, at least of his old age; — he made the impression of being an old-fashioned man. I suppose every age has looked back on its predecessor, sometimes with truth, as a time of simpler faith and more strenuous habits. It does, indeed, seem odd enough to the eye of the modern reader, to see the page which Governor Bradford wrote in the rude settlement of Plymouth, half-wrested from the wilderness, where, after describing the plain garb of one of the Congregational confessors of his early youth, he asks,[1] "What would such professors, if they were now living, say to the excesses of our times?" The question is wellnigh as old as humanity. But, undoubtedly, Eliot seemed to the men of the third generation on New England soil kin to a simpler, as he certainly was to a more heroic, age. His great moderation at the table was noticeable even in those days of plain living; his strict observance of the Sabbath, and his careful preparation for it, were remarked as unusual even in that age of Puritan strenuousness;[2] and Cotton

[1] Dialogue, in Young, *Chronicles of the Pilgrims*, p. 447.
[2] *Magnalia*, i., pp. 535, 538.

Mather, whose full wig showed his conformity to the supposedly becoming fashions of his age, records that such was Eliot's preference for the natural and unsupplemented covering of the head, which the Puritan custom of the Roxbury teacher's youth had preferred, that " he would express himself continually with a boiling zeal " at sight of examples of what he deemed a heaven-provoking excess.[1] But Eliot was no intolerant bigot; on the contrary, few in New England at that day would have shown the charity that he did, in 1650, in inviting a visiting French Jesuit missionary, Gabriel Druillettes, to spend the winter as an inmate of his house.[2]

Eliot's interest in public and ecclesiastical concerns was always marked. His share in the preparation of the *Bay Psalm Book* of 1640 has already been pointed out in treating of Richard Mather. But regarding his more ambitious attempts to suggest an improved organization of political and religious society it is no dishonor to his memory to suggest that an undue insistence on the permanent and binding authority of the institutions of the Jewish state, and a want of any considerable degree of statesman-like insight into the conditions of the political life in which his lot was cast, rendered his speculations more curious than valuable. This is conspicuously true of his tract on government,

[1] *Magnalia*, i., p. 540.
[2] Palfrey, *History of New England*, ii., p. 308. See *ante* p. 41.

published, in 1659,[1] at London, under the title of *The Christian Commonwealth*, though written seven or eight years earlier.[2] In this essay he lays down the basal principle[3] that

"the Lord Jesus will bring down all people, to be ruled by the Institutions, Laws, and Directions of the Word of God, not only in Church Government and Administrations but also in the Government and Administration of all affairs in the Commonwealth."

The organic rule for the appointment of civil officers he finds in Exodus xviii. 25; and from that passage he deduces the principle that rulers of tens, of fifties, of hundreds, of thousands, of ten thousands, of fifty thousands, and so on should be appointed, each with judicial and administrative authority over his subdivision; and that each, together with the officers of the next grade immediately under him, should constitute a court of justice — the lowest court being that of the ruler of tens, the next higher being that of the ruler of fifties, together with the five rulers of tens included in his fifty, and so on till over all the " Chief Ruler," chosen by the people, and assisted by his " Supreme Council," was reached. Of this reconstructed state the Bible was to be the sole statute book. The plan

[1] J. H. Trumbull, *Brinley Sale Catalogue*, No. 570.

[2] See *Records of* . . . *Mass.*, iv., part ii., 6. The whole tract is reprinted in 3 *Coll. Mass. Hist. Soc.*, ix., pp. 127-164.

[3] *Christian Commonwealth*, Preface.

was fantastic enough as applied to a country of complex social organization and ancient political traditions like England, though Eliot carried it out as far as possible in the regulation of the political affairs of his Indian converts. But the Massachusetts government, anxious for its own liberties which were imperilled by the restoration of the Stuarts, condemned the book in May, 1661, and ordered its suppression "as justly offencive . . . to kingly government in England."[1] Eliot expressed his disavowal of certain expressions in the book that seemed to reflect on the restored monarchy in a manly letter,[2] which speaks the tone of sincerity.

But though Eliot might renounce the full application of his theories to civil affairs, he was much enamored of his plan of subdivisions and graded courts therein outlined, so that, in 1665, he printed his *Communion of Churches*, in which he carried very similar principles over to the realm of ecclesiastical affairs. Perhaps his experiences with the Massachusetts legislature already narrated inclined Eliot now to caution, for the volume was not published, and is accounted the first "privately printed American book."[3] In this tract Eliot proposed that every twelve churches should unite in a "first council," composed of pastors and delegates, and meeting once a month at least; twelve "first councils" should, in turn, send a chosen pastor and a

[1] *Records of . . . Mass.*, iv., part ii., p. 5.   [2] *Ibid.*, p. 6.
[3] J. H. Trumbull, in *Brinley Sale Catalogue*, No. 760.

delegate to a quarterly " provincial council "; twelve " provincial councils " should in the same way send representatives to a yearly " national council," and twelve " national councils" might be represented in the same fashion in an " œcumenical council," the deliberations of which might be conducted in Hebrew.[1] It is needless to say that this fanciful outline of church polity found as scanty acceptance as Eliot's proposed reconstitution of civil government. He could not have done the work of Thomas Hooker or of John Cotton.

Eliot's fame rests on none of the publications just described, but primarily on his labors as a missionary, though as a pastor he would well have deserved commemoration had he never preached to the Indians. The thought of labor for the Indians of the New World did not originate with Eliot. To say nothing of the missionary efforts of the Spaniards to which all America from California southward bears witness to this day, or of that bright page of heroism and sacrifice which French Jesuits wrote as the chief glory of the early history of Canada, the English colonists, both of Pilgrim and of Puritan antecedents, had it as one of their main aims in coming to America to carry

[1] I have taken this epitome from Dexter, *Cong. as Seen*, pp. 509, 510. Eliot would provide for fractions by counting each group of more than twelve and less than twenty-four, as twelve ; a device that had already appeared in his *Christian Commonwealth*, where, for instance, a " ruler of ten " may rule over any number from ten to nineteen.

the Gospel to the native inhabitants. But no systematic plan had been adopted for so doing, and the task of founding homes in the new country proved of such difficulty that little attention could be given at first to the Christianization of the Indians. The language, moreover, was a formidable barrier, and even more the dissimilarity of thought between a civilized and a barbarous race. The Indians were accessible with difficulty save on the side of trade; to go among them, to become acquainted with them in any sense that would render an Englishman familiar with their thoughts, and permit the impartation of religious truth, implied days and nights in filthy wigwams, loathsome fare, and deprivations not merely of the comforts but of the decencies of life, such as few, however willing to make the sacrifices involved in setting up a home in the new land, cared to undergo. The Puritans from the first treated the Indians with consideration and tried to protect them by law. In spite of the short, sharp struggle with the Pequots in 1637, New England feeling did not turn strongly upon the Indians as a race to be guarded against, as against the wolf and the lynx, till after the outbreak of Philip's War in 1675. But the two peoples were apart, mutually misunderstanding each other, and finding any terms of intercourse difficult save those on the level of the exchange of the skins of the beaver and the otter, for the cloth, the knives, the kettles, and too often the muskets and the rum, of newcomers to New England soil.

The first New Englander who made protracted and successful effort to master the language of the Indians of eastern Massachusetts was that eccentric, opinionated, yet in many ways far-seeing and devotedly Christian man, Roger Williams.[1] As early as 1632, it would appear that Williams had begun to acquire an Indian vocabulary. On this task he labored while ministering at Plymouth, and he continued the work after his removal to Salem, so that by the time of his settlement at Providence in 1636, after his banishment from Massachusetts, he had a considerable command of the dialects of the tribes of the region — a linguistic acquaintance which proved of great value to the colonies, as a whole, in the negotiations consequent upon the Pequot war the year following. The fruit of these studies was the publication, in 1643, of Williams's *Key into the Language of America*, a word and phrase list, principally in the Narragansett dialect, that is our best monument of the colloquial speech of the aboriginal inhabitants of southeastern New England. Williams's purpose in all this labor was to carry the Gospel to the Indians; but though he preached to them, as he tells his readers, many hundred times, and not without results, he did not undertake systematic missionary work in the exec-

[1] See the Preface, by J. Hammond Trumbull, to Williams's *Key into the Language of America*, in *Publ. Narragansett Club*, i.

utive and organizing spirit that the situation demanded for any permanent success.[1]

Now it was just this patient, persistent, consecrated endeavor that Eliot gave. Just what circumstances induced him to undertake his work among the Indians it is hard to say. The time was not blind to the missionary duty, for on November 13, 1644, the Massachusetts legislature had directed the county courts to see to it that the Indians in their several jurisdictions were " instructed in ye knowledge & worship of God."[2] Henry Dunster, the first president of Harvard, had been interested in efforts for the Indians certainly since 1641.[3] Some instances of the conversion of Indians had already occurred and had been narrated in *New Englands First Fruits*, published in 1643. But there is no reason to question Eliot's own belief, whatever earthly causes may have conduced to the result, that " God first put into [his] my heart a compassion for their poor souls and a desire to teach them to know Christ and to bring them into his Kingdom."[4] His first step in preparation was the reception into his household of a young Indian servant, who had acquired some knowledge of English, that by his aid he might

[1] In 1674 Daniel Gookin wrote : " God hath not yet honored him [Williams], or any other in that colony [Rhode Island] that I can hear of, with being instrumental to convert any of the Indians."—Palfrey, *Hist. N. E.*, ii., 195, 196.

[2] *Records of* . . . *Mass.*, ii., p. 84.

[3] Lechford, *Plaine Dealing*, pp. 152, 153.

[4] Quoted by A. C. Thompson, *Protestant Missions*, p. 57.

JOHN ELIOT

master the dialect of the Massachusetts tribe.[1] By this help the Lord's Prayer and the Ten Commandments were translated; and Eliot was ready to begin his missionary work.

His first attempt, of which we know little, appears to have been discouraging. About the middle of September, 1646, he sought out some Indians under Chutchamaquin in Dorchester; but they showed little interest in his message, and asked him questions as to the cause of thunder, the nature of the tides, and the source of the wind, instead of those more spiritual interrogations which he hoped to awaken.[2] But Eliot was not discouraged and soon repeated his missionary efforts in another quarter; this time with success.

An account of those beginnings, probably from the pen of Rev. Thomas Shepard, of Cambridge, was printed in London in 1647,[3] and though very familiar, is of such interest and importance that I shall not hesitate to quote freely from it.

It was " upon October 28, 1646," the narrative states, that " four of us " went to Waaubon's wigwam, at Nonantum, in the northern part of what is now

[1] Eliot, *Indian Grammar*, p. 66.

[2] *The Day-Breaking*, p. 3 (see following note).

[3] The story of this first missionary undertaking is told in *The Day-Breaking, if not the Sun-Rising of the Gospell with the Indians in New-England*, London, 1647. Dr. J. H. Trumbull ascribed its authorship to Shepard, *Brinley Sale Cat.*, No. 445 ; Palfrey thought the author Rev. John Wilson of Boston, *Hist. of New England*, ii., p. 191 ; and it has been attributed to Eliot himself, though page 18 of the tract shows that this is incorrect.

Newton, and " found many . . . Indians, men, women, children, gathered together," at Waaubon's invitation. In their hearing Eliot, or one of his companions, began the work with prayer, " which now was in English, being not so farre acquainted with the Indian language as to expresse our hearts herein before God." Then Eliot, using the scarce familiar speech of the Massachusetts aborigines, preached " for about an houre and a quarter "—a time none too long for the contents of the sermon for the narrative records that

" he ran through all the principall matter of religion, beginning first with a repetition of the ten Commandments, and a briefe explication of them, then shewing the curse and dreadfull wrath of God against all those who brake them . . . and then preached Jesus Christ to them the onely meanes of recovery from sinne and wrath and eternall death, and what Christ was, and whither he was now gone; and how hee will one day come againe to judge the world in flaming fire; and of the blessed estate of all those that by faith beleeve in Christ . . . the creation and fall of man, about the greatnesse and infinite being of God, . . . about the joyes of heaven, and the terrours and horrours of wicked men in hell, perswading them to repentance for severall sins which they live in, and many things of the like nature; not medling with any matters more difficult."

Questions being asked for at the end of the sermon, the four companions felt that six queries that were propounded by their Indian auditors were so serious and pertinent as to indicate some special directing influence of God. The first inquiry was that fundamental question, "How may wee come to know Jesus Christ?" To which Eliot answered that such knowledge came by reading or hearing the Word of God, by meditation, and by prayer. This last-named suggestion led to the query, " Whether Jesus Christ did understand, or God did understand, Indian prayers"; to which Eliot gave the only answer possible to a Christian, that " Jesus Christ and God by him made all things, and makes all men, not onely English but Indian men, and if hee made them both . . . then hee knew all that was within man and came from man. . . . If hee made Indian men, then he knows all Indian prayers also." Next came that query, so often asked of missionaries the world over, and so difficult to answer: " Whether English men were ever at any time so ignorant of God and Jesus Christ as themselves?" To this Eliot replied " that there are two sorts of English men, some are bad and naught . . . and in a manner as ignorant of Jesus Christ as the *Indians* now are; but there are a second sort of English men, who though for a time they lived wickedly also . . . yet repenting of their sinnes, and seeking after God and Jesus Christ, they are good men now." The remaining questions had to do with the nature of idols, the possibility of the acceptance by God of the good son of a bad father, and the peopling of the world after the Deluge.

I have entered thus fully into an account of this first meeting because it shows the type of preaching of these missionaries. Nor was it without speedy results. On November 28th, after a third meeting had been held at Waaubon's wigwam, some of his dusky hearers came to Eliot's house, confessing their sins, and offering their children for Christian education,[1] and Waaubon himself was reported to have begun the practice of prayer.

Eliot did not confine his efforts to these spiritual instructions alone. Like more modern missionaries in Central Africa or the Pacific islands, he felt that civilization and education must go hand in hand as inseparable companions with evangelization. At this first meeting the Indians had asked him that land be assigned them for a permanent town.[2] That request, seconded by Thomas Shepard of Cambridge and John Allin, the minister at Dedham, who were probably two of Eliot's three companions in his Nonantum visit, the Massachusetts legislature granted about a week after the missionary sermon just described, the purpose being " for ye incuragm^t of ye Indians to live in an orderly way amongst us."[3] At the same time the Massachusetts legislature practically became the first missionary society in the English colonies, directing the ministers to choose two of their number

[1] *Day-Breaking*, pp. 19, 20.
[2] *Ibid.*, p. 7.   [3] *Records of* . . . *Mass.*, ii., p. 166.

JOHN ELIOT 159

annually to labor among the Indians, and promising assistance in the work.[1] Six months later—May, 1647 —the legislature voted Eliot £10 " in respect of his greate paines & charge in instructing ye Indians in ye knowledg of God."[2] So generally interested were the ministers in the work that, on the occasion of the second session of the Cambridge Synod in June, 1647, Eliot preached in its presence, in their own language, to a large concourse of Indians.[3] Contributions began to come in from Puritan sympathizers in England. One donation had, indeed, anticipated Eliot's work, that of Lady Armine, a granddaughter of the Earl of Shrewsbury, who had given £20 a year as early as 1644, for the evangelization of the Indians — a sum which the Massachusetts legislature in May, 1647, appropriated to Eliot's enterprise.[4]

So strong was the interest excited in England by the printed accounts of these missionary beginnings, that, on July 19, 1649, less than six months after the execution of King Charles I., the Long Parliament passed an act incorporating the first English foreign missionary society, under the name of the " President and Society for the Propagation of the Gospel in New

[1] *Records of . . . Mass.*, ii., pp. 178, 179.
[2] *Ibid.*, ii., p. 189.
[3] Winthrop, ii., p. 376.
[4] See *Some Correspondence between the Governors and Treasurers of the New England Company*, etc., p. ix., London, 1896; also *Records of . . . Mass.*, ii., p. 189.

England," with power to hold lands to the yearly value of £2000, and the right to collect money throughout England and Wales.[1] The response amounted to the then unprecedented sum of £11,430, and the Society which thus came into being continues to the present day, though its principal labors since the war of American independence have been confined to Canada. This Society made the Commissioners by which the four Congregational colonies of Plymouth, Massachusetts, Connecticut, and New Haven were represented in the loose political confederacy in which they had been joined since 1643, its direct agents in superintending the work. By 1658 the Society was spending £520 a year in New England, of which Eliot received £50, as his salary.[2] That year the Society paid £190 for the education of nine Indian young men at Roxbury and Cambridge, and, besides the stipend to Eliot, seven inhabitants of New England of English parentage and seven Indians were paid, in 1658, for various forms of missionary labor.[3] All this activity implied wide interest in the work on the part of the people of England and of New England alike; but it was not without its vigorous opponents in both lands, as useless, resultless, and a waste of money needed for religious effort at home.

[1] See *History of the New England Company*, etc., pp. 1, 2, London, 1871; Palfrey, *History of New England*, ii., pp. 197-199.
[2] Palfrey, ii., pp. 332, 333.
[3] *Ibid.*

JOHN ELIOT

I have already pointed out that, with Eliot, Christianity, civilization, and learning were inseparably united, and that, at the beginning of his missionary endeavor he sought to gather his converts into a town on the English model. But Nonantum, where this settlement was first made, proved unsuitable, and therefore, in July, 1650, a more ambitious village was begun at Natick. Here houses were built, chiefly by Indian labor, gardens and orchards planted, and a combined schoolhouse and meeting-house erected. For the government of the little community the Indians were encouraged to choose, in 1651, rulers of tens, of fifties, and a ruler of a hundred; a pattern of civil government which, as we have already seen, Eliot urged upon England a little later as that prescribed by the Scriptures. Here, after long testing, a church was established, on the Congregational model, in 1660, which numbered fifty Indian members by 1674, and to which Eliot preached, while his health permitted, once in two weeks, though before the close of his life, it came under the charge of a native Indian pastor.[1]

Eliot felt keenly the need of education for the spiritual training of his disciples, and there is no more self-denying or more successful endeavor in the annals of American missionary labor than that he made to give to his pupils the Word of God. Save for the

---

[1] *Magnalia*, i., pp. 564–566; Palfrey, ii., pp. 336, 338, iii., p. 141. See also, *A Late and Further Manifestation*, pp. 1–6. London, 1655.

phrase-book of Roger Williams, the Indian dialects of New England were unwritten; their structure was peculiarly difficult from a grammatical point of view; their literature was wholly to be created. That one who was all his New England life a busy pastor of an English-speaking congregation, and, also, from 1646 onward, an active evangelist among the Indians not only at Nonantum and Natick but over a wide stretch of the eastern portion of Massachusetts, should find time also for such an immense labor in the study of the vocabulary, grammar, and idioms of the Massachusetts dialect, and for so prolific and creditable publication of translations into that tongue, is one of the marvels of missionary accomplishment. How he strengthened himself for such toil, he expressed in one of his volumes in a phrase that gives the key to his industry and courage: "Prayers and pains through faith in Christ Jesus will do anything."[1] And what Eliot accomplished as a translator alone constitutes a monument of which any scholar might be proud.

His first work in the Indian language was a Catechism which he published in 1654.[2] It enjoys the distinction of being the first volume in the Indian tongue to be printed in New England; though, unhappily for the collector, every copy has disappeared. But the volumes

[1] *Magnalia*, i., 562, from Eliot's *Indian Grammar*.

[2] Dexter, *Cong. as Seen*, Bibl., 1661. Was it the Catechism used at Roxbury, June 13, 1654, and printed in English in *A Late and Further Manifestation*, pp. 11-20?

on which Eliot's fame as a translator chiefly rests were his New Testament of 1661, and his complete Bible of 1663. I can, of course, express no personal estimate of the qualities of this version. So utterly has the Massachusetts race and its speech perished from among men, that few are able to read Eliot's Bible; though probably it is not quite true to say, as used to be said during the lifetime of the late Dr. J. Hammond Trumbull, that only he could do so. But Dr. Trumbull,[1] whose competency as a judge no one will criticise, affirmed regarding Eliot's Bible that it was

" a marvellous triumph of scholarship; achieved in the face of difficulties which might well have appeared insurmountable. It may be doubted if, in the two centuries which have elapsed since the Indian Bible was printed, any translation of the sacred volume has been made from the English to a foreign tongue of more literal accuracy and completeness. If a different impression has been popularly received, slight study of the Indian text will suffice to remove it."

It was deemed the great honor of William Carey that he was the translator of the Bible into the languages of India; can we give Eliot less meed of praise?

Eliot's Indian Bible was only the beginning of a series of translations and publications in the Indian speech. Bound up with the volume was a translation of the Psalms in meter. The year 1664 saw the

[1] Trumbull in *Pub. Narragansett Club.*, i., pp. 6, 7; see also regarding this Indian literature, Trumbull's chapter in *Memorial History of Boston*, i., pp. 465 *sqq.*

putting forth by Eliot, in Indian dress, of Baxter's *Call to the Unconverted;* in 1665, a translation of Bishop Bayly's *Practice of Piety* was issued; in 1666 there followed Eliot's *Indian Grammar Begun;* and, in 1669, his *Indian Primer;* the year 1680 saw a second edition of the New Testament, and in 1685 of the whole Bible; and, finally, in 1689, Eliot put forth a translation of Shepard's *Sincere Convert.* These volumes were printed at the New England Cambridge, and chiefly, if not entirely, at the expense of the English Society, which thus supplied Christian literature, as well as tools and other material instruments of civilization to the Indian converts.[1] Of course this literature demanded instruction in reading; and therefore Eliot made the schoolmaster as prominent as the minister in his Indian settlements.

It is evident that a movement of such widespread interest as that in which Eliot was a leader could be confined to no one portion of New England. He was indeed the foremost always in leadership and service; but many others were associated with him, or entered independently into the missionary enterprise moved by the secret promptings of the Divine Spirit. Of these the most conspicuous, perhaps, were the two Thomas Mayhews, father and son, of Martha's Vineyard. There the work had begun, almost without

---

[1] For an example of some expenditures of the Society, see *N. E. Hist. and Geneal. Register*, xxxvi., pp. 297-299.

effort, in 1643, by the awakening of Hiacoomes, one of the leading Indians; and in 1646, the same year that Eliot began his work at Nonantum, the younger Mayhew commenced systematic efforts for the Christianization of his Indian neighbors.[1] After the death of this missionary the undertaking was carried on by his father, and in turn by his son, grandson, and great-grandson, till the demise of the latter in 1806, making this record of five generations the longest chain of hereditary endeavor in the annals of missions.[2] This labor on Martha's Vineyard and Nantucket was remarkably successful. By 1651 Mayhew could report one hundred and ninety-nine converts, and in 1670, a church was formed on Martha's Vineyard,[3] that was soon followed by several others on the islands of this group. In all this work the same English Society that aided Eliot lent its assistance from 1651 onward. Other, though smaller centers of activity developed on Cape Cod, at Marshpee, where a church was formed under Richard Bourne about 1670,[4] and at Eastham, where Rev. Samuel Treat long labored for the spiritual good of the Indians.[5] At Plymouth, the pastor of the old Pilgrim church from 1669 to 1697, John Cotton,

---

[1] See Mayhew's letter in *A Farther Discovery of the Present State of the Indians*, pp. 3-13. London, 1651.

[2] A. C. Thompson, *Protestant Missions*, p. 87.

[3] *Magnalia*, ii., p. 431.

[4] *Ibid.*, i., p. 567.

[5] Sibley, *Graduates of Harvard*, ii., pp. 305-307.

son of the more famous John, did much for the Indians, and helped to revise Eliot's Bible for its second edition.¹ Branford, in Connecticut colony, saw some work for its Indian inhabitants by its pastor, Abraham Pierson, father of the first president of Yale.² Eliot's own immediate mission grew, so that by 1654 a second town, on the plan of Natick, was organized at Punkapog, now known as Stoughton.³ And he had the assistance of consecrated and self-denying men, like Daniel Gookin, whom the Massachusetts government made, from 1656 to 1687, the "ruler" or superintendent of its Indian subjects.⁴ Eliot had the satisfaction, before his death, of seeing that his work would be carried on by those in the New England ministry who were in hearty sympathy with it, like Grindall Rawson of Mendon, and Samuel Danforth of Taunton.⁵

The missionary endeavor was crowned with undeniable success. In spite of its difficulties, by 1674 those Indians who had been brought in some measure under the influence of the Gospel, or "Praying Indians" as they were called, numbered four thousand, of whom nearly one half were on the islands of the

¹ Sibley, i., pp. 496–508; *Magnalia*, i., p. 568.
² Palfrey, ii., p. 340.
³ *Late and Further Manifestation of the Progress of the Gospel*, p. 2. London, 1655.
⁴ Palfrey, ii., p. 338.
⁵ Sibley, iii., pp. 163–168, 244–249.

Martha's Vineyard group.[1] About eleven hundred were in Eliot's villages. They were gathered into six churches, numbering in all one hundred and seventy-five members, and in at least twenty places preaching and schools were regularly maintained, chiefly by educated Indians. The villages of the "Praying Indians" numbered thirty-three. But the stronger tribes of southern New England, the Narragansetts and Wampanoags, were scarcely touched by Christianity, and probably wholly misunderstood the intentions of the missionaries.[2] They probably conceived the purpose of settlements like those at Natick and Marshpee as an attempt to render more formidable the white man's tribe by the familiar Indian method of the adoption of weaker neighbors; and doubtless the fear thus excited in these stronger Indian confederations had something to do with bringing on the terrific struggle for the possession of southeastern New England, known as Philip's war. That awful experience of murder, fire, and robbery cost New England six hundred men in 1675 and 1676 — to say nothing of the complete or partial destruction of more than forty towns. It cost the Indians far more, and permanently removed the Indian menace from southern New England. But it was a staggering blow for the missionary enterprise.

[1] Palfrey, iii., pp. 141, 142 ; see Eliot's report for 1673 in 1 *Coll. Mass. Hist. Soc.*, x., 124. The churches were Natick, Grafton (Hassanamisitt), Marshpee, Nantucket, and two on Martha's Vineyard.

[2] See Fiske, *Beginnings of New England*, pp. 208-210.

168   *JOHN ELIOT*

While most of the converts remained faithful to the English, and some, like those on Martha's Vineyard, were even trusted to guard captives of their own race, many of those who had come merely into external connection with the missionary movement went back to their savage companions, and some even of the converts vied with their heathen associates in the cruelties which they inflicted on the settlers. Even those of Eliot's disciples who remained faithful, as most of them did, were regarded with such suspicion that they were compelled to leave their villages and live under the surveillance of the colonial authorities.[1] And when the war was over there remained a bitter and often undiscriminating feeling of resentment that rose against every Indian as a natural enemy. Yet the work went on. Eliot, Gookin, Mayhew, and their associates faltered not; and, had it been the war alone that hindered, Indian missions in New England would have suffered only a temporary check. As late as 1698, more than twenty years after the war, Rawson and Danforth could report seven churches of Indians, and twenty stations where preaching was maintained and schools were taught. Before Eliot died in 1690, twenty-four Indians had been ordained to the Gospel ministry. His own first colony of Natick was under the pastorate of a devoted convert, Tackawompbait, who served the spiritual interests of the community

[1] Palfrey, iii., pp. 199-202, 220.

JOHN ELIOT 169

till death came in 1716; and some traces of this work of Indian evangelization, especially on Cape Cod and Martha's Vineyard, continued till far into the nineteenth century.

But it was a dying race for which Eliot labored, and even the Gospel could not greatly check its decline. Devoted as the missionaries were, the story of these Indian churches is one of rapid decay — a decay not owing to a spiritual exhaustion, but to the fading away of the Indian race itself. From Philip's war onward it rapidly dwindled, its decrease being well illustrated in the story of Natick, where the population of Eliot's time diminished to one hundred and sixty-six in 1749, to about twenty in 1797, and in 1855 to one.[1] From the standpoint of permanency it must be confessed that Eliot's work has not endured the test of time; but its failure was not due to any inherent lack of spiritual power; and I suspect that the historian, two hundred years in the future, who writes the story of the missions of the nineteenth century, will have much the same tale to narrate of that success of the Gospel in the islands of the Pacific in which our fathers saw the hand of God almost visibly displayed, and whose real power and significance no passing slurs by politicians anxious to assert the authority of a stronger race can wholly obscure. Like Eliot's, it is a work for a dying race; and like his, its only permanent record will

[1] 1 *Coll. Mass. Hist. Soc.*, x., p. 136; Bacon, *Hist. of Natick*, p. 21.

probably be in that book of those whose names are written in heaven. But was it less worth doing? Only he who values a soul at less than the Master's estimate can answer in the negative.

Eliot's life was long, far beyond that of any other conspicuous in the founding of New England. Cotton died at sixty-seven; Richard Mather at seventy-three; Hooker was sixty-one; Davenport was seventy-two. Eliot had nearly reached eighty-six when death came on May 20, 1690. He saw the passing away of the generations who were the leaders in his early manhood and the companions of his maturer years so completely as to come to remark, with that cheerful humor that never deserted him, that " his old acquaintances had been gone to heaven so long before him that he was afraid they would think he was gone the wrong way because he stayed so long behind." But, happily, he did not see the fatal decline of the mission work in which he had been so long engaged. He " was shortly going to heaven " he would say in his last days; " he would carry a deal of good news thither with him . . . to the old founders of New England, which were now in glory."[1] And the taking down of the mortal house, timber by timber, so trying an experience oftentimes in old age, was for him a kindly process. Infirmities crept upon him. But, as late as 1687, he was able to preach to the Indians perhaps once in two

[1] *Magnalia*, i., p. 579.

months;[1] and when weakness would no longer permit even this labor, his strong missionary spirit turned toward some effort for the despised negro slaves,— for Massachusetts had slavery in those days,— and he gathered those of his vicinity once a week for catechetical and spiritual instruction.[2] As the sands of the glass of his life ran out, and he was confined to his house, so that even this endeavor was beyond his powers, he took the blind son of a neighbor into his own home, as Cotton Mather says, " with some intentions to make a scholar of him."[3] It is a fitting picture that the worn-out missionary presents to us in his last days, seated by the fireside in his Roxbury home, teaching a crippled boy to repeat by heart that Bible which he had long before translated with such diligent fidelity into the Indian tongue. And we may well leave him there, with his own characteristic remark to those who asked him " how he did " ? " My understanding leaves me, my memory fails me, my utterance fails me; but, I thank God, my charity holds out still."[4]

[1] Letter of Increase Mather, *Magnalia*, i., pp. 566, 567.
[2] *Magnalia*, i., p. 576.
[3] *Ibid.*, i., pp. 576, 577.
[4] *Ibid.*, i., 541.

INCREASE MATHER

V.

INCREASE MATHER

THE leaders of Congregationalism whose lives and services we have thus far considered may all be said to have belonged to the generation of the founders. They were called away from their work by death at very different periods, it is true. Eliot survived Cotton — to take the extreme illustrations which are afforded by the four men at whom we have glanced — by more than thirty-seven years. Yet all four were born and trained in England, all were exiles for beliefs embraced while still in the mother country, and all were pioneers in some feature or other of New England's origins. All of them felt, in their various ways, the glow and the enthusiasm of the work in which they were engaged; and all looked back with fondness of recollection to that English home of their youth, as a land in whose struggles they had a personal and a permanent interest.

The man to whose career we shall turn our attention to-day shared, indeed, many of these traits of the founders; but he was unlike them in much also. Born in New England, educated in the New England schools, he was a true son of the New England soil. And strong as was his attachment to the ways of the founders, his work was cast in a more provincial, less heroic age, when the great religious impulse which had made New England possible had largely spent its fever, and the land had reached the rather humdrum status of an isolated colonial existence. We love to study the genesis of countries and of institutions; and I presume most of us turn by preference to the beginnings of New England rather than to what we deem the more prosaic annals of its second and third generations. Yet so conspicuously was the subject of our present lecture the leader and the epitome of his own age, so gifted was he in talents, so serviceable was he to the Congregational churches, and so fully does he deserve the description, "the greatest of the native Puritans,"[1] that few men in New England history are more worthy of the careful attention of the student of Congregationalism than Increase Mather.

Increase Mather was born on June 21, 1639, in that home in Dorchester into which we have already glanced in considering the career of his father, Richard. Popular tradition represents Puritan names as Biblical or fantastically religious to a degree not true of them in general. If one looks over a list of Puritan emigrants or a catalogue of early church members, one finds it made up chiefly, in reality, of the Williams, the Johns,

[1] Wendell, *Cotton Mather*, p. 287.

the Edwards, the Henrys, the Richards, the Thomases, in which Anglo-Saxon parents have delighted certainly since the Norman conquest. But occasionally you will meet an odd exception, and the child whose story we are beginning received his name, we are told, "because of the never-to-be-forgotten *Increase*, of every sort, wherewith GOD favored the Country, about the time of his Nativity."[1] The boy whose name was thus bestowed was the youngest of six children,— all sons,— five of whom grew to maturity, and four of whom entered the ministry, doing service of much more than ordinary conspicuity. The household atmosphere into which he was ushered, that subtle environment which determines for so many of us what we are to be, made the path of scholarship and of Christian service easy for him. His father's character and studious habits we have already considered; and his mother had no lower ideals for her boy. "Child," she was wont to say to him, "if GOD make thee a Good Christian and a Good Scholar, thou hast all that ever thy Mother Asked for thee."[2] The mother's desires for his scholarship were early fulfilled, for, at the age of twelve, the son entered Harvard.

The college of which he became a member was, indeed, already an honor to New England; but it was a

---

[1] Cotton Mather, *Parentator: Memoirs of Remarkables in the Life and the Death of . . . Increase Mather*, p. 5. Boston, 1724.
[2] *Ibid.*, p. 3.

tiny plant as compared with what it has since become. Founded by the Massachusetts legislature in October, 1636, by an appropriation—£400—not now adequate to endow a first-class scholarship, and encouraged two years later by the gift of John Harvard, it graduated its first class in 1642. It was a monument to the desire of the leaders of New England colonization to perpetuate a learned ministry, and no portion of their work is more remarkable than this early endeavor to reproduce the educational institutions of the home land. The college when Increase Mather entered was under the able presidency of Henry Dunster, who was compelled to resign on account of Baptist opinions, when the young student was half-way through his course, and was succeeded by Charles Chauncy, under whom Mather graduated in 1656. Its further instruction was conducted by two or three tutors or "fellows" taken from its recent graduates.[1] While the class of 1653 had reached the high-water mark of seventeen, only one graduated in 1654, two in 1655, and eight in Mather s own class of 1656. The one college building was already in a " ruinous condition," and the president's salary was largely in arrears; while the " fellows" had to divide £12 between them as their compensation.[2] Students were admitted, as has already been noted, when "able to understand *Tully*, or

[1] Quincy, *History of Harvard University*, i., p. 273.
[2] *Information of 1655*, *Ibid.*,i., p. 463.

such like classicall Latin Author *ex tempore*, and make and speake true Latine in Verse and Prose . . . and decline perfectly the Paradigim's of *Nounes* and *Verbes* in the *Greek* tongue."[1] Once matriculated in the college each student was required to attend prayers " in his Tutors chamber " at seven in the morning and five in the afternoon, there not merely to worship, but to give an account of his further study of the Scriptures twice a day in private. Any student under age was liable to corporal punishment for infractions of the college discipline. Monday and Tuesday were days of lectures and discussions in Logic, Physics, Ethics, Politics, Arithmetic, Geometry, and Astronomy, for the various classes. Wednesday was devoted to Greek. Thursday was spent on Hebrew, Chaldee, and Syriac. Friday was the time for Declamations. Saturday was devoted to catechetical and expository instruction in Theology, and to History and Botany.[2] The students boarded in commons, and so simple and frugal were the habits of the time that the total expense, aside from books and clothing, of the entire four years in college of those who graduated between 1653 and 1659 was from $100 to $200. Even this modest sum was usually paid in corn, malt, wheat, beef, eggs, cider, sheep, or some other commodity of the home farm rather than in coin.[3]

[1] Sibley, *Graduates of Harvard*, i., p. 11.
[2] *Ibid.*, pp. 11-14. [3] *Proc. Mass. Hist. Soc.*, p. 60. 1860.

In Mather's case, however, his residence at Harvard was interrupted by ill-health, and probably half his college course, if not more, was pursued in the household and under the instruction of that ablest dialectician among the early New England ministers, Rev. John Norton, at first at Ipswich, and then at Boston, where Norton succeeded Cotton in the care of the First Church.[1] Here at Boston, and in Norton's home, occurred, in 1654, the spiritual turning-point in Increase Mather's history. That experience was strenuous enough. Illness had laid its hand on the fifteen-year-old boy, and turned his thoughts Godward; but a sense of his own sinfulness overcame him. He prayed, he fasted, he wrote out a catalogue of his particular offenses; but he felt no peace of mind. He feared that he "Was Guilty of the Unpardonable Sin." At length in his distress the boy made use of the absence of his fellow pupils from Norton's house on election day, in a way that he later described in the following words:[2]

"I took this Opportunity of a Private Chamber; and shutting the Door, I spent all the Day, in Pouring out my Complaints unto the Lord. Towards the Close of the Day, being full of Extremity of Anguish in my Soul because of my Sin, it was put into my Heart, that I must go and throw myself down at the Feet of my Saviour, and see

[1] *Parentator*, p. 6.
[2] *Ibid.*, pp. 7-12; Chandler Robbins, *History of the Second Church . . . Boston*, pp. 18-19.

whether He would Accept of me, or no; . . . So I came before Him with those Words of *Esther*, *If I Perish, I Perish, Yet*, (I said) *Lord, if it must be so, I am resolved to Perish at the Feet of thy Mercy. It is true, I am a Dog, and indeed unworthy of so much as a Crumb; I have been a great Sinner; Yet I am resolved, I will not Offend any more, but be Thine, and be Thine only, and be Thine forever.* And while I was thus Praying and Pleading, those Words of CHRIST were darted into my Mind, *Him that cometh unto me I will in no wise Cast out.* . . . After that I had some *Comfortable Perswasion* that my Sins were Pardoned."

But the poor boy's hard-won peace of mind was soon shaken, for Norton preached a sermon in which he advanced the view often inculcated by the founders of New England, and notably by Thomas Hooker, "That a man might *Forsake* his Sins, and have been in some *Sorrow of Heart* for them, and yet not be *truly Converted* unto GOD." That was a staggering thought, and it was not till he had heard other sermons, from his father and from the "matchless" Jonathan Mitchell, that comfort came to him at last. Nor was there anything unusual in this intensity of struggle, this sense of guilt, or this self-distrust even in a schoolboy. We have already observed something similar in the case of others whose story we have considered. The preaching of early New England taught it as the normal mode of entrance into the Kingdom of God, and represented not merely that the path of conversion was difficult and open to but few, but that it was surrounded by pitfalls of self-deception, which only the most rigid scrutiny of the motives and intents of the heart could guard against.

Graduation came in 1656, and on his eighteenth birthday, in 1657, Mather preached his first sermon.[1] But the favor shown to New Englanders by Cromwell made the home country very attractive to Harvard graduates desirous of a career.[2] Many had gone thither; among them Increase Mather's two older brothers, Samuel, who had settled over an important congregation in Dublin, and Nathanael, who had obtained a living at Barnstaple in Devonshire. At Samuel's invitation, Increase now sailed for England, on July 3, 1657, less than two weeks after the delivery of his first sermon; and, on reaching Dublin, entered Trinity College, where he graduated Master of Arts in 1658.[3] His decided pulpit gifts brought him into notice, and the succeeding winter was spent by Mather in supplying the congregation left temporarily vacant at Great Torrington by the absence of its pastor, John Howe, on chaplain's duty at the court of Richard Cromwell. The spring of 1659 saw his appointment, at less than twenty years of age, as garrison chaplain on the island of Guernsey, a post which he held till the Restoration made it untenable in March, 1661. The young preacher was popular.

[1] *Parentator*, p. 15.
[2] See letter of Nathanael Mather, March, 1651, in Sibley, i., p. 157.
[3] *Parentator*, pp. 15-17.

He was urged to conform, as some of his fellow graduates of Harvard had done. A living of £400, at least four-fold any salary he could hope for in New England, was offered him; but his conscience would not allow him to use the Prayer Book, and on June 29, 1661, he left England, surprising his father by his unheralded arrival in the Dorchester home on August 31st, and his father's congregation by preaching to them the next morning.[1] A sermon before the Second Church in Boston a week later was followed by a call to its charge; but the young minister's deliberations were distracted by invitations from eleven other congregations,[2] and by the strongly cherished hope that the political situation in the home land would permit him to resume his ministry there, so that it was not till May 27, 1664, that he was ordained, by his father, Richard Mather, and his colleague, Rev. John Mayo, to the teachership of the Second, or, as it was generally called, the North, Church in Boston, which was to be his post of influence till his death, fifty-nine years later. The site of this meeting-house, now North Square, is in the densely populated foreign section of modern Boston, where Puritan or even Anglo-Saxon occupants of ancient days have scarcely left a trace behind; but under Mather's leadership, it was then the most largely

[1] *Parentator*, pp. 17–23.
[2] *Ibid.*, pp. 23, 24; Chandler Robbins, *Hist. of the Second Church*, pp. 21, 22.

frequented place of worship in the little colonial seaport.

While Increase Mather was debating this call, he had his first experience of public service for the churches, being sent by his father's church at Dorchester as a delegate to the Synod of 1662, where the Half-Way Covenant was approved, as has already been described in narrating the life of Richard Mather. It will be recalled that the youthful delegate opposed the result reached by the majority, and defended by his father; but on the point at issue he speedily changed his mind, and, certainly from 1671 onward, there was in New England no more devoted champion than Increase Mather of the rather dubious spiritual expedient for benefiting the young which the Synod had approved and he had originally opposed.[1]

It was in this time of waiting, also, on March 6, 1662, that Increase Mather married his stepsister, Mary, daughter of John Cotton, whose widow, the mother of the bride of twenty years of age, had married his father, Richard Mather. She bore him ten children; and when death took her from him, in his old age, after fifty-two years of life together, he married, in 1715, the widow of her nephew, the third to bear the name of John Cotton in the New England ministry.[2]

[1] Though Increase Mather's *First Principles of New England Concerning the Subject of Baptism* was printed in 1675, its Preface is dated 1671.
[2] Sibley, *Graduates of Harvard*, i., p. 437.

But, though settled over a growing church, the early years of his ministry were a trying time for the young teacher and his household. As we have already seen was the case with his father, serious religious doubts, even to the extent of questioning the existence of God, assailed him. His ill-paid salary, in the earlier years of his ministry, left him under a constant burden of anxiety by reason of debt. " I could be Content to be *Poor*, I care not how *Poor*," he wrote in his journal; " But to be *in Debt*, to the Dishonour of the Gospel, is a *Wounding, Killing* Thought to me; Yea, so Grievous as that if it be not Remedied, in a little time it will bring me with Sorrow to my Grave."

But as time went on his spiritual perplexities vanished, and the increase of his congregation under his successful ministry, together with the generosity of a few friends, at length placed him in circumstances of pecuniary comfort.[1]

As a pastor Increase Mather was most laborious; though we should probably think as some did in his own day, disproportionately devoted to his study rather than to the visitation of his flock. But Mather always believed the pulpit the seat of ministerial power, and he made most elaborate preparation for its duties. His son Cotton records,[2] that sixteen hours of the twenty-four were usually devoted to mental labor.

---

[1] On these troubles, see *Parentator*, pp. 26–36, and Chandler Robbins, *Second Church*, pp. 29–31.

[2] *Parentator*, p. 181.

"His *Daily Course* was This. . . . In the Morning repairing to his Study, (where his Custom was to sit up very late, even *until* Midnight, and perhaps *after* it) he deliberately Read a *Chapter*, and made a *Prayer*, and then plied what of Reading and Writing he had before him. At Nine a Clock he came down, and Read a *Chapter* and made a *Prayer*, with his Family. He then returned unto the *Work of the Study*. Coming down to *Dinner*, he quickly went up again, and begun the Afternoon with another *Prayer*. Then he went on with the *Work of the Study* till the Evening. Then with another *Prayer* he went again unto his Father; after which he did more at the *Work of the Study*. At Nine a Clock he came down to his *Family-Sacrifices*. Then he went up again to the *Work of the Study;* which anon he Concluded with another *Prayer;* and so betook himself unto his Repose."

It makes one ache with sympathy to think of this Puritan scholar, toiling over his plain desk, by daylight or by the dim light of a candle, without exercise, and with scanty interruption for the necessary food, the laborious round broken only by his frequent and methodical devotions. No wonder that, under the special strain of his father's death, in 1669, he so fell into what Cotton Mather calls " that Comprehensive Mischief which they call *The Hypocondriac Affection*, that," for a time, " his Recovery to any Service, was by many very much Despaired of." [1]

But perhaps you would like to know a little more in detail how Increase Mather mapped out his toilsome

[1] *Parentator*, p. 68.

week. He has left a record of its allotment of time.[1]
On Sundays he preached, and catechised his family.
Monday was dedicated to the study of his coming sermons, with a slight break, devoted to general reading
after dinner. Tuesday saw the sermons continued
through the morning, while in the afternoon he sought
" to *Instruct Personally* some or other"; Wednesday
was again devoted to his sermons and his books; a
labor which was resumed the next morning; though
a respite came on Thursday afternoon by the necessity
of attending, and frequently conducting, the Thursday
lecture, which was then the sole midweek service of
the Boston churches. After the lecture Mather was
accustomed to hold, with the other pastors of Boston
and vicinity, what would now be called a ministers'
meeting. Friday was again spent on the sermons and
in general reading; and Saturday was largely devoted
to memorizing the discourses to which so large a part
of the week had been dedicated, for, though Mather
wrote out all that he preached with painstaking minuteness, he left his manuscript behind him when he went
into the pulpit. His delivery was clear, his strong,
sonorous voice was used with deliberate gravity, and
his manner, though powerfully impressive, was extremely simple and non-oratorical. In the pulpit he
was deemed a master always.

It would be natural to imagine, from what I have

[1] Quoted, *Parentator*, p. 38.

just said, that Increase Mather was a recluse, persuasive in the pulpit, perhaps, but dwelling apart from men, shut away in his study from the concerns of the world about it. No conclusion could be more mistaken. Certain it is that he labored with almost the persistence of a bookworm in the room in which most of his waking hours were spent; but it is equally undeniable that no man in the New England ministry of his day had so great an influence over his professional brethren, the churches that they served, the educational interests that they held dear, or the political fortunes of the commonwealth as Increase Mather, nor could all his weeks have been mapped out like that just recorded. A brief consideration of four or five of the most striking instances of this activity for what he deemed the general good will illustrate the leadership which it was possible for a minister to attain in early New England.

Mather's first conspicuous appearance as the leader of the Massachusetts churches was in connection with the so-called "Reforming Synod" of 1679 and 1680.[1] To a man of his warm spiritual nature, pastoral zeal, and conservative devotion to the ideals of early New England, the spiritual tendencies of the age in which his ministry was cast were distressing. The old Puritan movement had largely spent its force. The

[1] A more minute account of the Reforming Synod and its work is given in Walker, *Creeds and Platforms*, pp. 409-439.

spiritual life of the second New England generation was distinctly lower in vitality than that of its fathers. Men looked back on the years of colonial beginnings with their fresh enthusiasms, their self-sacrifice and their spiritual power as a golden age of better things, and not wholly without reason. The decline was undeniable. Preaching in 1668, for instance, William Stoughton,[1] later Lieutenant-Governor, exclaimed in his election sermon:

"O what a sad Metamorphosis hath there of later years passed upon us in these Churches and Plantations. The first generation have been ripened time after time, and most of them geathred in as shocks of corn in their season. . . . Whilest they lived their Piety and Zeal, their Light and Life, their Counsels and Authority, their Examples and Awe kept us right . . . but now that they are dead and gone, Ah how doth the unsoundness, the rottenness and hypocrisie of too many amongst us make it self known."

Ten years later Increase Mather told his Boston congregation:[2]

"Prayer is needful on this Account, in that Conversions are becoming rare in this Age of the World. They that have their thoughts exercised in discerning things of this Nature have had sad apprehensions with reference to this Matter; that the Work of Conversion hath been at a great Stand in the World."

Nor was it only the decay of active piety that

[1] *New Englands True Interest; Not to Lie*, etc. Cambridge, 1670.
[2] *Pray for the Rising Generation*, etc. Cambridge, 1678.

caused concern. The rough contact with the wilderness lowered the tone of the sons and daughters of the emigrants; the passion for land led the settlers to spread themselves over the country in a way that made education and the maintenance of religious institutions difficult problems. And the eighth decade of the seventeenth century was marked by losses and distresses heretofore unexampled in colonial history. In 1675 and 1676 the struggle known as Philip's war, which we have noted already in treating of Eliot's missionary activities, took its ghastly toll of property and life; in November, 1676, just after this struggle, Boston had its first great fire, Mather's own church and dwelling, together with the section of the town adjacent, being destroyed. This calamitous loss was followed by an even more disastrous fire in the business portion of the chief colonial seaport three years later. Epidemics of smallpox, failure of crops, and shipwrecks added to the general sense of calamity, and, as the Puritan divines interpreted these things, of divine displeasure.[1]

Under these circumstances Increase Mather persuaded eighteen of his ministerial associates, doubtless those assembled at the annual convention then held at the time of the election, to unite with him in a petition to the Massachusetts legislature for a Synod.

---

[1] See Preface to Increase Mather's *Returning unto God . . . A Sermon*, etc., Boston, 1680; and *Magnalia*, ii., p. 316.

The prayer was granted, the summons issued,[1] and on September 10, 1679, the body met at Boston. Though not the moderator at this session, Increase Mather was the life of the assembly. His pen formulated the conclusions, and when those results were presented to the legislature and by it commended to the attention of the churches, his voice preached " a very Potent Sermon, on the Danger of not being *Reformed by these things.*"[2] The pamphlet embodying the Synod's conclusions, known as the *Necessity of Reformation*, is a most interesting witness to the religious state of New England, and to the questions which then awakened pastoral solicitude. Undoubtedly the picture it presents is too somber. It was designed to awaken and alarm. But enough of truth remains after all necessary deductions are made to make one query whether, indeed, the former days were better than these. Besides the general complaints of the " decay of the power of Godliness," pride, contention, intemperance, profaneness, lack of public spirit, untruthfulness, and " inordinate affection to the world," the catalogue of provocations to divine judgment enumerates certain special offenses, some of which, as charged on our ancestors of those supposedly stern and simple days, sound rather strangely.

" Pride in respect to Apparel," the Synod through

[1] *Records . . . of Mass.*, v., p. 215.
[2] *Parentator*, p. 85; *Records . . . of Mass.*, v., p. 244.

Mather[1] declared, "hath greatly abounded. Servants, and the poorer sort of People are notoriously guilty in the matter, who (too generally) goe above their estates and degrees, thereby transgressing the Laws both of God and man. . . . There is much Sabbath-breaking. . . . Walking abroad, and Travelling . . . being a common practice on the Sabbath day, which is contrary unto that Rest enjoyned by the Commandment. Yea, some that attend their particular servile callings and employments after the Sabbath is begun, or before it is ended. . . . There are many Familyes that doe not pray to God constantly morning and evening, and many more wherein the Scriptures are not daily read. . . . Nay, children & Servants . . . are not kept in due subjection; their Masters, and Parents especially, being sinfully indulgent towards them."

The remedies proposed, in order that God's anger might be averted from the suffering land, included a general "Renewal of the Covenant" in the churches, the enforcement of discipline, the better support of schools, a more efficient regulation of the liquor traffic, and "a full supply of Officers in the Churches, according to Christ's Institution." This last-named suggestion of amendment reminds us that, by 1679, the elaborate and supposedly exclusively Scriptural officering of churches with pastor, teacher, ruling elder and deacons, had largely given place to the more economical service of a single paid officer, the pastor, and the assistance of the deacons. In a few churches teachers and ruling elders were long to survive, but in

[1] *Necessity of Reformation*, pp. 4-15.

most they had disappeared already when this Synod met.

The evils against which the Synod labored were too deep-seated to be cured by any such palliative as it had to offer, though undoubtedly some good was accomplished. In general, the same state of religious decline continued till after Mather's death. But one more act of the Reforming Synod must be noted, in which, as in the work already described, Mather bore large share. The Cambridge Synod had approved the doctrinal portions of the Westminster Confession in 1648; but a generation had passed since that event and though no doctrinal discussion had intervened, the Reforming Synod, at its first session in 1679, appointed a committee, of which Mather was a member, to " draw up a Confession of faith," to be reported at a second session in May, 1680.[1] Mather and one other of this committee had been in England, when, in 1658, the representatives of the Congregational churches of that land had adopted a slight modification of the Westminster standard, known from their place of assembly in London as the " Savoy Confession." This creed, with one or two trifling emendations, was now adopted by the ministers and delegates, with a unanimity and an absence of debate which reveal clearly how little of departure from, or indeed of discussion of, the common Calvinism of the Puritan founders had

[1] See Walker, *Creeds and Platforms*, p. 419.

yet developed in New England. Cotton Mather thus records[1] his father's share in its approval:

"Though there were many Elder, and some Famous, Persons in that Venerable Assembly, yet Mr. *Mather* was chosen their *Moderator*. He was then Ill, under the Approaches & Beginnings of a *Fever ;* but so Intense was he on the *Business* to be done, that he forgot his *Illness ;* and he kept them so close to their *Business*, that in *Two Days* they dispatch'd it: and he also Composed the *Præface* to the *Confession.*"

So came into being the creed known usually as the "Confession of 1680," long regarded as the standard of the Massachusetts churches, though never imposed on them by governmental or ecclesiastical authority, and so venerated, in name at least, that it is referred to as one of the standards of Congregational belief in so comparatively recent a symbol as the " Burial Hill Declaration," adopted by the National Council of these churches in 1865.

Already the most conspicuous minister in New England, it was but natural that the trustees of Harvard College should turn to Mather when the presidency of that institution became vacant by the death of Urian Oakes in 1681. He declined at that time. But when death once more emptied the president's chair, he accepted the post; though continuing his Boston pastorate, a labor which was made lighter by the settlement of his eldest son, Cotton Mather, the same year, as

[1] *Parentator*, p. 87 ; see also *Magnalia*, ii., p. 180.

colleague pastor of the church of which he was in title "teacher"—an intimate and almost fraternal association that was to last for more than thirty-eight years, and to be broken only by death.

The college of which Increase Mather thus became president was, as we have already seen, but a feeble plant, and his aid, though granted necessarily for but a fragment of his time, seems to have been of real value. Undoubtedly he considered his services to the college more indispensable than they were judged by others; but unquestionably, also, no man in the Massachusetts of that day was so well fitted to carry the institution safely through the troublous fifteen years during which he was its head. The actual work of instruction was largely in the hands of the tutors, John Leverett and William Brattle,[1] with whom, as we shall see later, Mather did not sympathize theologically. But the credit of bringing the college safely, and with increasing classes, through the crisis which deprived the institution, as well as the colony, of its charter, and left it long without a legal basis, as well as of securing for it the important gifts of Thomas Hollis, must be ascribed to Increase Mather. And the influence of this position on the churches can only be estimated when we remember that nearly all ministerial candidates in New England then received the training of the one New England college.

[1] Sibley, *Graduates of Harvard*, iii., p. 181.

The time of Mather's accession to the presidency of Harvard was, indeed, one of concern for Massachusetts. The charter of 1629, conferring upon it, as interpreted by the colonists, nearly the powers of an independent state, had long been looked upon with disfavor by the Stuart sovereigns; and, in 1683, that opponent of the colonial liberties, Edward Randolph, had a writ served on the Massachusetts government summoning it to defend its charter from annulment by the English courts. Increase Mather vigorously encouraged resistance; and through his influence the lower house of the legislature and the Boston town meeting alike strenuously opposed the royal demand. The blow fell, nevertheless, for in June, 1684, the Court of Chancery at London vacated the charter. All Massachusetts institutions, the legislature, the courts, the college, the churches, even the tenure of private property, were deprived of their legal basis by this decision; and with the reign of James II., which began in February of the next year, Massachusetts soon chafed under the rule of the younger Dudley and of Sir Edmund Andros, and trembled with apprehension or realization at the abolition of personal, political, and property rights long held sacred.

To those in Massachusetts who looked with regret at the passing away of the old order it seemed that something might possibly be effected by a personal appeal to James II., whose undisguised Catholic sympathies disposed him to seek the support of all other English Non-conformists.[1] No man in the colony was so fitted for such a mission as Increase Mather, by reason of his conspicuity in the pulpit, his political principles, his acquaintance in England, where he had been an acceptable preacher, and his capacity to appear to advantage at court. His errand was suspected, and Randolph tried his best to arrest him; but on April 7, 1688, after more than a week of hiding, he got safely on shipboard,[2] and twenty-nine days later landed at the English Weymouth. James received Mather graciously, though he granted none of his requests;[3] but Mather cultivated the friendship of the chief of the Non-conformists and of the Whig leaders with such diligence that when, in the winter of 1688–1689, the throne of England passed to William and Mary he was in a position to present the case of the colonies to the new sovereigns. It needed all the persuasive arts of the colonial ambassador-in-chief, for William was jealous of colonial independence, and the two associates whom the Massachusetts legislature had sent over to assist Mather complicated his efforts

[1] For Mather's mission to England, see *The Andros Tracts*, ii. (Prince Society), Boston, 1869, edited by W. H. Whitmore. I have described this incident in *Papers of the American Society of Church History*, v., pp. 72–77, and in picturing it here have to some extent reproduced the language in which I have there told the story.

[2] Sewall, *Diary*, v. *Coll. Mass. Hist. Soc.*, v., pp. 209, 210.

[3] For these requests, see Hutchinson, *Hist. Mass. Bay*, pp. 367–369. London, 1765.

by staking all on a restoration of the old charter, to which the King would not agree. So Mather fought out the battle single-handed, and on the whole very successfully. The charter which he obtained in the summer of 1691 was not all that he desired. It gave to the King, instead of to the colony, the right to appoint the highest officers of state; it reserved to him a right to reject distasteful laws; it allowed appeals to his higher English courts, and it granted freedom of worship to all Protestants. But though Mather would gladly have had these provisions other than they were, the new charter united Plymouth colony to Massachusetts, thus permanently preventing its dreaded annexation to New York; it left the legislature under the control of the people; reserved to it the public purse; preserved the local governments of the towns; and, by comfirming all grants heretofore made by the General Court, assured to individuals and the churches the possession of their property, and largely the maintenance of their ancient constitution.

Though Mather could not escape the criticism of those who wished the restoration of the old semi-independent and ecclesiastically exclusive government, many of whom looked upon him as a traitor for not securing more than he did, there can be no doubt that no Massachusetts man of that age could have obtained as much. It is not extravagant to affirm that he did more than any other man of his generation to maintain essentially operative, and to hand down to his successors, the civil and ecclesiastical institutions of New England, which without his efforts could not have escaped far more serious modification than they actually underwent in this trying time.

Mather's influence in this negotiation, and the impression of leadership among the citizens of Massachusetts which he made upon the English authorities is perhaps best illustrated by the fact that the royal government left the crown appointments at the initiation of the new provincial administration largely to his nomination.[1] The extent to which he used this influence to secure office for his friends and parishioners was unwise, and was the source of much later hostility to him. And, in general, it may be said that, while Mather did a work for Massachusetts of almost inestimable importance in this troubled time, he made more enemies than he could possibly have aroused in any other way, and the jealousies and antagonisms now engendered embittered his later life.

Increase Mather was not a man to forget his mission as a minister in the excitement of politics, and one incident of his English sojourn illustrates at once his freedom from ecclesiastical partisanship and his interest in religious affairs. The Toleration Act of 1689, passed during Mather's time of waiting in London, gave to Trinitarian Protestant Non-conformists a legal,

[1] *Parentator*, p. 144.

though restricted, right to worship. Of the Non-conformist bodies the Presbyterian, of which Richard Baxter and John Howe were the guiding spirits, was the largest, the Congregationalists ranking next in size and counting about one half as many adherents. It was natural that this new-found freedom should awaken desire for the union of bodies so long under persecution, and this desire found expression primarily, it would appear, in London, where Increase Mather labored with his characteristic activity to bring Congregationalists and Presbyterians into confederation. To his efforts, more than to those of any other man, was due the union effected on April 6, 1691, by which these Dissenters in London became one body, and through the efforts of Flavel and others the movement spread rapidly to other parts of England. It had, indeed, no lasting history.[1] Closely related as Presbyterianism and Congregationalism are, they seem impossible of amalgamation, and this confederation was ruptured in 1694, two years after Mather's return to New England; but its written basis, the so-called "Heads of Agreement," crossed the Atlantic by Mather's influence, and, in 1708, was adopted, together with the *Saybrook Platform* of that year, as a legal basis of the churches of Connecticut—a position of political authority which it sustained in that commonwealth till 1784.

[1] The story is told at length in Walker, *Creeds and Platforms*, 440-462.

One event, closely connected in time with Mather's return from England, cannot be passed by in any estimate of his influence in New England — the grim witchcraft tragedy at Salem. Increase Mather's connection with it was, indeed, much more remote than that of his son Cotton. The excitement in the household of Rev. Samuel Parris, of what is now Danvers, with which the fanatic outburst opened, had begun in March, 1692, two months before Mather's return. But Cotton and Increase Mather were so one in spirit, that, in the public eye, all that the former did carried the sanction of the latter. There can be no doubt, also, that Increase Mather's *Illustrious Providences*, of 1684, contributed to the popular belief in witchcraft, if not so powerfully as his son's *Memorable Providences, Relating to Witchcrafts and Possessions*, of 1689 and 1691. Increase Mather certainly could have done much, had he been so disposed, to check the witchcraft excitement, and he was enlightened enough to argue against the adequacy of several of the popularly accepted evidences of witchcraft in his *Cases of Conscience Concerning Evil Spirits;* but he as certainly believed in the possibility of compacts with the devil, and, as late as 1694, the Harvard trustees, under his leadership, issued an appeal to the ministers of New England for the collection of narratives of enchantments. He and his son Cotton tried their best to suppress that influential, if exceedingly personal, volume, the *More*

Wonders of the Invisible World, of 1700, in which Robert Calef of Boston expressed a skepticism regarding witchcraft which all intelligent persons have since come to share. But there can be no doubt that Mather's belief in the reality of satanic possession was conscientious; and it had the support of many of the best men of his age on both sides of the Atlantic. Such a man as Richard Baxter, for instance, was no less strongly a believer in these supposedly supernatural manifestations. Yet, however we may excuse Increase Mather, the witchcraft episode is not a pleasant page in his story.

Mather may be said to have been at the height of his influence and popularity in 1692, the year of his return from England. In that year, the colonial legislature granted to Harvard College a new charter permitting the bestowment of the higher academic degrees, and under this charter, which was speedily annulled by the King, Harvard gave to Increase Mather the first doctorate of divinity ever granted in New England, and the title of Bachelor of Divinity to the two tutors, Brattle and Leverett, who had been associated with him. Not till 1771 was the doctor's degree given by Harvard again.[1]

But, as has been pointed out, Mather's great services to the colony had given offense no less than

[1] *Parentator*, pp. 170-172; Sibley, *Graduates of Harvard*, i., pp. 424, 425.

satisfaction, and the popular awakening from the witchcraft delusion reacted in considerable measure upon him. His friend and nominee for Governor, Sir William Phips, proved an unsuccessful administrator, and the difficulties of securing a proper charter for Harvard grew rather than decreased as successive efforts to this end were frustrated in 1692, 1696, 1697, 1699, and 1700. Mather's parish and his publications demanded so much of his time that he could only " Visit it [the college] once or twice every Week, and Continue there a Night or two ";[1] and his opponents now made the very natural desire that Harvard should have a resident president the basis for an attack upon him. At successive sessions of the legislature, in 1693, 1695, and 1698, the wish was expressed by formal vote,[2] that Mather should remove from Boston to Cambridge; but he did nothing in the way of compliance, being naturally reluctant to leave the pulpit of the largest church in the colony for an exclusive devotion to the headship of a charterless college of two tutors and perhaps sixty students.

As the last decade of the seventeenth century drew to a close, however, the situation was further complicated by the rise of what may be styled a liberal movement in Boston and in Cambridge, though the modifications of usage and thought were so slight that

[1] So Vice-President Willard summarized the duties, Sibley, ii., p. 22.
[2] Sibley, i., pp. 425-427.

it hardly deserves so pretentious a name.[1] Increase Mather, as has been pointed out, was strongly a conservative. Sincerely alarmed by the declining state of religion in the New England of his time, he considered a return to the old ways, an enforcement of discipline, and the perpetuation of the ideals of his early ministry the true method of fostering the religious life. How dark the situation of New England then seemed to him may be judged from a sentence or two in a sermon[2] preached before Harvard College on December 6, 1696:

"There is call to fear lest suddenly there will be no Colledge in New England; and this is a sign that ere long there will be no Churches there. I know there is a blessed day to the visible Church not far off; but it is the Judgment of very Learned men that in the Glorious Times promised to the Church on Earth, America will be Hell."

But there were others who regarded a modification of the usages of early New England as desirable. Most intimately connected with Mather of any of these were John Leverett and William Brattle, who, we have already seen, were long associated with him as tutors under his presidency, and had become trustees of the college in 1692. Leverett was a political force. In 1698 he had entered the legislature, where he rose to the speakership, and his classes, to accommodate

[1] I have told this story at some length in the *Yale Review* for May, 1892; and in *Creeds and Platforms*, pp. 465-483.

[2] Quoted in Sibley, i., p. 453, from *A Discourse Concerning the Uncertainty of the Times of Men*. Boston, 1697.

his political duties, had had to meet at five in the morning.[1] William Brattle had become pastor of the Cambridge church in 1696. In hearty sympathy with his brother was Thomas Brattle, the Harvard treasurer, and with them stood Ebenezer Pemberton, a younger tutor at Harvard, and Benjamin Colman, a young ministerial candidate of the class of 1692. Probably the most significant change desired by these innovators was an abandonment of the early New England custom of requiring a public account, or relation, as it was styled, of religious experience from all who united with a church — a requirement consonant enough with the intense and conscious piety of the founders, but which the lowered tone of spiritual life had rendered irksome to many. They also wished that all baptized adults who contributed to a minister's support should share in his selection, and that any children presented by a Christian sponsor, whether parent or not, should be admitted to baptism. They furthermore desired an enrichment of the service by the devotional reading of some portion of the Scriptures, without explanatory comment, — a kind of Prayer-Book-like reading which the early Puritans had stigmatized as dumb reading,—and the occasional liturgical use of the Lord's Prayer. These modifications do not seem very radical to us, but to Mather they appeared full of peril. In 1697, he attacked the innovators'

[1] Sibley, iii., p. 183.

view of the needlessness of relations in a letter to the church at Cambridge of which Brattle was pastor, and to the students of the college; and three months later followed this charge into the enemy's camp by a protest from his church to that of Charlestown, which had chosen its minister in the way the innovators desired.

All this seemed dictatorial, and though undoubtedly conscientious, was none the less irritating. The result was that Thomas Brattle and some Boston sympathizers constructed a new meeting-house in Boston in 1698, called Benjamin Colman home from England to its pulpit, requesting him to procure ordination before sailing from more sympathetic hands than he would find among Mather's friends in Boston, and, on December 12, 1699, organized a new church — Brattle Church — without summoning the advice of any council, to occupy the meeting-house and to practice the innovations. These acts had the approval of the other members of the liberal party, and they called out from Increase Mather, in March, 1700, his most interesting contribution to Congregational history and polity—his *Order of the Gospel.* In this tract he condemned the Brattle Church principles, and declared that to approve them was to " give away the whole Congregational cause at once, and a great part of the Presbyterian Discipline also." He remarked, with pointed reference to Colman's English ordination, that, " to say that a Wandering Levite who has no Flock is a

Pastor, is as good sense as to say, that he that has no Children is a Father"; and the allusion to his subordinates at the college was unmistakable in his exhortation, " Let the Churches Pray for the Colledge particularly, that God may ever Bless that Society with faithful Tutors that will be true to Christ's Interests and theirs, and not Hanker after new and loose wayes."[1]

Two ecclesiastical parties had evidently developed, and Mather's opponents were strong enough to have the question of his non-residence reopened by the legislature in July, 1700. Thus alarmed, he actually removed to Cambridge for a few months; but the absence from his family distressed him, and he proposed to the legislature that he continue on the non-residential basis on which his presidency had been actually placed so long. But while the representatives of the country towns supported him loyally in the lower house, sympathetic with his conservative position, the upper house, largely from Boston and vicinity, and hostile to him for many reasons, personal, political, and religious, on September 6, 1701, declined to approve Mather's continuance as president, and thus dropped him from the office which he had filled for sixteen years. How largely personal the action of the legislature was is shown by the fact that it immediately made Samuel Willard of the Boston Old South Church his successor on precisely the same terms of non-resi-

[1] *Order of the Gospel*, pp. 8, 11, 12, 102.

dence — the court keeping a show of consistency by calling him vice-president, instead of president.

To Mather the defeat was a bitter disappointment, and its gall and wormwood continued as long as he, and his son Cotton, his associate in the struggle, lived. Nor was it only the pain of a personal discomfiture or the disregard of services which Mather was conscious were well rendered and which seemed to him to deserve a better recompense. For, besides the personal motives which had entered into the struggle, his had been a serious and honest attempt to save the college from what he deemed essential spiritual harm, and defeat seemed the ruin of a cause which he believed to be that of the Gospel. But the defeat was none the less final. When Willard died, in 1707, Mather hoped that the office would come to him or to his son Cotton, but he hoped in vain. His innovating former subordinate, John Leverett, was the choice, and the bitterness of the disappointment was shown in a violent attack by father and son on Governor Joseph Dudley, whom they looked upon as responsible for this second shattering of their hopes.

Increase Mather was sixty-two years of age when he lost the presidency of Harvard, and what was to him far more important, when he saw in his own rejection the defeat of the conservative party for whose predominance in Church and State he labored. He had twenty-two years of life yet before him. Though he was to some extent passed by in the current of the age, though he felt the bitterness of disappointment always, and a sense that his services to the colony had not received the appreciation that their worth deserved, and thus his old age became in some considerable degree one of repining, it was a time of usefulness, fruitfulness, and honor to the end. The estimate in which he was held by his clerical brethren is shown by their unanimous choice of him in April, 1715, to bear the congratulatory address, then expected at the accession of a sovereign, to George I. — an honor which his age compelled him to decline.[1] His church valued his services and listened to him with pleasure so long as he was in physical strength to preach. His wisdom was much sought at councils and other ecclesiastical gatherings. And his activity with his pen was constant. In the case of the other leaders of early Congregationalism whom we have already considered I have attempted to give a fairly complete account of their writings. With Mather their number and variety make such a treatment impossible. Though the productions of his pen are far from equaling in number the four hundred and fifty-one titles attributed to his son, Cotton, they reach the sufficiently remarkable total of one hundred and fifty-nine.[2] Of these, more than one half were written after

[1] *Parentator*, p. 194.
[2] A full list may be found in Sibley, i., pp. 438-469.

his retirement from the presidency of Harvard in 1701. Most are small in size, but many are considerable volumes, and the range of topics which they cover is as wide as their number is surprising. Some are sermons on events of public interest, fires, earthquakes, storms, comets, executions. Others are biographical sketches of deceased worthies, or narratives of important public events, like the Indian wars; yet others are political tracts, designed to present the New England cause, as he saw it, to New England's critics. Religious controversy has its ample place, of course, but by far the larger part of these volumes, great and small, have a distinctly edificatory aim, their prime purpose being to upbuild the spiritual life. Increase Mather's style, as compared with the curiously pedantic, whimsical diction of his son Cotton, was simple and direct, though with some tendencies toward the same aberrations that appear in the latter's writings. He reveals himself everywhere the man of learning and of wide observation of the world. Yet much of this literature is trite and uninteresting to modern readers. Much is commonplace. But it did not seem so then. The first New England newspaper that had any duration was not printed till 1704; few non-ministerial households had any volumes, save perhaps a Bible, an almanac, and a few treatises of the older Puritan divines. To such a generation writings like those of Mather came with all the freshness, timeliness, and interest of the modern religious newspaper. They met a real need; and in a way that made the New England of that day truly debtor to him who wrote.

Mather's tolerance grew with his years. In 1679, when he framed the conclusions of the Reforming Synod, he wrote of the Dissenters then in New England:[1]

"Men have set up their Threshold by Gods Threshold, and their Posts by his Post. Quakers are false Worshippers; and such Anabaptists as have risen up amongst us . . . do no better than set up an Altar against the Lords Altar."

But, in 1718, he shared in the ordination of Elisha Callender over the Baptist church in Boston; and in the Preface to the sermon which his son Cotton preached on the occasion he bore testimony that " all of the brethren of that church with whom I have any acquaintance . . . are, in the judgment of rational charity, godly persons."[2] His pecuniary generosity was unfailing. Besides the tenth of his income which he devoted to benevolence as a matter of conscience, he stood ready to render aid to the deserving; and the church over which he was pastor was noted for its liberality in gifts in that day when contributions for other than home expenses were unusual.

On entering the fiftieth year of his ministry, in 1713,

[1] *Necessity of Reformation*, p. 3.
[2] Backus, *Hist. of New England*, i., p. 421. 1871.

Mather proffered his resignation to his people. Its acceptance was refused, though the church speedily voted that he should preach " only when he should feel himself able and inclin'd."[1] So, blessed in the kindly regard of his own congregation, and in the continued association of his son with him in his ministry and labors, whatever disappointments he may have felt over other circumstances of his later life, he gradually relaxed his hold on the world of which he had been so conspicuous a citizen. His enfeebled condition confined him to the house after September, 1719; the thought of his approaching rest in the presence of his Lord seemed increasingly attractive to him. To his London friend, Thomas Hollis, who had inquired if he were still in " the land of the living," he sent the message: " No! Tell him, I am going to it; This Poor World is the Land of the Dying. 'T is Heaven that is the true Land of the Living."[2] But, as in his father's case, his suffering was prolonged, and he died, after a distressing illness, but rejoicing in confidence of entrance into the eternal city, on August 23, 1723, at the ripe age of eighty-five. They honored him, so his son recorded, " with a Greater *Funeral* than had ever been seen for any *Divine*, in *these* . . . parts of the World ";[3] and it was fitting that they should, for the Massachusetts of that day had lost its most gifted son.

[1] *Parentator*, p. 197.   [2] *Ibid.*, p. 209.   [3] *Ibid.*, p. 211.

Last summer, toward evening, I walked through the crowded and foreign streets, where once his congregation dwelt, to the simple tomb in Copp's Hill burying-ground where he sleeps. The grateful air blowing across the open hilltop as the hot summer sun sank had drawn many from the crowded tenements of the North End to the cemetery. Many of the faces were unmistakably Hebrew or Italian; the boy who pointed out the tomb to me was of Irish birth. I did not see one who seemed of the old Puritan race for which Mather labored. The thought was inevitable that as the scene of his life work had altered, so the age in which he lived, its struggles, its endeavors, its disappointments, and its achievements had vanished without leaving a trace behind. But no! as one looked over the city, in its strength and stateliness, as one glanced at the shaft on Bunker Hill and remembered the spirit and the deeds of which it stands the symbol, and as one thought of the great university beyond, the truer feeling came, that these strong men so built themselves into the New England that they loved as to make the more populous, more cosmopolitan, more generous, and more tolerant New England of to-day possible. Whatever strength New England has to-day she draws from the molding power of men of whom Increase Mather was a conspicuous example.

JONATHAN EDWARDS

VI.

JONATHAN EDWARDS

TO come to Andover with a lecture on Jonathan Edwards seems wellnigh an impertinence. Here, where his name has been honored more, if it be possible, than anywhere else in New England, where his life and works have long been familiarly and affectionately studied, where most of his unpublished manuscripts are guarded, there is nothing novel that a lecturer can offer; nor can he expect his knowledge of his theme to compare in thoroughness with that of several of his hearers. Yet the lecturer is reminded that this is a course on Congregationalism, not on unfamiliar Congregationalists; and to treat of the eighteenth century without glancing up, at least for a few moments, at the towering figure of our most original New England theologian, is like shutting out from memory the Presidential Range as one thinks of the White Mountains.

Passing along the sandy road that skirts the edge of the low bluff above the level meadowland, that borders the east bank of the Connecticut River, in the town of South Windsor, one sees by the roadside the site where stood, till the beginning of the nineteenth century, the " plain two-story house "[1] in which Jonathan Edwards was born. Though pleasant farming country, there is little in the immediate surroundings to detain the eye; but the blue hills beyond the river to the westward stretch away into the distance as attractively now as they did then when, if tradition is to be trusted, Jonathan's autocratic father, the parish minister, warned a neighbor whose refusal to remove a wide-spreading tree annoyed him, that if this disrespectful conduct was continued he would not baptize that contumacious neighbor's child. Behind the house, to the eastward a few rods, rises a low, tree-covered hill, cutting off the view in that direction, and affording a retreat to which father and son were accustomed to withdraw in pleasant weather for meditation or for prayer.[2] Here at what is now South Windsor, Timothy Edwards, Jonathan's father, exercised an able, spiritual, and conspicuously learned ministry from 1694 to his death in 1758.[3] Grandson of William Edwards, an early settler of Hartford, and son of Richard Edwards, a prominent merchant of Hartford, and of his erratic wife, Elisabeth Tuthill,[4] Timothy Edwards had graduated with distinction from

[1] See J. A. Stoughton, *Windsor Farmes*, p. 46, Hartford, 1883, and H. R. Stiles, *History and Genealogies of Ancient Windsor*, i., p. 556, Hartford, 1891. The house stood till 1813.

[2] Stoughton, *ibid.*, pp. 46, 47.

[3] *Ibid., passim.*

[4] See *Colonial Records of Connecticut*, iv., p. 59 ; Stoughton, *ibid.*, pp. 39, 69.

Harvard College in 1691, and was always a man of marked intellectual power. The considerable list of boys fitted in his home for college [1] bears witness to his abilities as a teacher, and the judgment of his congregation that he was a more learned man and a more animated preacher than his son, Jonathan,[2] reflects the esteem in which he was held by the people of his charge. His wife, Jonathan's mother, was a daughter of Solomon Stoddard, of Northampton, the ablest minister of the Connecticut valley when the seventeenth century passed into the eighteenth, and granddaughter of John Warham, the first pastor of Windsor.

Into this intellectual, strenuous, and yet cheerful home in this bit of rural New England Jonathan Edwards was born on October 5, 1703. Here he grew up, the fifth among eleven children and the only brother among ten tall sisters. Here he was fitted for college in his father's study, and the intellectual sympathy thus begun between father and son was to be a lifelong bond.

Youthful precocity is by no means an infallible prophecy of mature strength, but with Jonathan Edwards the mind received an early development and manifested a grasp that was little less than marvelous at an age when most schoolboys are scarcely emerging from childhood. His observations on nature,

---

[1] For some of these names see Stoughton, *Windsor Farmes*, pp. 77, 78, 101-103.

[2] S. E. Dwight, *Life of Pres. Edwards*, p. 17. New York, 1830.

notably the well-known paper on the habits of the spider, apparently written when Edwards was about the age of twelve; and even more his notes on the mind, some at least of which seem to have been the immediate fruit of his reflections upon Locke's famous *Essay*, which he had read when fourteen, witness to his early intellectual maturity. The same precocious strength of mind is apparent in his less easily dated, but youthful, attainment of some of the positions of Berkeley or Malebranche — an attainment that seems to have been due to an independent development, rather than to acquaintance with their writings.[1]

Naturally, such a boy went early to college; and we find Edwards entering Yale in September, 1716, about a month before the close of his thirteenth year. The institution whose distinguished graduate he was to become was far enough removed from the university of the present. Founded in 1701, and therefore only two years older than Edwards himself, its precarious existence had thus far been spent at Saybrook; but the question of removal to New Haven was in heated debate just at the time that Edwards entered,[2] and a month after the beginning of his Freshman year was

[1] Dwight, *Life*, pp. 22-63, 664-702; G. P. Fisher, *Discussions in History and Theology*, pp. 228-232; Allen, *Jonathan Edwards*, pp. 3-31; E. C. Smyth, in *Proceedings of the American Antiquarian Society* for 1895, pp. 212-236; Fisher, *History of Christian Doctrine*, pp. 396, 403. H. N. Gardiner, *Jonathan Edwards: A Retrospect*, pp. 115-160, Boston, 1901.

[2] F. B. Dexter, *Biographical Sketches of the Graduates of Yale*, i., pp. 159, 160.

decided by the trustees. Their decision in favor of New Haven was unpopular in the section of the colony in which Edwards's home was situated; and, before the close of 1716, a considerable portion of the students of the distracted college had gathered at Wethersfield under the instruction of two tutors, one, a recent graduate of Harvard, the other, three years an alumnus of Yale.[1] Of these emigrating dissenters Edwards was one; and at Wethersfield he remained till the healing of the division in the early summer of 1719 carried him to New Haven.[2] Here he lived in the newly erected hall and dormitory, then known distinctively as Yale College, in a room rented at the moderate rate of twenty shillings a year; and here, too, he boarded in commons at a charge of five shillings—$83\frac{1}{3}$ cents—a week. These prices were in no way exceptionally moderate, nor is there any evidence of which I am aware that Edwards's student days were not as comfortable from a pecuniary standpoint as those of any of his position in the commonwealth. Here at New Haven he graduated, in September, 1720, at the head of a class of ten, after a course involving little more than an acquaintance with a few books of Virgil and orations of Cicero, the Greek Testament, the Psalms in Hebrew, the elements of Logic, Ames's *Theology*

[1] Elisha Williams, Harvard, 1711, afterward president of Yale, speaker of the Connecticut lower house, judge of the Superior Court, and colonel of the Connecticut troops; and Samuel Smith, Yale, 1713.

[2] See Edwards's letter of March 26, 1719, Dwight, *Life*, pp. 29, 30.

and *Cases of Conscience*, and a smattering of Physics, Mathematics, Geography, and Astronomy.[1] In Edwards's case, however, this course had been greatly supplemented by the reading at Wethersfield of such books as he could borrow or purchase, and at New Haven by the use of the largest and best selected library then in Connecticut, which the diligence of Jeremiah Dummer and of other friends in England had procured for the college. It was doubtless the opportunity afforded by this library that kept Edwards at New Haven engaged in the study of theology till the summer of 1722, when, it seems probable, he was licensed to preach.[2]

Somewhere in this period of study, probably about the time of his graduation,[3] Edwards passed through the deepest experience that can come to a human soul, a conscious change in its relations to God. As John Wesley was a Christian and a minister before he was "converted," and yet was wrought upon mightily by that spiritual experience that came to him as he heard Luther's Preface to the *Commentary on Romans* read in the Moravian Chapel in Aldersgate Street, London, at a quarter before nine on the evening of May

---

[1] Dexter, *Biographical Sketches*, pp. 115, 141-143, 177, 200, 203; Dwight, *Life*, p. 32.

[2] Hopkins, *Life and Character of* . . . *Jonathan Edwards* (Boston, 1765), ed. Northampton, 1804, p. 4; Dwight, *Life*, p. 63.

[3] Dwight, *Life*, p. 58. He is supposed to have joined the church of which his father was pastor soon after his graduation.

24, 1738, so Edwards, moved by religious convictions when a boy and again when in college, yet rebellious against the absoluteness of the divine sovereignty which his theology and his philosophy alike demanded, came in an instant to a "sense of the glory of the divine Being"[1]—to quote his own words—which thenceforth changed the entire conscious attitude of his soul toward God. And as Calvin, after the severe struggle involved in the submission of his will to that of God, made the divine sovereignty the corner-stone of his system, so Edwards now found that doctrine "exceedingly pleasant, bright, and sweet." But it was not, as with Calvin, a submission to an infinite authority that was the central thought of the experience that came to Edwards as he read the words "Now unto the King eternal, immortal, invisible, the only wise God, be honor and glory forever and ever, Amen." Rather it was the high-wrought, mystic conception of the excellence of the God to whom his heart went out in a flood of devotion that mastered him with an overwhelming sense of the divine presence and majesty. With true mystic outflowing of affection he seems to have had relatively little sense of a burden of the guilt of sin; he was above the plane which makes the question of one's own interests central. By him sin was felt chiefly in a profoundly humiliating sense of his own infinite unlikeness to God. But he longed with

[1] See Hopkins, *Life*, pp. 24-42; Dwight, *Life*, pp. 60, 61.

all the power of an ardent nature to " enjoy that God, and be rapt up to him in heaven, and be, as it were, swallowed up in him forever." And this new apprehension of " the glorious majesty and grace of God " found poetic satisfaction in enjoyment of Solomon's Song, in sympathy with external nature, the sky, clouds, " grass, flowers, trees," or the majesty of the lightning and the power of the storm.

This new sense of the divine glory, almost a pure intuition of the majesty, holiness, and power of God, satisfied the mystic and imaginative side of Edwards's nature, no less than the speculations which found in all being but the manifestation of spirit, and especially of the potent Spirit of God operating directly on the human spirit, satisfied the philosophic tendency so strangely joined with an almost oriental wealth of fancy in this remarkable man. And from both sides of his thinking his theology flowed: rock-ribbed in its speculative logic, in its limitation of the power of human freedom, in its recognition of the immediate agency of God in all events, in its emphasis on the absolute and arbitrary sovereignty of the Creator over his creatures; yet insistent on a " conversion " the chief resultant of which was an affectionate delight in God, and finding the highest Christian experience in a mystical and almost incomprehensible sense of the divine glory manifested to the loving human soul.

This experience, no less than Edwards's belief in the

immediacy and power of the operations of the divine Spirit on the soul of man, led him to emphasize a struggling and conscious " conversion," rather than a scarce-observed process of growth, as the normal instead of the occasional method of entrance into the Kingdom of God. This is a view always widely prevalent in times of deep religious quickening. It was preached in early New England by Hooker, Cotton, Shepard, and the founders generally. Wesley and Whitefield taught it. And it was set forth with such persuasiveness by Edwards as an underlying principle of his conception of the religious life as profoundly to affect New England for a century after his death. Emphasizing as it does the great truth of the divine origin of all Christian life, its overemphasis as a necessary law tends to rob baptism of significance, to minimize the covenant relationships of Christian households, and to leave the children of the truest servants of God presumptively outside the Christian fold till consciously touched by the transforming power of the Spirit. Edwards's own son and namesake could write years later:[1] " Though I had, during my father's life, some convictions of sin and danger, yet I have no reason to believe I had any real religion, till some years after his death."

In the power of these thoughts Edwards entered on

---

[1] Letter of March 30, 1789, in Hawksley, *Memoirs of the Rev. Jonathan Edwards*, p. 255. London, 1815.

his first pastoral experience, taking charge of a small Presbyterian church in New York City from August, 1722, to April, 1723 — a relation which the congregation would gladly have made permanent. This practical experience but deepened his previous aspirations and convictions into a remarkable series of seventy resolutions. Some are the familiar maxims of earnest men, as " To live with all my might while I do live"; but more represent the peculiar coloring of Edwards's religious life, as " Never to do any manner of thing, whether in soul or body, less or more, but what tends to the glory of God, nor be, nor suffer it, if I can possibly avoid it."[1]

New York, though pleasant, did not seem to Edwards a hopeful field for his life work, and in May, 1723, he was back in his father's house in South Windsor. But other churches speedily sought his services. North Haven called him in vain in September, 1723; and, in November of that year, he accepted an invitation to the pastorate at Bolton, a little eastward of his home. Yet, for some reason now unknown he did not enter upon this ministry, and June, 1724, found him, instead, in a tutorship at Yale College.[2]

The period was one of great distraction in that much vexed institution. Without a president since the defection of Rector Cutler to Episcopacy in 1722, its

[1] In full in Dwight, *Life*, pp. 68–73.
[2] Dexter, *Biographical Sketches*, pp. 218, 219.

government and instruction were in the hands of two young and frequently changed tutors. During Edwards's incumbency, begun when he was not yet twenty-two, the work was done with credit to himself and benefit to the college; and he might have continued in it for several years longer had not a most attractive invitation come to him from the people of Northampton to become the colleague of his grandfather, the venerable Solomon Stoddard. Induced by family ties, drawn by the prominence of the congregation, then esteemed the largest in Massachusetts outside of Boston, and by that repute for a certain aristocratic and social charm which Northampton then, as now, enjoyed, he resigned his tutorship and, on February 15, 1727, was ordained to the colleague pastorate of the Northampton church. The death of Stoddard two years later [1] left him in sole charge.

The establishment of these ties was speedily followed by the formation of others of a more personal character. On July 28, 1727, he married Sarah Pierpont, daughter of Rev. James Pierpont of New Haven, and great-granddaughter of Thomas Hooker, the founder of Hartford. Our New England ancestors married early,—the bride and groom were seventeen and twenty-four,— but Edwards had long been attracted by the character, even more than by the beauty, of the young woman who thus linked her life

[1] February 11, 1729.

with his; and his description of her at the age of thirteen is one of the few striking bits of poetic prose which the rather arid literature of eighteenth-century New England produced.[1] Mrs. Edwards was well worthy of his regard. Hers was a nature not only of remarkable susceptibility to religious impression, but of executive force, cheerful courage, social grace, and sweet, womanly leadership.[2] She added cheer to his house, supplemented his shyness and want of small talk, and it was no inapt, though facetious, tribute to her general repute that affirmed " that she had learned a shorter road to heaven than her husband."[3] Devoted to that husband, whose frail health required constant care, administering a large part of the business affairs of the home with cheerful forgetfulness of her own disabilities that he might be free to spend his accustomed thirteen hours daily in his study, or to take his solitary meditative walks and rides,[4] she brought up eight daughters and three sons and bore her full share of labor in the vicissitudes of Edwards's life. Warmly attached to each other, husband and wife were but

[1] In full, Dwight, *Life*, pp. 114, 115 ; Allen, pp. 45, 46.

[2] Sketch by Hopkins in his *Life and Character of the late Rev. Mr. Jonathan Edwards*, Boston, 1765 ; see also Dwight, *Life*, pp. 113-115, 127-131, 171-190 ; Allen, pp. 44-49.

[3] Allen, pp. 47, 48.

[4] Hopkins, p. 43 ; Dwight, *Life*, 110-113. Prof. F. B. Dexter informs me that an examination of Edwards's unpublished correspondence shows that he was more of a man of business than his older biographers believed him to be. He certainly left a larger estate than most New England ministers of his time.

briefly separated by death, she surviving him less than seven months.[1] Every recollection of Edwards's achievements should also involve a remembrance of the devoted and solicitous care which made much of his work possible.

Edwards's ministry was marked from the first; and it was not long before the Northampton pulpit was strongly felt in Massachusetts and Connecticut in a direction largely counter to the religious tendencies of the time. Taken as a whole, no century in American religious history has been so barren as the eighteenth. The fire and enthusiasm of Puritanism had died out on both sides of the Atlantic. In this country the inevitable provincialism of the narrow colonial life, the deadening influence of its hard grapple with the rude forces of nature, and the Indian and Canadian wars rendered each generation less actively religious than its predecessor; and, while New England shone as compared with the spiritual deadness of Old England in the years preceding Wesley, the old fervor and sense of a national mission were gone, conscious conversion, once so common, was unusual, and religion was becoming more formal and external.

Then, too, it seems to be the law of the development of a declining Calvinism everywhere, whether in Switzerland, France, Holland, England, or America, that it passes through three or four stages. Beginning

[1] Died October 2, 1758.

with an intense assertion of divine sovereignty and human inability, it ascribes all to the grace of God, a grace granting common mercies to all men, and special salvatory mercy to the elect. This special grace has its evident illustrations in struggling spiritual births, lives of high consecration, and conscious regeneration. In seasons of intense spiritual feeling, like the Reformation or the Puritan struggle in England, it is easy to ascribe all religious life to the special, selective, irresistible, transforming power of God. But, in time, the high pressure of the spiritual life of a community or of a nation, which has passed through such a crisis-experience as had the founders of New England, abates. Men desirous of serving God do not feel so evidently the conscious workings of the divine Spirit, and they ask what they can do, not indeed to save themselves, — this second stage of Calvinism with no less emphasis than the first asserts that God alone can accomplish salvation by special grace,— but what they can do to put themselves in a position where God is more likely to save them. And the answer from the pulpit and in Christian thought is an increased emphasis on the habitual practice of prayer, faithful attendance at church, and the reading of God's Word, not as of themselves salvatory but as "means" by which a man can put himself in a more probable way of salvation. From this the path to the third stage is easy; to the belief that religion is a habit of careful attention to the duties of the house of God and observance of the precepts of the Gospel in relation to one's neighbors—a habit possible of attainment by all men, and justifying the confidence that though men cannot render an adequate service to God, yet if each man labors sincerely to do what he can under the impulse of the grace that God sends to all men God will accept his sincere though imperfect obedience as satisfactory. This stage was known in Edwards's day on both sides of the Atlantic as "Arminianism," and it was accompanied by an unstrenuous or negative attitude toward the doctrines which the first stage of Calvinism had made chief. From this position it was an easy transition for some to the fourth stage, in which the essence of the Christian life is made to consist in the practice of morality, and the need of man is represented to be education and culture, not rescue and fundamental transformation. English Puritanism had reached the fourth stage in some of its representatives when Edwards began his ministry; New England had not gone farther than the third as yet, and was chiefly in the second; but an "Arminian" point of view was rapidly spreading, even among those who would warmly have resented classification as "Arminians." Rev. Samuel Phillips of Andover, who was certainly thought a Calvinist, thus expressed a prevalent feeling in 1738:[1]

[1] *Orthodox Christian*, p. 75. 1738.

"I can't suppose, that any one . . . who at all Times, faithfully improves the *common Grace* he has, *that is to say*, is diligent in attending on the appointed Means of Grace with a Desire to profit thereby; . . . and in a Word, who walks up to his Light, to the utmost of his Power, shall perish for want of *special* and saving Grace."

Now it was Edwards's great work as a religious leader to be the chief human instrument in turning back the current for over a century in the larger part of New England to the theory of the method of salvation and of man's dependence on God which marked the earlier types of Calvinism. Yet it was not wholly a return. While he emphasized the arbitrary and absolute character of the divine election as positively as the older Calvinists, and even more strenuously asserted the immediacy of the divine operations in dealing with the human soul, he tried to find place for a real and still existent, if unused and unusable, natural human power to turn to God, and hence a present, as well as an Adamic and racial, responsibility for not so doing.

Edwards's stimulating preaching soon had a marked effect on the little Northampton community of two hundred families.[1] The town was not unfamiliar with religious quickenings. At least five had occurred under the able ministry of Solomon Stoddard. But Edwards's sermons were on themes calculated to stir a

[1] Edwards gave a full account of these events in his *Narrative of Surprising Conversions* (1736-37) in *Works*, ed. Worcester, 1808-09, iii., pp. 9-62, from which the statements in this paragraph are taken.

community, and especially an isolated rural community. Two sudden deaths in the spring of 1734 excited the concern of the little town—a concern which was deepened by a vague alarm lest the spreading Arminianism which the Northampton pulpit denounced was a token of the withdrawal of God's redemptive mercy from sinful men. And the preacher set forth, in sermons which read with power after a lapse of more than a hundred and sixty years, the complete right of God to deal with his creatures as he saw fit, the enmity of human hearts against God, the terrors of the world to come, and the blessedness of acceptance with God. " I have found," said Edwards, " that no sermons have been more remarkably blessed, than those in which the doctrine of God's absolute sovereignty with regard to the salvation of sinners, and his just liberty with regard to answering the prayers or succeeding the pains of mere natural men, continuing such, have been insisted on." By December, 1734, a movement of spiritual power was manifest in the community which resulted in six months' time in " more than three hundred " conversions. The experience of those wrought upon, in large measure, corresponded to the type of preaching to which they had listened; and Edwards describes it as normally involving three definite stages. Of these the first was an " awful apprehension " of the condition in which men stand by nature, so overwhelming as to produce oftentimes painful physical effects. Next followed, in cases which Edwards believed to be the genuine work of the Spirit of God, a conviction that they justly deserved the divine wrath, not infrequently leading to expressions of wonder that " God has not cast them into hell long ago." And from this valley of humiliation the converts emerged, often suddenly, into " a holy repose of soul in God through Christ, and a secret disposition to fear and love him, and to hope for blessings from him," and into such " a sense of the greatness of his grace " as to lead, in many instances, to laughter, tears, or even to a " sinking " of the physical frame, as if the inward vision of God's glory were too much for mortal spirits to endure.

This type of Christian experience is foreign to the altered and unemotional age in which we live, but it was not peculiar to Edwards's congregation. The Puritan founders of New England had entered the Kingdom of Heaven by the same door; and one finds in the sermons of Hooker or of Shepard the same analysis of the inmost feelings of the sinful human heart, the same sense of the exceeding difficulty and relative infrequency of salvation, and the same consciousness of desert of the divine. wrath. It was to appear again not merely in the " Great Awakening " of 1740-42, but in the remarkable series of revivals which, beginning in the last decade of the eighteenth century, lasted nearly to the Civil War. But in

Edwards's sermons the view of conversion of which this experience is the normal accompaniment is put with a relentlessness of logic and a fertility of imagination that have never been surpassed. We trace his steps as he argues, in terms in which no parent would estimate the misdeeds of his child, that sin is infinite in its guilt because committed against an infinite object.[1] We follow his reasoning with a recoil that amounts to incredulity that such is the latent hatred of the unregenerate human mind that it would kill God if it could.[2] We revolt as we read Edwards's contention that the wicked are useful simply as objects of the destructive wrath of God;[3] as he beholds the unconverted members of the congregation before him withheld for a brief period by the restraining hand of God from the hell into which they are to fall in their appointed time;[4] as he pictures the damned glow in endless burning agony like a spider in the flame;[5] and heightens the happiness of the redeemed by the contrast between the felicities of heaven and the eternal torments of the lost, visible forever to the saints in glory.[6] No wonder one of his congregation was led to suicide and others felt themselves grievously tempted.[7]

[1] Sermon on Romans iv., 5, *Works*, vii., pp. 27, 28.
[2] *Ibid.* v., 10, *Works*, vii., pp. 168, 175.
[3] Sermon on Ezekiel xv., 2-4, *Works*, viii., pp. 129-150.
[4] Sermon on Deuteronomy xxxii., 35, *Works*, vii., pp. 487, 491, 496, 502.
[5] Sermon on Ezekiel xxii., 14, *Works*, vii., p. 393.
[6] *Ibid.*, xv., 2-4, *Works*, viii., pp. 141-143.
[7] *Narrative of Surprising Conversions*, *Works*, iii., pp. 77, 78.

Repulsive as this presentation is, it is but fair to Edwards to remember that it seemed to him to be demanded no less by his philosophic principles than by his interpretation of the Bible. And it is merely justice to recall, also, that though the terrors of the law fill a large place in his pulpit utterances, no man of his age pictured more glowingly than Edwards the joys of the redeemed,[1] the blessedness of union with Christ, or the felicities of the knowledge of God. When all deductions have been made from his presentation of Christian truth—and much must be made —he remains a preacher such as few have been of the eternal verities of sin, redemption, holiness, judgment, and enjoyment of God.

It is evidence that this awakening at Northampton was not the effect of Edwards's preaching alone, that a similar stirring took place within a few months throughout that section of Massachusetts and in a number of towns of Connecticut.[2] The news of this then unusual work drew attention to the young Northampton minister, not only from all parts of New England but from across the Atlantic. His sermons and methods brought some enemies, but many friends; and, at the request of the Rev. Drs. Isaac Watts and John Guyse, the leading Congregational ministers of England, Edwards prepared, and these ministers

[1] *E. g.*, his sermon on John xiv., 27, *Works*, viii., pp. 230-247.
[2] *Narrative of Surprising Conversions*, *Works*, iii., pp. 77, 78.

published at London, in 1737, an extended account of the revival.[1]

Known thus far and wide as one whose ministry had been signally distinguished by dramatic manifestations of spiritual power, it was natural that when the coming of Whitefield to the Congregational colonies, in the autumn of 1740, gave the human impetus to the marvellous religious overturning known as the " Great Awakening," Edwards should be regarded as the best American representative of the revival spirit which then had its most extensive manifestation. The story of that momentous stirring will be told in the next lecture more fully than our time will permit to-day. To Edwards it seemed at first the very dawning of the millennial age, and the visible manifestation of the divine glory.[2] It appeared but the repetition, not merely in Edwards's own parish, but on a scale coextensive with the American colonies, of the revival of his early ministry. He welcomed the youthful Whitefield to his pulpit; who, in turn, recorded an approval of the occupants of the Northampton parsonage in the words: " He is a Son himself, and hath also a Daughter of *Abraham* for his wife "; and said of Edwards, " I think

[1] *A Faithful Narrative of the Surprizing Work of God in the Conversion of Many Hundred Souls in Northampton and the Neighbouring Towns*, London, 1737. Generally known as the *Narrative of Surprising Conversions*. A briefer account by Edwards had been published at Boston late in 1736.

[2] *Some Thoughts Concerning the Present Revival of Religion in New England*, pp. 96-103. Boston, 1742.

I have not seen his Fellow in all *New England.*"[1] Edwards himself preached as an evangelist in many pulpits besides his own. And when criticism arose and waxed to denunciation in many quarters as the more radical elements of the movement ran their violent and divisive course, he defended the revival as a true work of the Spirit of God, which every Christian ought to favor to the utmost of his power, while deprecating the excesses of many of the exhorters, in his treatise of 1742, entitled *Some Thoughts Concerning the Present Revival of Religion in New England.*

But though Edwards distrusted, in this volume, the weight laid by many of the friends of the revival on the bodily effects which so frequently accompanied the preaching of Whitefield, Tennent, Parsons, Bellamy, or his own, he nevertheless insisted that they were oftentimes a real product of the Spirit of God, and he cites in proof an experience of his wife begun probably near the close of 1738 and reaching its culmination in the revival scenes of 1742. In so doing he gave a part of one of the most interesting chapters in mystic biography anywhere recorded [2]— the complement to it being contained in Mrs. Edwards's own account published by Dr. Dwight.[3] It is one which shows how Edward's thought had in it the germ of a development of his theology fully reached by his disciples as

[1] Whitefield's *Seventh Journal*, pp. 47, 48.
[2] *Thoughts*, pp. 62–78.   [3] Dwight, *Life*, pp. 171–186.

to the extent to which a Christian must be cordially submissive to the divine disposal. Edwards did, indeed, deprecate the statements of converts that they were willing to be damned, if God so chose. " They had not clear and distinct ideas of damnation," he says; " nor does any word in the Bible require such self-denial as this." [1] And he also held that an impenitent man might rightfully pray for God's mercy.[2] But Edwards taught that the essence of virtue is the preference of the glory of God to any personal interests. And the burden of Mrs. Edwards's struggle was this crucial problem of submission. It is illustrative of the wifely devotion of this remarkable woman that the very crises of her trial were her willingness to endure, if necessary, the disapproval of her husband, and to see another more successful than he in his Northampton pulpit, if God so desired. After these battles had been won, it was easy to go on to a sense of readiness to " die on the rack, or at the stake," or " in horror " of soul, rising at last to a willingness to suffer the torments of hell in body and soul "if it be most for the honour of God."[3]

These experiences were accompanied not once, but repeatedly by such a sense of the divine glory that [4]

---

[1] *Narrative of Surprising Conversions, Works*, iii., p. 37.

[2] Letter of 1741, in Dwight, *Life*, p. 150: " There are very few requests that are proper for an impenitent man, that are not also, in some sense, proper for the godly."

[3] Dwight, *Life*, p. 182.

[4] *Thoughts*, pp. 63, 76.

"the Strength of the Body [was] taken away, so as to deprive of all Ability to stand or speak; sometimes the Hands clinch'd, and the Flesh cold, but Senses still remaining";

and the result was

"all former Troubles and Sorrows of Life forgotten, and all Sorrow and Sighing fled away, excepting Grief for past Sins, and for remaining Corruption . . . a daily sensible doing and suffering every Thing for GOD, . . . eating for GOD, and working for GOD, and sleeping for GOD, and bearing Pain and Trouble for GOD, and doing all as the Service of Love."

What shall we say to these things? Not that they are not the real experiences of sensible men and women, in a period of high-wrought religious feeling. They are; or we must deny the Christian consciousness of Paul, of Bernhard, of Francis. But they are not the experiences of the normal religious life, and to insist on them as such is to make a great mistake.

And Edwards also came to feel that it was in some sense a mistake. When the "Great Awakening" was over, he published, in the light of that tremendous wave of excitement and its disappointing results, his noblest purely religious exposition, the *Treatise Concerning Religious Affections*, of 1746. None but a man of remarkable poise of judgment could have written it. It betrays no reaction against the movement which had so come short of what he hoped. It sees the good and the bad in it; and, rising above the temporary occasion, seeks to answer the question, "What is the Nature of True Religion?"[1]

Edwards,[2] unlike modern psychologists, divided the soul into two "faculties," understanding and affections—the latter including, but not separating, the will and the inclinations. Each faculty is the realm of religion, but that of the affections most of all—that is to say, no religion can be genuine which remains merely a matter of intellectual knowledge of truth without prompting to acts of will and outgoings of emotion.

But to be moved by strong emotions, Edwards perceived, is not necessarily to be religious. This was the mistake that many had made in the recent revival, and it was as great an error, Edwards thought, as the denial that the affections had to do with religion, which reaction from the excesses of the revival had produced in some. That emotion is greatly stirred, or that bodily effects are produced, are no signs that men are truly religious — though Edwards here sticks to his guns and declares that to affirm that bodily effects are not of themselves evidences of religion is not to affirm that true religious emotion may never have bodily effects. Nor are we to trust to a fluent tongue, a ready recollection of Scripture, an "appearance of love," a peculiar sequence of religious experiences, a sense of assurance,

[1] *Religious Affections*, Preface.
[2] In this paragraph I have tried to give a brief synopsis of the book.

a zeal for attending meetings, or an ability to give a well-sounding account of an alleged work of grace, as proving a man a Christian. Rather, true Christian affections involve a "new spiritual sense," which comes not by nature, but by the indwelling power of the Holy Spirit, inducing a new attitude of the heart toward God; an unselfish love for divine things because they are holy; a spiritual enlightenment which leads to a conviction of the certainty of divine truth and a humiliating sense of unworthiness; and a change of disposition which shows itself in love, meekness, tenderness of spirit, producing symmetry of character, increasing longing for spiritual attainments, and a life of Christian conduct in our relations to our fellow-men.

The ideal that Edwards held up is of exceeding loftiness—too high to be made, as he and his followers made it, the test of all Christian discipleship. But it is a noble ideal for a Christian man, and especially for a Christian minister, to hold before himself as that toward the realization of which his Christian life is striving in feeling and animating purpose.

It is as a personal illustration of the *Religious Affections*, I think, that we should view the biographical edition of the diary of his young friend, David Brainerd, the missionary to the Indians, which Edwards published in 1749.[1] Betrothed to Edwards's daughter

---

[1] "There are two Ways of representing and recommending true Religion and Virtue to the World, which GOD hath made Use of : The one

Jerusha, and dying at Edwards's house, in 1747, at the age of twenty-nine, Brainerd's story has the pathetic interest always attaching to frustrated promise; and his missionary zeal has made his consecration a stimulus to others. But, though one of the most popular of Edwards's books at the time of its publication, his *Life of Brainerd* is a distressing volume to read. The morbid, introspective self-examinations and the elevations and depressions of the poor consumptive are but a sorry illustration at best of the noble ideal of the full-rounded, healthful Christian life.

Edwards shared with Brainerd what our generation looks upon as the young sufferer's most winsome trait — his missionary sympathy; but opportunities for manifesting it in a rural New England parish in the middle of the eighteenth century were few. One such came in 1746, when a proposition reached New England from a number of Scotch ministers that Christians unite in a "concert of prayer for the coming of our Lord's kingdom" throughout the earth.[1] Edwards welcomed it eagerly, and, in 1747, published an extensive treatise in furtherance of the suggestion.[2] In

is by Doctrine and Precept; the other is by Instance and Example."— *An Account of the Life of the late Reverend Mr. David Brainerd*, Preface. Boston, 1749.

[1] *Works*, iii., pp. 370–372.

[2] *An Humble Attempt to promote Explicit Agreement and Visible Union of God's People in Extraordinary Prayer for the Revival of Religion and the Advancement of Christ's Kingdom on Earth.* Boston, 1747.

the course of this essay he took occasion not only to urge the desirability of united prayer and to answer some objections to union which seem rather absurd to our age, though they were then regarded as real difficulties, but to set forth his interpretation of prophecy and his ardent hope for the speedy coming of a brighter religious day.

Edwards's own personal trials were thickening in the years following the revival at which we have just been glancing. Some of the causes of growing estrangement between him and his Northampton people are patent enough ; some are obscure. Two are distinctly in evidence. The first was a case of discipline, apparently of the year 1744, wherein proceedings against a number of young people in his congregation for circulating what he deemed, doubtless truly, impure books, were so managed or mismanaged, as to alienate from him nearly all the young people of the town.[1]

The other evident cause was the controversy over the terms of church membership, which was the ostensible ground of his dismission.[2] In a former lecture some account was given of the rise of the "Half-Way Covenant" — that system approved by the second generation on New England soil, by which the

[1] Dwight, *Life*, pp. 299, 300.
[2] Dwight gives a full and documentary account of this controversy, *ibid.*, pp. 300-448.

children of church members, though themselves not consciously regenerate, were admitted to sufficient standing in the church to bring their children in turn to baptism, although themselves barred from the Lord's table. Hence the nickname " Half-Way Covenant," indicating that those who stood in this relation were members enough to enjoy the privileges of the one sacrament for their children, but not members enough to participate in the other.

This system became general in New England by the beginning of the eighteenth century; but in some places the earlier practice was yet further modified. Some argued that if earnest-minded though unregenerate children of church members were themselves sufficiently church members, by reason of the divine promise, " to be a God unto thee, and to thy seed after thee,"[1] to bring their children in turn to baptism, they were sufficiently members to come to the Lord's Supper. Indeed, it was their duty to come thither, if sincerely desirous of leading a Christian life, for they would find the communion, like prayer and public worship, a means tending to conversion. This view was made popular in the upper Connecticut valley by the great influence of Edwards's grandfather and predecessor, Solomon Stoddard. Held by him as early as 1679, he did not introduce the practice into the Northampton church till after 1700; but it

[1] Genesis xvii., 7.

soon after became the custom in that church and in most of its immediate neighbors.[1] Edwards was settled under it and practiced it for nearly twenty years.

Edwards's own lofty conceptions of the Christian life and his emphasis on conversion as its beginning led him gradually, however, to the conclusion that no church privileges should be given to those not conscious, in some degree, of a work of the Spirit of God in their own souls. He intimated this change of view in his *Religious Affections* of 1746;[2] but it illustrates the spiritual torpor that followed the fever of the "Great Awakening," and possibly the alienation between Edwards and his young people, that he waited from 1744 to December, 1748, for a single candidate for church membership to come forward even under the easy terms of the Northampton church. When an applicant at last appeared he made known his change of opinion, and intended change of practice, temperately and moderately. There was, indeed, a good deal to be said against such a modification as the pastor proposed. His honored grandfather had introduced the existing system; he had been settled, well knowing what it was; he had practiced it. It might be urged that it was a breach of contract for

---

[1] Some account may be found in Walker's *Creeds and Platforms*, pp. 279-282.

[2] Edwards's own statement, in Dwight, *Life*, p. 314.

him to abandon it. But, even granting this, one hardly understands the virulence of the opposition which Edwards encountered from those who must almost all have been his spiritual children. One hardly sees sufficient ground for the hostility that led to charges that Edwards planned a Separatist congregation; that refused to hear his arguments; that sought to induce prominent ministers to answer the admirable book which he published in 1749 in defense of his position;[1] that appears in the long wrangle over the composition of the council which should consider his further relations to the Northampton congregation; or in the bitter enmity of some of his kinsfolk in and out of the ministry of the county. Edwards himself once declared that he had little skill in conversation; " he was thought by some . . . to be stiff and unsociable "; he held himself aloof from pastoral calling save in cases of real need;[2] and one can but suspect that he lacked the art of leading men. Honest and conscientious to the core—in this change of practice, as in the case of discipline, he seems to have taken none of the preparatory measures which often make all the difference between success and failure in swaying a democratic body. Stoddard had certainly held his peculiar views for nearly thirty years before

[1] *An Humble Inquiry into the Rules of the Word of God, concerning the Qualifications Requisite to a compleat Standing and full Communion in the Visible Christian Church.* Boston, 1749.

[2] Hopkins, *Life*, pp. 44-46, 54.

they became the practice of his congregation, but such careful nurturing of a desired measure was apparently foreign to Edwards's nature. That the matter was intellectually clear to him was sufficient; it ought to be so to others.

But, however explainable, the fact remains that in this crisis Edwards had the support of no considerable portion of his congregation, nor did the strong sense of professional unity characteristic of the clergy of the eighteenth century prevent a majority of his neighboring ministers from opposing him. A council of nine churches met on June 19, 1750.[1] That advisory body having decided that Edwards's dismission was necessary if his people still desired it, the Northampton church voted by more than two hundred to twenty-three to dismiss its pastor. That action the council approved by a majority of one on June 22d. And the town added what was an insult to the burdens of the deposed pastor by voting, probably in November, 1750, that Edwards should not preach in the community. It is interesting to note that one, at least, of those of Edwards's congregation prominent in procuring his removal, and esteemed by the Northampton pastor his most energetic opponent, Joseph Hawley, Edwards's cousin, and a leading lawyer and politician,

---

[1] Dwight gives the documents, *Life*, pp. 398–403; Edwards wrote a most interesting account in letters of July 5, 1750, to Erskine, and of July 1, 1751, to Gillespie, Dwight, *ibid.*, pp. 405–413, 462–468.

afterward not only privately but publicly avowed his regret and repentance for what had been done.¹ And Edwards's contention in the principal subject of this controversy was not without abundant ultimate fruitage. His friends, notably his pupil, Rev. Dr. Joseph Bellamy, carried forward his attack on Stoddardeanism and the Half-Way Covenant, with the result that, by the first decade of the nineteenth century, when Edwards had been fifty years in his grave, the system had been generally set aside by the Congregational churches.

Turned out from his pastorate thus, at the age of forty-seven, with a family of ten living children,² he had to look about for a new charge. His friend, Rev. Dr. John Erskine, suggested a settlement in Scotland, where Erskine was a leader in the Church;³ the people of Canaan, Conn., heard him with approval;⁴ but the place of his next seven-years' sojourn was determined by a two-fold call that came to him through the efforts of his friend and pupil, Samuel Hopkins, in December, 1750, from the church in the little frontier village of Stockbridge to become its minister, and from the English "Society for the Propaga-

¹ Letter of May 9, 1760, Dwight, *ibid.*, pp. 421-427. See Edwards's characterization of him, *ibid.*, pp. 410, 411.

² Two daughters, however, were married in the year of Edwards's dismission.

³ Edwards's letter of July 5, 1750, Dwight, *Life*, p. 412.

⁴ Dexter, *Biographical Sketches of the Graduates of Yale College*, i., pp. 219, 220.

tion of the Gospel in New England," which had grown out of Eliot's labors a century before, to become its missionary to the Housatonic Indians at the same place.[1] Thither he and his household removed in the summer of 1751. But Stockbridge was not without its serious controversies between the new pastor and missionary and those who were exploiting the Indians for pecuniary advantage; and the chief of his new foes was a relative of some of his leading opponents in the Northampton separation. These disputes distressed the first years of his new settlement, but Edwards's position was so manifestly just that, with the support of the Commissioners whose missionary agent he was, victory and peace came to him.[2]

Edwards doubtless conscientiously fulfilled his stipulated duty of preaching to the Indians once a week through an interpreter,[3] besides ministering to the English-speaking Stockbridge congregation, but he was too settled in scholastic ways to make a successful missionary. His own judgment of himself he expressed when he wrote to Erskine, in 1750, that he was "fitted for no other business but study."[4] And

[1] Dwight, *Life*, p. 449; see also Hopkins's statement, West, *Sketches of the Life of the Late Rev. Samuel Hopkins*, pp. 53–57. Hartford, 1805.

[2] For some aspects of this controversy, see Dwight, *Life*, pp. 450–541.

[3] There is an outline of one of these sermons in Grosart, *Selections from the Unpublished Writings of Jonathan Edwards*, pp. 191–196. Privately printed (Edinburgh), 1865.

[4] Dwight, *Life*, p. 412.

at Stockbridge opportunity came to him, even amid the distractions of the great military struggle between France and England in which little Stockbridge was at times a turmoiled frontier outpost,[1] for studies which produced the four treatises by which he is best known —his *Careful and Strict Enquiry into the modern prevailing Notions of Freedom of Will*,[2] his *End for which God created the World*, his *Nature of True Virtue*,[3] and his *Great Christian Doctrine of Original Sin defended*.[4]

This is not the time and place, even if the lecturer possessed the ability, to enter on any thorough criticism, or even on any elaborate exposition, of these works. Viewed simply as feats of intellectual achievement they present the highest reach of the New England mind and have given their author a permanent place among the philosophers of the eighteenth century. Were Edwards's writings subtracted from the literature of colonial New England the residue would embrace little more than the discussions of a narrow and provincial society, aside from the course of the world's affairs. It was Edwards who gave to the thought of eighteenth-century New England about whatever interest and lasting repute it bears in other lands. Edwards's treatises involved no changes in his

[1] Compare Edwards's letter of April 10, 1756, to McCulloch, in Dwight, *Life*, p. 555.
[2] First edition, Boston, 1754.
[3] These two treatises were first published at Boston in 1765.
[4] First edition, Boston, 1758.

theology. Rather they were the logical formulation of what he had long taught.

Edwards's volume on the *Will*, usually esteemed his crowning work, was long planned,[1] but was not written till 1753. It was his supreme effort against the Arminianism which had been the horror of his early ministry. Calvinism, in this feature of its strenuous creed, had fallen low. Its contemporary defenders in England, like Watts and Doddridge, had been compelled, as Edwards's son Jonathan phrased it, to "bow in the house of Rimmon, and admit the *Self-Determining Power*" of the will.[2] In the *Discourse* published by Daniel Whitby, rector at the English Salisbury, in 1710, predestination in the Calvinistic sense was widely believed to have received its deathblow; and we may imagine that the arguments therein advanced had often been pressed upon Edwards's attention by his keen-minded kinsman and opponent in Northampton, Joseph Hawley, when the latter was a student in his household.[3] But whatever of local and personal interest there may have been for Edwards in the theme, the general defense of what he deemed the truth against widely prevalent error was motive enough to rouse a man of his temperament to utmost endeavor.

[1] Dwight, *Life*, p. 507.
[2] "Improvements in Theology," *ibid.*, p. 614.
[3] *Ibid.*, pp. 410, 411.

To Edwards's thinking,[1] human freedom signifies no more than a natural power to act in accordance with the choice of the mind. With the origin of that choice the will has nothing to do. Man is free to do as he chooses, but not free to determine in what direction his choice shall lie. His will always moves, and moves freely, in the line of his strongest inclination, but what that inclination will be depends on what man deems his highest good. While man has full natural power to serve God,— that is, could freely follow a choice to serve God if he had such an inclination,—he will not serve God till God reveals himself to man as his highest good and thus renders obedience to God man's strongest motive. Moral responsibility lies in his choice, not in the cause of the choice; and hence a man of evil inclination deserves condemnation, since each choice is his own act, even though the direction in which the choices are exercised is not in his control. Man cannot choose between various choices, nor can his choice originate without some impelling cause external to the will; but his will acts in the direction in which he desires to move, and is free in the sense that it is not forced to act counter to its inclination.

In this treatise Edwards took up conceptions essentially resembling those advanced by Hobbes, Locke,

[1] In describing Edwards's books I have borrowed some sentences from my *History of the Congregational Churches in the United States*, pp. 283-286. New York, 1894.

and Collins, with whose religious speculations he had no sympathy; but his use of these ideas was profoundly original. He appears to have been acquainted with the writings of Locke only, and his grasp of the points involved is far surer than that of the English philosopher. The volume was, till comparatively recent times, in extensive use, being esteemed by Calvinists generally an unanswerable critique of the Arminian position. It has met, however, with growing dissent, and though not often directly opposed of late years, is largely felt to lie outside the conceptions of modern religious thought; but it has acceptance still, especially with those who hold a necessitarian view of the universe, and may be said never to have had a positive and complete refutation, though suffering a constantly increasing neglect.

The preparation of this treatise on the *Will* was followed by the composition of two smaller essays, probably in 1755 [1]—that *Concerning the End for which God created the World*, and that on the *Nature of True Virtue*. Of the former investigation into a profound and mysterious theme it may be sufficient to say that Edwards's immediate interpreters, notably his son Jonathan, regarded it as uniting the two heretofore supposedly mutually exclusive explanations of the universe as created either for the happiness of finite beings or as a manifestation of the glory of the Creator.

[1] Dwight, *Life*, p. 542.

This union Edwards would effect by showing that both results " were the ultimate end of the creation," and that, far from being incompatible, " they are really one and the same thing." The universe in its highest possible state of happiness is the ultimate exhibition of the divine glory.[1]

The second of these treatises,—that on the *Nature of True Virtue*,— though incomplete, expresses in metaphysical form the feature of the teaching of Edwards that has probably most affected New England thought. He asserted that the elemental principle in virtue is benevolence, or love to intelligent being in proportion to the amount of being which each personality possesses.[2] Other things being equal, the worth of each personality is measured by the amount of being which it has. To use Edwards's illustration, " an *Archangel* must be supposed to have more existence, and to be every way further removed from *nonentity*, than a *worm*."[3] And the benevolence which constitutes virtue must go out to all in proportion to their value thus measured in the scale of being. Closely connected with this benevolence toward being in general is a feeling of love and attraction toward other beings who are actuated by a similar spirit of benevolence. But any love for being less wide than

---

[1] " Improvements in Theology," Dwight, *Life*, pp. 613, 614.
[2] *Nature of True Virtue*, *Works*, ii., pp. 394-401.
[3] *Ibid.*, p. 401.

this, or springing from any motive narrower than general benevolence cannot be true virtue.

This theory profoundly influenced New England theology. Reduced to popular thought, it taught that selfishness is sin, and that disinterested love to God and to one's fellow-men is righteousness. It seemed to furnish a self-evident demonstration of the necessity of a divinely wrought change of heart. It gave a ground also for holding that virtue is identical in its nature in God and man by showing that benevolence toward intelligent personalities in proportion to the amount of being that each possesses leads God, as the Infinite Being in comparison with whom the rest of the universe is infinitesimal, to seek first his own glory, while man, if actuated by the same motive of general benevolence, seeks first the glory of God. Nor was this doctrine less effective in giving a basis for philanthropy. It was no accident that classed Samuel Hopkins, sternest of the pupils of Edwards, or Jonathan Edwards the younger, clearest-minded expounder of the Edwardean system, among the earliest New England opponents of negro slavery, or drew the earliest missionaries of the American Board from Edwardean ranks. Like the treatise on the *Religious Affections*, this essay holds love to be the basal element in piety; but in its banishment of self-interest it left room for the assertion by some of Edwards's successors that no true benevolence could be present till the soul was ready to submit willingly to any disposition of itself which God saw was for the best good of the universe, even if that disposition was the soul's damnation. We have already noted that though Edwards never asserted this necessity, Mrs. Edwards reached this degree of self-renunciation in the revival of 1742.

The fourth important fruit of Edwards's studies was a volume that was passing through the press at the time of his death—that on *Original Sin*. Of all his works none is more ingenious or intellectually acute, but none has met so little acceptance. The subject of original sin, like that of the powers of the will, was one on which the eighteenth-century opponents of the historic Augustinian view were widely supposed to have got much the better of its defenders. Chief among these opponents in popular regard was John Taylor, a Presbyterian Arian minister at Norwich, England, whose *Scripture Doctrine of Original Sin*, of 1738, argued that sorrow, labor, and physical death are consequences to us of Adam's transgression, but we are in no sense guilty of Adam's sin, our rational powers are in no way disabled, nor are we on account of that sin in any state of natural corruption so as to be now without capacity fully to serve God.

These opinions were reflected in eastern Massachusetts; and, in 1757 and 1758, a lively exchange of pamphlets took place in which Rev. Samuel Webster of Salisbury and Rev. Charles Chauncy of Boston attacked the doctrine of original sin, while Edwards's friend, Rev. Peter Clark of Danvers, and his pupil, Rev. Joseph Bellamy, defended it. Edwards had probably written most of his volume when this American discussion opened; but though he had Taylor primarily in mind, it was doubtless hastened through the press in view of the debate on this side of the Atlantic.[1]

In his volume on original sin Edwards argued, with great wealth of illustration, the innate corruption of mankind at whatever stage of their existence from earliest infancy to old age, with proofs drawn from Scripture and experience. This corruption amounts in all, of whatever age, to utter ruin. It has its root in Adam's sin, and that sin is ours, but not by any Augustinian presence of humanity in Adam.[2] On the contrary, Edwards explained our guilt of that far-off transgression by a curious theory of the preservation of personal or racial continuity—a theory drawn in part from Locke's speculations on Identity and Diversity.[3] That which makes you and me to-day the same beings that thought or walked or studied yesterday is the constant creative activity of God. God, by a "constitution," or appointment of things, that is

[1] Some account of this controversy may be found in my *History of the Congregational Churches*, pp. 273-276.

[2] Here again I borrow from the volume above cited.

[3] Compare Fisher, *History of Christian Doctrine*, p. 403.

"arbitrary" in the sense that it depends on his will alone, sees fit to appoint that the acts and thoughts of the present moment shall be consciously continuous of those of the past ; and it is this ever-renewed creation that gives all personal identity to the individual.[1] What is true of each man is also true of the race. God has constituted all men one with Adam, so that his primal sin is really theirs, and they are viewed as "*Sinners*, truly guilty, and *Children of Wrath* on that *Account*."[2]

Mr. Lecky has characterized this volume as " one of the most revolting books that have ever proceeded from the pen of man."[3] Without at all sharing the severity of his criticism, it may fairly be said to be a work that renders more difficult, if anything, one of the most mysterious problems of religion—the origin and universal pervasiveness of evil.

Our glance at Edwards's principal writings has necessarily been fleeting; but it has sufficed to show that he impressed several principles on the minds of his contemporaries and successors. Teaching that the sinner possesses the natural power, but not the inclination, to do the will of God, he held that a change of disposition, wrought by a conversion through the

[1] See *Original Sin*, pp. 338-346. 1758.

[2] *Ibid.*, p. 355.

[3] *History of the Rise and Influence of the Spirit of Rationalism in Europe*, i., p. 368, New York, 1866; see also Allen, *Jonathan Edwards*, p. 312.

transforming work of the Spirit of God, was not merely the primary, but the only important, thing in beginning a Christian life. He taught, also, that the essential characteristic of that life was love to God and to his creatures rather than to self, and that there could be no true religious life which did not have its seat in the emotions and will even more than in the intellect. Edwards did not live long enough to work out a full-rounded system. But besides the evident features of his teachings at which we have glanced, he dropped many hints and half-elaborated suggestions which made his work not merely the beginning of a development carried much farther by his followers, but have led to the claim that he was the father of most various tendencies in later New England thought.

Edwards's pastorate at Stockbridge was the harvest-time of his intellectual activity; but it was followed by a brief episode that had the promise of usefulness for him as a former of character and a leader of young men. The death of Rev. Aaron Burr, the husband of Edwards's third daughter, Esther, in September, 1757, left vacant the presidency of Princeton College, which Burr had occupied since 1748. The "College of New Jersey" had been founded, in 1746, as an institution in more hearty sympathy with the revival movement to which Edwards was attached than were Harvard or Yale. Nine of its trustees were graduates of Yale.[1]

[1] Dexter, *Biographical Sketches*, i., p. 220.

The college had recently been permitted (1753) by the Connecticut legislature to raise funds in Edwards's native colony by means of a lottery, " for the encouragement of religion and learning," as the act read.[1] It appealed to New England as much as to the Middle States, and represented what was then freshest and most spiritually warm-hearted in New England thought. Naturally the trustees looked to Edwards; and, two days after Burr's death, elected him to the vacant presidency.[2]

Edwards hesitated. He wished to complete his *History of the Work of Redemption*, which should set forth his conceptions of theology as a whole.[3] Yet the call was one he felt to be pressing, and with the supporting advice of an ecclesiastical council which met at Stockbridge early in January, 1758, he accepted the appointment. But he was destined to assume the work of the proffered office only to lay it down. Inoculated with smallpox as a protective measure, on February 13, 1758, the disease, usually mild under such circumstances, took an unfavorable turn, and he died at Princeton, March 22d, in his fifty-fifth year, leaving his work, from a human point of view, incomplete.

Jonathan Edwards the controversialist, the revival

[1] *Colonial Records*, x., pp. 217, 218.
[2] Dwight, *Life*, p. 565.
[3] Letter to the Princeton trustees, *ibid.*, p. 569.

preacher, and the metaphysician is the figure oftenest in our thought. It is necessary that it should be so, for in all these respects he was a leader of men. But as we think of him in these attributes he seems remote. His controversies are over questions in which our age takes languid interest, his denunciatory sermons we read with reluctance, his explanations of the will, of the constitution of the human race, or of the end for which God created the world we admire as feats of intellectual strength; but they do not move our hearts or altogether command the assent of our understandings. The thought I wish to leave with you is rather of the man who walked with God. No stain marred his personal character, no consideration of personal disadvantage swayed him from what he deemed his duty to the truth in the controversy at Northampton which led to his dismission. He was the type of a fearless, patient, loyal scholar. But this steadfast-mindedness was based on more than personal uprightness. To him God was the nearest and truest of friends, as well as the strongest of sovereigns. In his narrative of his religious experience he noted the delight and the strength that he found in the saying of the old Hebrew prophet regarding the Saviour:[1] " A man shall be as an hiding place from the wind, and a covert from the tempest; as rivers of water in a dry place, as the shadow of a great rock in a weary

[1] Isaiah xxxii., 2 ; see Hopkins, *Life*, p. 36 ; Dwight, *Life*, p. 132.

land." Above all his other gifts and acquisitions he had, and he made men feel that he had, a vision of the glory of God that transfigured his life with a beauty of spirit that makes his memory reverenced even more than his endowments of mind are respected.

CHARLES CHAUNCY

VII.

CHARLES CHAUNCY

AS one walks up Beacon Street from King's Chapel in Boston one passes, at the crown of the hill, two handsome buildings, each devoted to the interests of a religious body calling itself Congregational. Almost opposite each other, Channing Hall and the new Congregational House bear witness in brown-stone, or in granite, marble, and brick, to the division of the historic churches of colonial New England into two separate, and probably permanently antagonistic, camps,— those nicknamed "Orthodox" and "Liberal." The visible manifestation of this separation dates only from the opening decades of the nineteenth century; but the causes of this parting run back at least sixty years before, and reveal themselves in the sharp antagonisms of pre-Revolutionary Massachusetts.

In the last lecture we considered the life and work of Jonathan Edwards, chief leader among our native New England ministry in a revived and intenser Calvinism, in a warmer spiritual life, and in an insistent and awakening type of preaching. To-day we shall turn to the story of one who was often Edwards's opponent, who had no sympathy with Edwards's theology, who doubted the wisdom of the revival movement which Edwards championed, and who largely helped to give an impetus in the direction which Edwards stigmatized as "Arminian," or even toward more "Liberal" views beyond, to a considerable section of the New England churches.

The name Charles Chauncy has been twice borne by men eminently distinguished in the New England ministry. The first to wear it was a Puritan exile, who had been born in 1592, had graduated from Trinity College, Cambridge, in 1613, had enjoyed a fellowship at that university, and had been vicar at the English town of Ware for ten stormy years when the policy of Laud drove him to New England in 1637.[1] After preaching three years to the Pilgrim congregation at Plymouth, where he was recognized as a man of learning and power, in spite of some criticism caused by his insistence on the immersion of infants and the celebration of the Lord's Supper in the evening as the only rightful modes of observing the sacraments,[2] he was called to Scituate in 1641; and in November, 1654, became the second president of

---

[1] For sketches of President Chauncy, see Mather, *Magnalia*, i., pp. 463-476, 1853-55; and W. C. Fowler, in *New England Historical and Genealogical Register*, x., pp. 105-120, 251-262.

[2] Winthrop's *Journal*, i., pp. 397-399; ii., pp. 86, 87, 1853.

Harvard, a post that he filled with conspicuous ability till his death in February, 1672.

President Chauncy's eldest son, Isaac, after graduating at the infant Harvard in 1651, discharged a learned, controversial, and unpopular ministry in England, chiefly in London, till his death in 1712.[1] This Isaac had, in turn, a son, named Charles for his distinguished grandfather, who in early life followed the grandfather's example by emigrating to America, and died, a merchant, at Boston, in May, 1711.[2] To the merchant a son was born at Boston, on New Year's day, 1705, to whom the name Charles was given in turn, and who is the subject of the present lecture.[3]

Left an orphan at six years of age, Charles grew up at Boston, and in 1717, when scarcely twelve, entered Harvard, being a few months younger at the time he began his college course than was Jonathan Edwards when the latter entered Yale a year before. Graduating

[1] Sibley, *Graduates of Harvard*, i., pp. 302-307.
[2] *N. E. Hist. and Gen. Register*, x., p. 324.
[3] No full biography of Rev. Dr. Charles Chauncy has been published. His colleague, Rev. John Clarke, published a *Discourse . . . at the Interment of the Reverend Charles Chauncy*, at Boston in 1787, which has some biographic facts. Brief sketches may be found in Emerson, *Historical Sketch of the First Church in Boston*, pp. 173-214, Boston, 1812; by Fowler, in *N. E. Hist. and Gen. Register*, x., pp. 324-336; in *Memorials of the Chauncys*, pp. 49-70, Boston, 1858; in Sprague, *Annals of the American Pulpit*, "Unitarians," pp. 8-13, New York, 1865; and in Ellis, *History of the First Church in Boston*, pp. 187-208, Boston, 1881. An appreciation of his literary work may be found in Tyler, *History of American Literature*, ii., pp. 199-203, New York, 1879.

in 1721 with a distinguished record for scholarship, he studied theology at Boston or at Cambridge; and, on June 12, 1727, was chosen by a vote of sixty-four to forty-five to the colleague pastorate of the old First Church of Boston at a salary of four pounds and ten shillings a week and firewood for his household use.[1] On October 25th, following, he was ordained[2]; as was the custom, preaching the sermon himself,[3] for New England had not yet wholly outgrown the feeling that such a service was a test of the candidate's pulpit abilities, as essential to enable the council to judge of his fitness as his examination in theology or his relation of Christian experience.

Chauncy's elder associate in the charge of the Boston First Church was Thomas Foxcroft, who had occupied that post with eminent repute as a preacher since 1717, and was to labor side by side with Chauncy till death separated the colleagues in 1769.[4] It illustrates the fundamental kindliness of spirit of the two men thus joined in a common work, that though they took diametrically opposite positions regarding the questions raised by the "Great Awakening," and wrote, the one in defense and the other in disapproval,

---

[1] Emerson, p. 176; Ellis, p. 187.　　　　[2] Ellis, p. 187.

[3] His text was Matt. xxviii., 20.

[4] Foxcroft died June 18, 1769, in his seventy-third year. Though he continued in the pastorate of the Boston First Church till his death, he was thought to have lost something of his early fire and pulpit power, owing to a paralytic shock experienced in 1736.

of that hotly contested movement, this disagreement never affected their personal good-fellowship. " He was a real good Christian," said Chauncy of Foxcroft as he preached that colleague's funeral sermon, " a partaker of the Holy Ghost; uniform in his walk with God . . . fixing his dependence . . . on the mercy of God and the atoning blood and perfect righteousness of Jesus Christ "; [1] and this spiritual appreciation one for the other seems to have underlain the sharp diversities of view of these long-associated ministers.

Naturally, as the younger colleague of a preacher of reputed eloquence, and even more because he was marked, as a sermonizer, by a studious simplicity of speech that avoided all rhetorical adornment as a species of intellectual dishonesty, Chauncy's early ministry attracted little notice. Indeed, this simplicity of pulpit composition, which always characterized him, led a hearer, to whom it was reported that Chauncy had prayed that God would never make him an orator, to observe that "his prayer was unequivocally granted." [2] Something of this lack of rhetorical adornment may have been due to a rapidity of composition which frequently enabled him to write his afternoon sermon in full during the noon-day intermission between the two Sunday services. But the same qualities of style appear in his

[1] Sermon on the *Death of Rev. Thomas Foxcroft*, Boston, 1769, quoted in Ellis, p. 183.   [2] Emerson, p. 184.

most labored treatises; and in the investigation of a doctrinal or political theme Chauncy was capable of most protracted study. He had none of the intuitive grasp or metaphysical genius of Edwards, but in patient scholarly investigation he had not a superior, and probably not an equal, in eighteenth-century New England. The ornate taste of the period immediately following the American Revolution was inclined to ridicule Chauncy's style a little;[1] but men always respected his thought. Yet his very simplicity and directness make his sermons easy reading; and a modern reader deems it not the least of merits that one is never at a loss as to Chauncy's meaning. What he has to say is always worthy of attention, and the thought frequently stands out all the more strikingly by reason of the plainness of its verbal garb.

This directness of public utterance in the pulpit or by the written page was accompanied by a similar bluntness of private address. Chauncy would not flatter.[2] Yet, though deemed rather formidable when he called on his parishioners, as he was accustomed to do on Monday mornings,[3] he always had a kindly heart, and his family life was always cheerful and helpful. A friend of his later years has thus drawn his portrait:[4]

[1] John Clarke, *Discourse*, p. 28; Emerson, p. 205.
[2] John Clarke, *ibid.*, p. 25.
[3] Ellis, p. 194.
[4] Letter of Rev. Dr. Bezaleel Howard, dated January 22, 1833, in Sprague, *Annals*, "Unitarians," p. 12.

"He was, like Zaccheus, little of stature. God gave him a slender, feeble body, a very powerful, vigorous mind, and strong passions; and he managed them all exceedingly well. His manners were plain and downright,—dignified, bold, and imposing. In conversation with his friends he was pleasant, social, and very instructive."

In his home-life he was the cheerful and friendly companion. A student by habit, he yet found the time to be much with his household. But he had to endure the discipline of much personal sorrow. His own health was long precarious. Three times he had to mourn the death of a wife. His declining years were spent in the comparative wreck of the town of his ministry consequent upon the struggles for American independence, — for Boston did not recover its population or its full prosperity till near the time of Chauncy's death.

The little colonial seaport capital of Chauncy's early ministry had altered much since the days of John Cotton.[1] Though still largely Puritan, the Puritan ascendancy had been more broken there than elsewhere in New England. Its inhabitants numbered about fifteen thousand at Chauncy's settlement, and did not increase to more than twenty thousand during the period covered by his long ministry. But they

[1] See the *Memorial History of Boston*, Boston, 1882, *passim*, especially ii., pp. 187-268, 437-490; iii., pp. 189-191, for the facts presented in this paragraph.

included the wealthy and the political administrators of the colony; and the officers of government combined with the more prosperous merchants and shipowners to form an aristocracy of much pretensions to fashion and of much desire to reflect, in a distant way, London social life. English books were more widely read than in rural New England. English philosophical and religious thought found a ready response. The cosmopolitan spirit characteristic of a seaport was more manifest in ideals and habits of life than elsewhere in New England. Congregationalism was the predominant religious polity, being represented by seven churches at the time of Chauncy's settlement; but two Episcopal churches drew upon the elements of the community which were by reason of crown appointments or by taste most in sympathy with England; while the French Huguenot exiles, the Quakers, the Baptists, and the Presbyterians were represented by single congregations.

If the provincial town had its questions of wealth, politics, and fashion beyond any other in New England, it had also in a peculiar degree its problems of poverty. In spite of a cheapness of many articles of food as surprising to a Londoner of that time as to any present New England householder, a report prepared fifteen years after Chauncy's settlement enumerated a thousand poor widows, sure testimony to the tribute of life wrung by the ocean from the commerce of the seaport, and fifteen hundred negroes; and as early as 1735, the town authorities declared to the provincial legislature that Boston had become "the resort of all sorts of poor people, which instead of adding to the wealth of the town, serve only as a burden and continual charge."[1]

Religiously estimated, Boston was not what it had been in the days of the founders. The old Puritan enthusiasm had departed, and though the Sunday congregations were large and Sunday was observed with a strictness that surprised English visitors, the Thursday Lecture, once so popular, was greatly neglected;[2] while wealth, commercial interests, and the presence of a foreign office-holding class had largely deprived religion of its original primacy in popular interest. "The Generality,"[3] wrote Whitefield in his journal of 1740, "seem to be too much conformed to the World. There's much of the Pride of Life to be seen in their Assemblies. Jewels, Patches, and gay Apparel are commonly worn by the Female Sex, and even the common People, I observed, dressed up in the Pride of Life."

Such was the general aspect of affairs when Boston, in common with the American colonies as a whole,

[1] *Boston Town Records*, January 1, 1735; in *Memorial History of Boston*, ii., p. 459.
[2] *Ibid.*, pp. 467, 468; see also Whitefield's characterization in his *Seventh Journal*, p. 44. 2d edition, London, 1744.
[3] Whitefield, *ibid.*

was shaken by the " Great Awakening "[1] in 1740. Premonitory evidences of an increased interest in religion had appeared in revival movements in many places in rural New England during the five years that had elapsed since the " surprising conversions " under Edwards's ministry at Northampton narrated in a previous lecture. But the chief human agency in the general spiritual overturning that began in 1740 was George Whitefield. That youthful evangelist came to New England in the height of his early fame. Not yet twenty-six at the time of his arrival in Boston, in September, 1740, his reputation for zeal, consecration, and an oratorical power probably unmatched in the history of the Anglo-Saxon pulpit, had preceded him, and produced an expectancy in the popular mind that well prepared the way for the deep impression that his actual presence caused. " My hearing how god was with him everywhere as he came along," wrote one of his humbler converts,[2] "it solumnized my mind & put me in a trembling fear before he began to preach for he looked as if he was Cloathed with authority from ye great god." His ecclesiastical position was one, moreover, to attract attention. In full sympathy with the type of religious thought characteristic of the Congregational and Presbyterian

[1] The best single account of this revival movement and its consequences is still that of Joseph Tracy, *The Great Awakening*, Boston, 1842.

[2] See Nathan Cole's Narrative, in G. L. Walker, *Some Aspects of the Religious Life of New England*, pp. 89-92. Boston, 1897.

Churches, he was yet a minister of the Church of England; and he represented also the spiritual power of the new Oxford movement in which he and the Wesleys were alike leaders. New England had never listened to such a preacher, and has never in its history bowed in such admiration before any proclaimer of the Gospel message.

At Boston Whitefield was greeted enthusiastically by all classes in the community. Governor Belcher welcomed him with effusion and was one of his most devoted and demonstrative hearers. On the Sunday following his arrival he preached for Foxcroft, Chauncy's colleague, with " great and visible effect ";[1] and this experience was repeated for ten days in most of the Congregational meeting-houses of Boston or with larger audiences on the Common. A brief journey to the eastward as far as York was followed by another week of similar pulpit success in Boston, and then the evangelist passed onward in his rapid flight by way of Concord and Worcester to Northampton, and thence, preaching at Westfield, Springfield, Hartford, New Haven, and at some of the smaller intermediate towns, to New York and the southern colonies. Everywhere his audiences were as wax under the spell of his eloquence. On repeated occasions men cried out and women fainted; many in the weeping congregations declared themselves converted. Massachusetts and

[1] Whitefield, *Seventh Journal*, p. 28.

Connecticut were profoundly stirred. And the message was, on the whole, one addressed to the real wants of sinful men. It was adapted not merely to excite the emotions of a passing hour, but to point out the need and the way of salvation. The movement thus inaugurated had upon it in some very considerable degree the blessing of God. The two or three years that followed Whitefield's preaching were the only marked period of general ingathering that our churches enjoyed between the passing away of the founders of New England and the last decade of the eighteenth century.

Yet, if the young evangelist was undoubtedly earnest and sincere, he was also opinionated and harsh in his judgments; and these qualities speedily made trouble. Speaking in the Old South Church during his stay in Boston he declared that " the Generality of Preachers talk of an unknown, unfelt Christ. And the Reason why Congregations have been so dead, is because dead Men preach to them."[1] This strain of criticism he reiterated throughout New England. In spite of Jonathan Edwards's protest,[2] he preached at Suffield, to the students at New Haven, and elsewhere on "the dreadful Ill-Consequences of an unconverted Ministry."[3] And, in summing up the impressions of his

---

[1] Whitefield, *Seventh Journal*, p. 40.
[2] Dwight, *Life of Pres. Edwards*, p. 147.
[3] Whitefield, *Seventh Journal*, pp. 50, 53, 55.

New England pilgrimage for publication, Whitefield wrote: " Many, nay most that preach, I fear do not experimentally know Christ ";[1] while of Harvard and Yale he recorded his impression that " their Light is become Darkness, Darkness that may be felt."[2]

A second characteristic of Whitefield which gave countenance to what was later to be the most extravagant feature of the "Awakening" was the weight which he put on the physical effects of his preaching as evidence of the presence of God in the congregation. Though Rev. Thomas Prince could witness that he did " not remember any crying out, or falling down, or fainting "[3] under Whitefield's preaching at Boston, such extreme physical manifestations took place during the delivery of his sermons elsewhere ;[4] and even at Boston Whitefield could record of his preaching in the New North Church that[5]

" Jesus Christ manifested forth his Glory. Many hearts melted within them. . . . Look where I would, the Word smote them, I believe, through and through, and my own Soul was very much carried out. Surely it was the Lord's Passover. I have not seen a greater Commotion since my Preaching at *Boston*."

So markedly was this over-valuation of the physical a trait of the young evangelist that Edwards, who, as

[1] Whitefield, *Seventh Journal*, p. 56.   [2] *Ibid.*, p. 57.
[3] Quoted in Tracy, *Great Awakening*, p. 116.
[4] Whitefield, *Seventh Journal*, pp. 59, 62, 63, 69, 74.
[5] *Ibid.*, p. 39.

we have seen, was not out of sympathy with such bodily manifestations of extreme feeling, remonstrated with Whitefield on the importance attached to them.[1]

These peculiarities of the English revivalist were exaggerated by those whom his preaching raised up to imitate his methods. Many of these itinerating pastors, like Edwards, Bellamy, Parsons, Wheelock, Pomeroy, or Graham, were men of the highest character and great usefulness to the churches. Yet, under Edwards's preaching at Northampton in 1741, as Edwards himself recorded, " it was a *very frequent* Thing to see an *House full of Out-Cries, Faintings, Convulsions*, and such like ";[2] and under Parsons's searching appeals, to quote the preacher's own words, " stout men fell as though a cannon had been discharged, and a ball had made its way through their hearts."[3] Men claimed to see heaven and hell in visions; and whole communities were thrown into excitement by these reports, as was Lebanon, Connecticut, by the assertions of a boy of thirteen and of a girl of eleven that Christ had shown them the Book of Life, and the names of some of their neighbors written therein, and that " the Book of Life was filled up, wanting about One Page . . . and when that was fill'd up, the Day of Judgment was to come."[4]

[1] Dwight, *Life of Pres. Edwards*, p. 147; Tracy, *Great Awakening*, p. 100. [2] *Christian History*, issue for January 21, 1743-44. [3] Tracy, p. 138.
[4] Solomon Williams, *The More Excellent Way*, Preface. New London, 1742.

And the more radical leaders in the movement were marked by yet more questionable methods. Of these extremists the most notorious was James Davenport, minister at Southold, Long Island, regarding whom Whitefield, whose judgments as to character were not penetrating, affirmed " that he never knew one keep so close a walk with God."[1] Preaching as an itinerant at Boston, in July, 1742, Davenport declared in prayer, " that most of the ministers of the town of Boston and of the country are unconverted, and are leading their people blindfold to hell."[2] At New London, in March, 1743, in a scene that was almost a riot, he heaped up the books of Flavel, Increase Mather, Colman, Sewall, his fellow-revivalist Parsons, and others held in esteem in the churches, and walked about the blazing pile, declaring that as the smoke of these volumes went upward, so the smoke of their authors was now rising from the torments of hell.[3] Davenport did, indeed, later modify his practices,[4] and a Boston jury, as well as the Connecticut Legislature, adjudged him insane. But he undoubtedly represented a certain phase of the "Awakening."

The effect of this turmoil was largely disastrous.

[1] Tracy, *Great Awakening*, p. 230.

[2] *Ibid.*, p. 247.

[3] *Ibid.*, p. 249. For further volumes burned, see Chauncy, *Seasonable Thoughts*, pp. 222, 223. Boston, 1743.

[4] See *Two Letters from the Rev. Mr. Williams & Wheelock of Lebanon, to the Rev. Mr. Davenport, which were the Principal Means of his late Conviction and Retraction.* Boston, 1744.

The "Awakening" ceased almost as speedily as it had begun, and was followed by a period of great spiritual deadness. Edwards himself, as before stated, waited from 1744 to 1748 for a candidate for church membership to appear. Churches were divided. In Connecticut severe measures were taken by the civil authorities to prevent itinerancy and any preaching undesired by the regular incumbent of the parish. In that colony, and to some extent in Massachusetts, the more extreme sympathizers with the revival formed Separatist churches that ran a stormy, spiritually distracted, and persecuted career. In general the ministry and the churches of New England and of the middle colonies were divided into two camps on the question whether the methods of the revival were to be praised or blamed, known as " New Lights " and " Old Lights " in New England and as " New Side " and " Old Side " in the colonies to the southward.

Of this " Old Light " party in New England Chauncy was the leader, and this leadership first brought him into prominence. Thoroughly convinced himself that the Whitefieldian revival was an outburst of ill-directed emotion that would do more harm than good to the abiding spiritual life of the churches, and averse by nature to what he deemed extravagance of method and appeal, he set himself to do what he could to check the evils of a movement that seemed to him dangerous to true religion.

Chauncy, though condemned by many as an "opposer of the work of God;"[1] was no denier of the necessity of a fundamental change of heart as essential to entrance on the Christian life. A brief extract from his sermon on *The New Creature*,[2] preached about eight months after Whitefield's visit to Boston may illustrate alike his views and his sermonic style.[3]

" Put the question to your own soul, Have I had experience of such a change, as that I can esteem myself a *new creature?* Have I indeed been *transform'd by the renewing of the* HOLY GHOST ? How is it with my APPREHENSIONS ? . . . What are my tho'ts of sin ? Does it seem a slight thing or an accursed evil ? What are my thoughts of holiness ? Do I entertain a low opinion of it, or does it appear a matter infinitely reasonable and important ? What are my thoughts of CHRIST ? Do I see no beauty in him for which he should be desired, or does he appear altogether lovely ? Can I, in my own apprehensions, do without him, or do I see the need, the absolute need I stand in of him, and that there is no other name given under heaven among men, whereby I can be saved ? And how is it with my PURPOSES ? What am I determin'd for, this world or another ? Is my resolution for GOD and CHRIST and *heaven* and *holiness*, a sudden, accidental, transient business, or the settled, permanent, habitual purpose of my heart ? And how is it with my AFFECTIONS ? On what are

[1] Edwards, *Thoughts Concerning the Present Revival*, pp. 143, 144, Boston, 1742 ; Chauncy, *Seasonable Thoughts*, pp. 392, 393.

[2] *The New Creature Describ'd, and consider'd as the sure Characteristic of a Man's being in Christ*, Boston, 1741. Preach'd at the Boston Thursday Lecture, June 4, 1741.

[3] *Ibid.*, pp. 21, 22.

they plac'd, and after what manner are they exercis'd? Whom do I love most, GOD or the world? Which do I fear most, the anger of GOD, or outward losses and crosses? What grieves me most, the frowns of the world, or the want of GOD's favour? Which do I place my hope most in, the things of time, or the things of eternity? And how is it as to my LIFE AND MANNERS? . . . Have I renounced my sins, all my sins, my most beloved sins, or do I still keep them? And if I have turn'd from sin, to whom have I turn'd? Have I turn'd to GOD in CHRIST? And is it my daily constant endeavour to live to GOD? What is my course and manner of life? Is it conducted by the will of GOD? Is it conform'd to the example of CHRIST? Is it a just transcript of the precepts of the gospel? Am I pious towards GOD? Am I righteous towards men? Am I sober in respect of myself?"

This is no low or mean conception of conversion. It is not unworthy of Edwards himself in its spiritual insight. But, all the more because Chauncy thus emphasized the patient manifestations of the renewed life as the true evidence of Christian character, he doubted the spiritual worth of the sudden emotions, the exciting sermons, the crowds, the outcries, and the visions of the Whitefieldian revival. Undoubtedly he discredited that revival too much. God's hand was in it more than he could see. But his motives in opposing it were no lower, or less directed to what he deemed the advancement of the kingdom of God, than those of its warmest advocates.

Chauncy preached a sermon having for its theme

the *Out-pouring of the Holy Ghost*, on May 13, 1742,[1] when his church held a fast to supplicate that divine blessing, and in the discourse he set forth with clearness and power what a permanent work of the divine Spirit would be; but by the autumn of that year the coming of Rev. James Davenport to Boston led him to a positive, rather than a predominantly negative, attack on what he deemed the errors of the "Awakening." Though he declared in his sermon on *Enthusiasm*,[2] or, as we should say, Fanaticism, that "the SPIRIT of GOD has wro't effectually on the hearts of many, from one time to another; and I make no question he has done so of late, in more numerous instances, it may be, than usual";[3] he now directly and powerfully attacked those methods of which the doings of James Davenport were an extreme instance.

Always a student, and intent on drawing from the past warnings against the excesses of the present, Chauncy published the same year an account of the fanatical manifestations among the persecuted Huguenots of the Cervennes,[4] and of English claimants to

---

[1] *The Out-pouring of the Holy Ghost. A Sermon Preach'd in Boston, May 13, 1742.* Boston, 1742.

[2] *Enthusiasm described and caution'd against*, Boston, 1742. Preached the "Lord's day after the Commencement, 1742." Text, 1 Cor. xiv., 37.

[3] *Ibid.*, pp. 25, 26.

[4] *The Wonderful Narrative, or a Faithful Account of the French Prophets*, Glasgow, 1742. The best account of these "prophets" is in Baird, *The Huguenots and the Revocation of the Edict of Nantes*, ii., pp. 183-190.

prophetic inspiration like John Lacy;[1] but his chief polemic treatise was called out by Edwards's defense of the revival, printed, as has been pointed out in a previous lecture,[2] in 1742, and entitled *Some Thoughts Concerning the present Revival of Religion in New England*. To Edwards, Chauncy replied, in 1743, in an elaborate volume, the *Seasonable Thoughts on the State of Religion in New England*,[3] imitating in title Edwards's work. In this book Chauncy gave an extensive and painstaking collection of evidence witnessing to the extravagances and disorders of the "Awakening," and prefaced the whole with a historical account of the Antinomian controversy of a hundred years before as affording in some sense a parallel. It was considered a most effective arraignment at the time of its publication, and it is indispensable to any present-day student of the revival.

This protracted controversy caused Chauncy great labor. How great, and with what physical results, can best be told in his own words.[4]

" Mr. Whitefield made his appearance among us. This kept me still to close and constant labor in my study. I

[1] These "prophecies" may be found in *The Prophetical Warnings of John Lacy, Esq., Pronounced under the Operation of the Spirit*, London, 1707; and several similar contemporary tracts.

[2] See *ante*, p. 238.

[3] Boston, 1743.

[4] From a manuscript letter of May 6, 1768, to Rev. Dr. Ezra Stiles, now in the possession of Yale University.

wrote and printed in that day more than two vol. in oct? A vast number of pieces were published also wrote by others; but y^r was scarce a piece . . . but was sent to me, and I had the labor sometimes of preparing it for the press, and always of correcting the press. I had also hundreds of letters to write in answer to letters received from all parts of the country. This labor, continued without interruption, for so many years, in addition to my ministerial work, wch I did not neglect in any part of the time, broke my constitution . . . and brot on an habitual cholic wch reduced me to a skeleton in opposition to the utmost skill of all the physicians in town. But by a resolute severity as to regimen, and a great number of journies of 7, 8, 9, and 10 hundred miles, in the course of three or four years, I so far recovered my health, as to be able to pursue my studies again."

Some features of this regimen, to which Chauncy attributed his restored health, were thus noted by a friend of his old age.[1]

" The Doctor was remarkably temperate in his diet and exercise. At twelve o'clock he took one pinch of snuff, and only one in twenty-four hours. At one o'clock, he dined on one dish of plain, wholesome food, and after dinner took one glass of wine, and one pipe of tobacco, and only one in twenty-four hours. And he was equally methodical in his exercise, which consisted chiefly or wholly in walking. I said, ' Doctor, you live by rule.' ' If I did not, I should not live at all.' "

Chauncy's attitude in the Whitefieldian controversy

[1] Letter of Rev. Dr. Bezaleel Howard, in Sprague, *Annals*, "Unitarians," p. 13.

brought him into prominence not only in New England but in Scotland. Whether for this eminence or on more personal grounds, he received the degree of Doctor of Divinity from the University of Edinburgh in 1742.[1]

This controversy showed him to be a man of courage in the expression of his convictions, and the same characteristic trait was exhibited in another arena in 1747. Massachusetts from 1690 to 1750, and again during the Revolutionary War was plagued with a depreciated paper currency, the story of which might prove instructive to those among us who wish to " expand " the circulating medium. At Chauncy's settlement about two and two thirds of a shilling in notes had been equivalent to a shilling in " hard money "; by 1747 it took six and a half of the paper issue to equal the coin it supposedly represented.[2] In his election sermon before the governor and legislature, on May 27, 1747,[3] Chauncy spoke temperately but unmistakably against this[4] and a number of other current abuses from the text, " He that ruleth over Men must be just, ruling in the Fear of God."[5] This plainness of speech angered not a few of the legislators, and

---

[1] It first appears on the title-page of his sermon on *Enthusiasm*; see *Historical and Genealogical Register*, x., p. 325.

[2] See the table given by Felt, *An Historical Account of Massachusetts Currency*, p. 135. Boston, 1839.

[3] *Election Sermon*, Boston, 1747.

[4] *Ibid*, pp. 19-23, 29-31, 37-42, 62-64.   [5] 2 Samuel, xxiii., 3.

a fruitless proposition was made that the legislature should express its displeasure by refusing the customary publication of the sermon. Chauncy thus answered the man who told him.[1]

" It shall be printed, whether the general court print it or not. And do you, sir, say from me, that, if I wanted to initiate and instruct a person into all kinds of iniquity and double dealing, I would send him to our general court."

The Whitefieldian controversy had interrupted a course of study which fitted Chauncy for the next great public discussion in which he engaged,—that on Episcopacy. In his account of his own life, Chauncy has written thus of the beginnings of his investigation of this theme.[2]

" The occasion was that Mr Davenport [3] [first rector of Trinity Church, Boston] who married my first wife's sister, declared for the Church, and went over [to England] for orders, . . . I imagined my connection wth him would naturally lead me into frequent conversations upon this point. And that I might be thoroughly qualified for a debate wth him or others he might be connected wth . . . I entered upon this study."

The studies thus begun for a domestic use were eventually employed in a much wider debate. To us the opposition of the Congregational ministry and

[1] Emerson, *Historical Sketch of the First Church in Boston*, p. 198.
[2] Letter of May 6, 1768, to Dr. Ezra Stiles, in possession of Yale University.
[3] Rev. Addington Davenport, Harvard, 1719, died in 1746.

churches of the eighteenth century to Episcopacy may seem undue and uncharitable. An examination of the situation will disabuse us of the thought. That opposition was not primarily to Episcopacy as a religious system, but to Episcopacy in its political consequences. The New England colonies had been planted by men and women anxious to get beyond the reach of the bishops and courts of the English Establishment. But these colonies were still subject to the authority of the British government, and should that government see fit to establish the religious institutions of England beyond the Atlantic, there was nothing to prevent the non-Episcopal churches of the colonies from suffering the disabilities imposed on " Dissenters " in England.

Doubtless there was much want of charity in both parties; but the interferences of the English government in the affairs of the Congregational churches of Massachusetts,— an interference incited by the few Episcopal ministers in the province,—was ominous of what might happen were Episcopacy to grow in power. Two instances may suffice. When the Congregational churches of Massachusetts sought to call a " Synod," in 1725, to take counsel as to how the prevailing religious decline could be arrested, the project, though approved by the Massachusetts Upper House, was blocked by the English government, aroused thereto by the Episcopal clergy of Boston and their superior, the Bishop of London.[1] When, to give a second example, some Congregational ministers procured a charter from the Massachusetts legislature, in 1762, for a "Society for Propagating Christian Knowledge among the Indians of North America," the Episcopal ministers of Massachusetts, fearing that the new enterprise would endanger the interests of the English "Society for the Propagation of the Gospel in Foreign Parts," of which most of them were paid missionaries, stirred up the English ecclesiastical authorities to procure the disallowance of the new society's charter by the "King in Council."[2] If such interferences with local self-government were brought about by a few scattered and but partially organized Episcopalians, what might not be feared in the way of parliamentary interference should a complete hierarchy be set up by act of Parliament in the colonies?

That an episcopate should be established was the ardent wish of the colonial Episcopalians. In 1724, 1725, 1727, 1749, and 1767,[3] and probably at frequent

[1] See W. S. Perry, *Papers Relating to the History of the Church in Massachusetts*, pp. 179-181, 184, 186-190, 351, privately printed, 1873; Hutchinson, *History of the Province of Massachusetts Bay*, ii., pp. 322, 323, ed. Boston, 1767: Palfrey, *History of New England*, iv., p. 454, 455.

[2] Perry, *Papers Relating to the History of the Church in Massachusetts*, pp. 471, 472, 476-481, 497; Chauncy, *Remarks on . . . the Bishop of Landaff's Society Sermon*, pp. 19, 20; see also Bradford, *Memoir . . . of Rev. Jonathan Mayhew*, pp. 197, 235, Boston, 1838.

[3] Perry, *Papers Relating to the History of the Church in Massachusetts*, pp. 143, 175, 176, 227, 433, 531, etc.

intervals between, the Massachusetts Episcopal clergy urged their desires on the English authorities. In 1749 it seemed probable that the British government would take the wished-for step, though there was hesitation about appointing resident bishops for New England.[1] This prospect was undoubtedly one of the causes that led that earnest defender of the validity of New England ordinations, Chief-Justice Paul Dudley, to found the Dudleian lectureship at Harvard. The danger passed by at the time, but only to recur again, in 1761,[2] in aggravated form, and to become chronic till the Revolution put an end to it forever. To the men of the generation before the Revolution the peril seemed very real; and one of the acutest and most learned of recent Massachusetts historians has pointed out that, in New England, fear of bishops imposed by Parliament was as potent a stimulus to the Revolutionary spirit, as fear of taxes imposed by Parliament.[3] It was a main cause in uniting the Congregational ministry almost to a man in defense of American liberties. And how largely this opposition to Episcopacy was political resistance to foreign aggression is shown by the fact that, when once American independence was achieved, New England

[1] Palfrey, *History of New England*, v., p. 95.
[2] See Mayhew's letter to Hollis, in Bradford, *Memoir*, p. 195.
[3] Mellen Chamberlain, *John Adams*, pp. 21-35, Boston, 1898, with valuable citation of authorities.

witnessed the introduction of an episcopate with its characteristic claims to exclusive divine authority, not only without united resistance such as had been protractedly manifested before the Revolution, but without more criticism than any innovating religious body has always to encounter.

Jonathan Mayhew, the brilliant, patriotic, contentious, and Arian pastor of the Boston West Church began an aggressive defense of American liberties, civil and ecclesiastical, as early as 1750;[1] and, in 1763, he plunged into a bitter discussion with Rev. East Apthorp of Cambridge over the aims and methods of the " Society for the Propagation of the Gospel in Foreign Parts," which was represented by Apthorp and other Episcopal missionaries in New England. Before this debate had run its two years' heated course it had involved the Archbishop of Canterbury himself.[2]

Chauncy's first participation in printed opposition to Episcopacy was in his publication of the Dudleian lecture in defence of non-Episcopal ordination in 1762. Five years later, in December, 1767, a sermon preached before the " Society for the Propagation of the Gospel in Foreign Parts " by the Bishop of Landaff,[3] in which

[1] His *Discourse on the Anniversary of the Death of Charles I.* was printed on both sides of the Atlantic and attracted much attention by its defense of liberty.

[2] An extended, though one-sided, account of this controversy may be found in Bradford, *Memoir of . . . Jonathan Mayhew*, pp. 243 *et seq.*

[3] Preached at London, February 20, 1767.

the American colonies were represented as lands of barbarism and heathenism, drew forth from Chauncy a noble, temperate, and unanswerable defense of the character of the founders of New England, their efforts to evangelize the Indians, and the then existing state of the religious and educational institutions that they had planted.[1]

The reply just noted was to a publication by an English prelate; Chauncy's next contribution to the Episcopal debate was an *Answer* to an able American Episcopalian, a graduate of Yale, and rector at Elizabeth, New Jersey, Thomas Bradbury Chandler. In 1767 Chandler had published *An Appeal to the Public in behalf of the Church of England in America*,—a sober-minded presentation of the well-known claims of Episcopacy as a method of church government, and of the advantages to Episcopacy to be derived from the establishment of bishops in the colonies. This *Appeal* Chauncy answered, in 1768,[2] with an elaborate pamphlet addressed to every point of Chandler's argument; and, as Chandler made rejoinder in 1769,[3] Chauncy replied a second time in 1770,[4] only to draw

[1] *A Letter to a Friend*, etc., the title on fly-leaf being, *Dr. Chauncy's Remarks on certain Passages in the Bishop of Landaff's Society Sermon.* Boston, 1767.

[2] *The Appeal to the Public Answered in Behalf of the Non-Episcopal Churches in America.* Boston, 1768.

[3] *The Appeal Defended*, etc. All Chandler's tracts in this debate were printed in New York.

[4] *Reply to Dr. Chandler's Appeal Defended.*

forth a third pamphlet from Chandler in 1771.¹ This controversy led, in 1771, to the publication of Chauncy's chief work on the Episcopal claim, the *Compleat View of Episcopacy, as Exhibited in the Fathers of the Christian Church, until the Close of the Second Century*—a volume largely based on the studies of his early ministry.² Probably no other New Englander of his day could have shown such an acquaintance with the fathers from Clement of Rome to Clement of Alexandria, and the work must be considered an able and successful attempt to give an ³

"ANSWER to those, who have represented it as a CERTAIN FACT, universally handed down, even from the Apostles Days, that GOVERNING and ORDAINING AUTHORITY was exercised by such Bishops only, as were of an ORDER SUPERIOR to Presbyters."

Chauncy's activities against the establishment of a British episcopate in America were by no means confined to the publications noted. Writing to a friend in 1766, he said:⁴

"We the ministers of this town have for a long course of years held a correspondence with the ' Committee of Deputation of Dissenters ' at London, and have found our account in it. They have been greatly serviceable to us

¹ *The Appeal Farther Defended.*
² Preface, p. iii.
³ Title-page.
⁴ Letter of September 29, 1766, to Rev. Dr. Ezra Stiles, now in the possession of Yale University.

many ways. It was owing to y' influence, under God, that the scheme for the mission of a Bishop into America about 20 years ago¹ was entirely disconcerted and defeated."

Chauncy's wisdom derived from this experience led him to fear that the annual joint convention of delegates from the Synod of New York and Philadelphia and from the Connecticut General Association, which met from 1766 to 1775 to guard against Episcopal encroachment, would defeat its object by arousing opposition in England to so visible a union of Congregational and Presbyterian forces. In his judgment, "Separate endeavours, suitably conducted, are the only ones that will serve our interest."² But to fears and efforts alike the Revolutionary War put an end.

Of that war the work of Chauncy in this Episcopal struggle was an important forerunner, and in the fortunes of the struggle when it came he felt a keen and patriotic interest. To him there seemed but one side that could possibly be right, and he told his friends, with a rhetorical exaggeration very unusual in him, that angelic aid would come to the Americans, so just was their cause, were the patriot strength to fail.³ The repeal of the Stamp Act and the sufferings of Boston under the repressive measures of Parliament called out vigorous publications from his prolific

---

¹ *I. e.*, the attempt of 1749–50.
² Letter to Rev. Dr. Ezra Stiles, of June 29, 1767.
³ Sprague, *Annals*, "Unitarians," p. 9.

pen.¹ When the war came, the siege of Boston drove him from the town till its capture by Washington's army, in March, 1776, enabled him to return. But his age and feebleness precluded any very active share in the patriot efforts. His own struggle for American liberty had been fought chiefly in the years before Lexington and Bunker Hill.

In considering Chauncy's relation to the "Great Awakening," it has been seen that his attitude was directly opposed to that of Edwards. But this disagreement was far from being the only point of unlikeness between the two men. During Chauncy's ministerial life eastern Massachusetts was largely moving in a doctrinal direction in striking discord with that of Edwards and his school, and scarcely less estranged from the view-point of the founders of New England. This "Liberal" direction was one, however, in which the development of English Puritanism had led the way. In the home land not merely Arminianism but Arianism had gained strong footing among Presbyterian Dissenters during the first quarter of the eighteenth century, and had become predominant among them before the year 1750 was reached. Arianism, as well as Arminianism, tinged the writings of some of the ablest English theologians of that period, both within and without the Church of England, and

¹ *Discourse on the Good News from a Far Country*, 1766 ; *A Just Representation of the Hardships and Sufferings of the Town of Boston*, 1774.

the books of Thomas Emlyn, William Whiston, Samuel Clarke, Daniel Whitby, and John Taylor, in which this doctrine is implied or expressly asserted, were among the most valued treatises in English Dissenting circles during the first half of the eighteenth century. They had strong opponents, indeed, but they were widely read; and though English Congregationalism resisted the Arminian and Arian inroad much more successfully than English Presbyterianism, its leaders, Watts and Doddridge, defended the historic Calvinism rather feebly.

These works crossed the Atlantic and naturally found most welcome in eastern Massachusetts, since that region, owing to its trade, the size of its seaports, and the acquaintance of its more prominent ministers, by correspondence at least, with the leading English Dissenters, was more susceptible to current English thought than southern and western New England. Arminian speculations, as they were then called, as to free will, original sin, and the value of human efforts in securing salvation had penetrated somewhat widely by the middle of the eighteenth century, as we have already had occasion to notice in treating of Edwards. And though Arianism was too radical a departure for any extensive rooting before the time of Edwards's death, it was distinctly advocated by Chauncy's neighbor in the Boston ministry, Jonathan Mayhew, in 1755, while his ministerial contemporaries, Lemuel

Briant of Braintree, Ebenezer Gay and Daniel Shute of Hingham, and John Brown of Cohassett were believed to sympathize with this denial of the Trinity. Elsewhere in eastern Massachusetts and New Hampshire Arian outcroppings had appeared before 1760; and, in 1768, Samuel Hopkins declared his "conviction that the doctrine of the Divinity of Christ was much neglected, if not disbelieved, by a number of ministers in Boston." This development was to go on silently, and for the most part unnoted, during the distractions of the Revolutionary struggle and of the political debates that followed it, till it burst forth in the Unitarian controversy soon after the beginning of the nineteenth century.

With this gradual modification of doctrine Chauncy sympathized; and in its spread his influence was as great as that of any man in eastern Massachusetts. It was all the more so because he was no radical or extremist and because the greater part of the writings of which he was the author were of a character to win the approval of Christians generally. This moderation of most of Chauncy's utterances renders him a hard man to classify. As his successor in the pulpit of the Boston First Church pointed out in 1811, his sermons contain much that is "calvinistick,"[1] as that term was later used by American Unitarians; but Chauncy

[1] William Emerson, *Historical Sketch of the First Church in Boston*, p. 186.

himself was no Calvinist, and some of his theories are not in accord with any historic presentation of the Evangelical faith. The "orthodox" and the "liberal" are inextricably intermixed in him, and in that characteristic he was probably typical of the contemporary stage of development of the movement which ultimately became Massachusetts Unitarianism.

Most of Chauncy's doctrinal writings were completed before 1768, though the more important were not published till after the Revolutionary War.[1] In a letter giving an account of them to a friend at the date just mentioned, he told something of the course of study by which he was led to them. After his recovery from the debility consequent on overwork during the Whitefieldian period, he said:[2]

"My next study was the bible, more particularly the epistles, more particularly still the epistles of the Apostle Paul. I spent seven years in this study. . . . The result of my studying the Scriptures . . . is a large parcel of material suted to answer several designs."

This labor left Chauncy with absolute confidence in the full and final authority and complete inspiration of the Bible; but as his investigations were largely through the lenses furnished by the works of Locke, Clarke, Taylor, and Whitby,[3] the results were in many

[1] See letter of May 6, 1768, to Dr. Ezra Stiles, in the possession of Yale University. [2] *Ibid.*

[3] See Chauncy's grateful acknowledgments of his indebtedness to Taylor, in his *Salvation of All Men*, pp. xi.-xiv. London, 1784.

points variant from current orthodoxy. Yet to Chauncy they undoubtedly seemed the teachings of the Bible as distinguished from man-made systems, and creeds of human composition.[1]

The first fruit of this study was a clever anonymous satirical pamphlet[2] which he contributed to the discussion on Original Sin in 1758 — a debate already noted in our account of Edwards. The dissent from current Calvinistic theories of imputation here indicated is further developed in his *Twelve Sermons* of 1765, and in the last important publication he set forth, the *Five Dissertations on the Fall and its Consequences*, printed in 1785, though written before 1768. In these discussions Chauncy maintained that all men capable of moral action are sinners; but though that universal sinfulness is a consequence of the primal lapse, it is an indirect consequence. No man is guilty of any but his personal sins, yet those personal sins are the result of the enfeeblement of his nature which the Scriptures include under the comprehensive term "death," and death was the penalty of the Adamic disobedience.[3]

"The judicial sentence of God, occasioned by the one offence of this one man, is that which fastens 'death,' with

[1] See *Salvation of All Men*, pp. viii., ix.; also his *Twelve Sermons*, p. iii.
[2] *The Opinion of One that has perused the Summer Morning's Conversation concerning Original Sin, wrote by the Rev. Mr. Peter Clark.* Boston, 1758. [3] *Twelve Sermons*, p. 23.

all its natural causes and appendages, upon the human kind; and tis IN CONSEQUENCE of this sentence, UPON men's coming into existence under the disadvantages arising from it, that they ' sin ' themselves."

This may not seem a wide departure from then current New England conceptions, yet the cleft between it and a theory like that of Edwards was deep. It enabled Chauncy to hold that men were not born sinners, while inevitably becoming offenders if they grew to years of moral responsibility.

The immediate occasion of the preparation of Chauncy's *Twelve Sermons*, just mentioned, was the preaching in Boston, in the autumn of 1764, of Robert Sandeman,[1] that curious disciple of the Scotch religious seceder, John Glas. Sandeman, who found some following in New England, especially in and about Danbury, Conn., held that " justifying faith is nothing more or less than the bare belief of the bare truth "[2]—that is, an accurate and undoubting intellectual acceptance of the precise facts which the Scriptures reveal concerning the life and work of the Saviour constitutes saving faith in Christ. Over against Sandeman, Chauncy asserted faith to be such an assent of the mind to the truths witnessed to us by the testimony of God in Revelation as causes them to

[1] Chauncy wrote to Stiles, November 19, 1764, "Mr. Sandeman went from this town last Friday P. M." Letter in possession of Yale University.

[2] See *Contributions to the Eccles. Hist. of Conn.*, p. 284. New Haven, 1861.

become a spring of right action in us, and leads us to repentance, good works, and holiness of life.[1] It need not be without admixture of error to be genuine. Some error, probably, is present in the conceptions of truth even of those of clearest spiritual vision.[2]

This discussion led Chauncy to ask how saving faith is obtained, and he answered in a way that Edwards and Hopkins greatly opposed as an irreligious exaltation of human powers, though his answer was not unlike that of the representatives of the older Calvinism in his day. He urged that while saving faith is the unmerited gift of the " Spirit of God," and while God is sometimes " found of those who sought him not,"[3] God " no more ordinarily BEGINS, than carries on, the work of faith, as it respects it's existence and operation in the hearts of sinners, without the concurring use of their powers and endeavours."[4] A man should be urged to use his rational powers to know what he can of God's ways, to discern good and evil, and to foresee future rewards and punishments. He ought, though unregenerate, to recognize the teachings of Revelation, to feel something of the " sinfulness of sin," to practise religious duties, to read and meditate on God's Word, to be present and attentive at public worship, and pray fervently and persistently to God for salvation.[5] These things are not saving faith, but,

[1] *Twelve Sermons*, sermons iii.–v.   [2] *Ibid.*, pp. 76-82.
[3] *Ibid.*, p. 192.   [4] *Ibid.*, p. 195.   [5] *Ibid.*, pp. 205-216.

Chauncy affirms, " 't is ' ordinarily ' in concurrence with ' these endeavours' of sinners that God bestows his Spirit to ' begin ' the work of faith " ' [1] " The plain truth is," says Chauncy, that " God, man, and means are all concerned in the formation of that character, without which we cannot inherit eternal life." [2]

Naturally, such coöperation as this in the process of salvation implies a very different degree of freedom in man than Edwards believed to exist; and, in his *Benevolence of the Deity*, published in 1784, but a work to which he could refer in 1768 as " wrote many years ago," [3] Chauncy treated of man's liberty at some length.[4] He declared that man is " an *intelligent moral agent;* having in him an *ability* and *freedom* to WILL as well as to *do*, in opposition to NECESSITY from any extraneous cause whatever." [5] In maintaining this self-determination he had Edwards evidently in mind as a principal antagonist.[6]

It is equally natural, also, that in the generally excellent series of sermons on the Lord's Supper which Chauncy published, in 1772, under the title of *Breaking of Bread*, he should uphold the Stoddardean view, denial of which had cost Edwards the Northampton pulpit, and urge that [7] " the ordinance of the supper is

[1] *Twelve Sermons*, p. 216. [2] *Ibid.*, p. 339.
[3] The letter of May 6, 1768, often cited.
[4] *Benevolence of the Deity*, pp. 128-144.
[5] *Ibid.*, title-page. [6] *Ibid.*, pp. 131,132.
[7] *Breaking of Bread*, p. 26 ; see also *ibid.*, pp. 191-113.

admirably well adapted to promote the edification of all that come to it in the serious exercise of faith, though their faith, at present, should not be such as to argue their being ' born from above.' "

But however much man can coöperate with God, Chauncy iterates and reiterates that "the worthiness of that glorious person, who ' once offered up himself a sacrifice to God for sin,' is the alone foundation of all spiritual bestowments, whether to saints or sinners." [1]

To the thought of an atonement Chauncy holds tenaciously. That atonement was due to the [2]

"good will of God, and [is] one of the glorious effects of it. . . . Some may have expressed themselves, so as to lead one to think, that the blood of Christ was shed to pacify the resentments of God, . . . But . . . so far was the blood of Christ from being intended to work upon the heart of God, and stir up compassion in him, that it was love, and because he delighted in mercy, that he ' spared him not, but delivered him up for us all.' The incarnation, obedience, sufferings, and death of Christ are therefore to be considered as the way, or method, in which the wisdom of God thought fit to bring into event the redemption of man. And a most wisely concerted method it is. In this way, mankind are obviously led into just sentiments of the vile nature, and destructive desert of sin; as also of that sacred regard, which God will forever show to the honor of his own governing authority: Nor could they,

[1] *Twelve Sermons*, pp. 267, 268 ; see also *Salvation of All Men*, pp. 19, 20.
[2] *Benevolence of the Deity*, pp. 166, 167.

in any way, have been more powerfully engaged to turn from their iniquities."

Surely this is not far from that governmental theory of the atonement which the younger Jonathan Edwards was to put forth in the autumn of 1785, a year after Chauncy's book was published, and to put forth with such acceptance that it was long regarded as a prime characteristic of New England theology.

In the biographical letter of 1768, from which we have repeatedly quoted, Chauncy said:[1]

"The materials for one design I have put together and they have layn by in a finished Quarto vol. for some years. This is wrote wth too much freedom to admit of a publication in this country. Some of my friends who have seen it have desired that I would send it home[2] for publication, and to have it printed wthout a name. I question whether it will ever see the light till after my death; and I am not yet determined, whether to permit its being y^n printed, or to order its being committed to flames. Tis a work that cost me much thot, and a great deal of hard labor. It is upon a most interesting subject."

The work thus tantalizingly indicated was issued at last by its author, though anonymously, at London, in 1784, under the title of *The Mystery hid from Ages and Generations, made manifest by the Gospel-Revelation: or, The Salvation of All Men the Grand Thing*

[1] Letter to Ezra Stiles, May 6, 1768.
[2] *i. e.*, to England, curiously illustrative of the pre-Revolutionary feeling.

aimed at in the Scheme of God. Though anonymous, its authorship was well known, and called forth speedy reply by name.[1]

In this volume Chauncy not merely declared himself a restorationist, but maintained with great ingenuity, learning, and evident sincerity of conviction that restorationism is the teaching of the New Testament, and especially of the Pauline epistles. No less positively than Edwards, Chauncy holds that the vast majority of intelligent mankind are on their way to hell.[2] But hell is not eternal; it is a place of frightful suffering, prolonged " God only knows how long ";[3] but it has an end; and the end will come when the Mediatorial King of this dispensation will have " put all enemies under his feet," even that last of enemies, the second death, and shall have delivered up the ransomed and purified universe to " him that put all things under him, that God may be all in all."[4]

" The *reign of Christ*, in his mediatory kingdom, is to make way for GOD'S BEING ALL IN ALL; and will accordingly *last*, till he has *ripened* and *prepared* things for the *commencement* of this *glorious period*. . . . He will [then] give up his *mediatory kingdom to the Father*, who will,

[1] *E. g.*, Jonathan Edwards, the younger, *The Salvation of All Men Strictly Examined, and the Endless Punishment of those who die Impenitent, Argued and Defended against the Objections and Reasonings of the late Rev. Doctor Chauncy, of Boston*, etc. New Haven, 1790.

[2] *Salvation of All Men*, p. 322; for Edwards's views, see *Works*, vii., pp. 417, 418: viii., pp. 202, 203. [3] *Salvation of All Men*, p. 343.

[4] See 1 Corinthians, xv., 21-28, a passage of which Chauncy makes much in his argument.

from this time, *reign* IMMEDIATELY *himself;* making the most glorious manifestations of his being a *God*, and *Father*, and *Friend to all, in all things, without end.*"[1]

The question naturally arises, in view of these and other passages which have been quoted, as to what conception Chauncy had of the person of Christ. Chauncy nowhere enters fully into this problem. His language regarding the Saviour is generally that of the New Testament, but as far as I have observed he employs only those descriptive terms of Holy Writ which may be held to imply subordination. Christ is the " Son of God," in Chauncy's sermons constantly. And when he passes from the words of Scripture he uses such phrases as " Saviour of Men," " prime minister of God's kingdom," and " grand commissioned trustee " of God's purposes.[2] He affirms " that, next to God, and in subordination to him, we should make *his Son*, whom he has authorized to be our King and Saviour, the beloved object of our faith and hope, our submission and obedience." These, and many similar proofs that could be adduced, make it evident that Chauncy was a high Arian. Christ to him was an object of worship; faith in Christ was the condition of our salvation. Our acceptance with God is founded on the " blood and righteousness " of Christ. Christ is the " all in all," the sovereign of this dispensation;[3] yet he is not God, nor equal with God.

[1] *Salvation of All Men*, pp. 217, 225. [2] *Ibid.*, pp. 195, 324, 364.
[3] *Ibid*, pp. 217, 358, 364.

It is evident that, in many points, Chauncy had departed not merely from the historic theology of New England, but from the presentations of truth historically characteristic of the Church Universal. But he was curiously unconscious of this departure. He believed himself " unorthodox " on the question of the ultimate fate of the wicked, and in his speculations concerning the consequences of the fall,[1] but he felt himself in sympathy not merely with historic Christianity but with the general Christianity of his own age. Writing in 1765, he had said:[2]

" The great fault of the faith of christians at this day . . . does not lie, as I imagine, unless in here and there a detached instance, in fatal mistakes about the truth. The incarnation, life, death, resurrection, and exaltation of Christ, and the great articles connected herewith, and dependent hereon, stand true in the minds of most christians, at least in this part of the world: Nor do they, as I conceive, commonly mix falsehood with them, at least in so gross a sense as to be justly chargeable with wholly subverting their real meaning. And yet, they are far from being the subjects of a faith that justifies. And the reason is because the assent of their minds to the report of the gospel, is not of the right kind. 'Tis the produce of education and tradition, rather than the testimony of God. 'Tis a feeble inoperative persuasion, little affecting their hearts or influencing their lives. They receive the great doctrines of christianity as speculations, not important realities."

I have quoted this passage as illustrative alike of

[1] Letter of May 6, 1768.   [2] *Twelve Sermons*, pp. 91, 92.

Chauncy's unconsciousness as to whither the movement in which he bore an influential part was tending, and of his piety of heart. And I take it that this unconsciousness was characteristic of the ministry of eastern Massachusetts in his day. The Unitarian outcome was as yet unsuspected. And, as for Chauncy himself, one can but feel that in piety, devotion to Christ, depth of consciousness of sin and knowledge of the way of salvation, in spite of all his serious modifications of the earlier theology, he stood in much nearer sympathy with the founders of New England than with Priestley, Lindsey, or their associates who then bore in England the Unitarian name.

Chauncy's ministry was prolonged to the close of its fifty-ninth year. Old age had somewhat limited his activities, but his mind was keenly alive to the last, and as his end drew near, he " was observed by those who were near him to be a great part of his time engaged in devotional exercises."[1] On February 10, 1787, he died at the age of eighty-two; and he left behind him the memory not merely of a strong man who greatly influenced New England thought, but of a good man, whose only place could be in that Redeemer's kingdom which he believed would ultimately include all men.

[1] Obituary notice, in *Massachusetts Gazette*, February 13, 1787.

SAMUEL HOPKINS

VIII.

SAMUEL HOPKINS

THE fundamental principles of New England Congregationalism have always encouraged independence of thought, however deficient the actual application of those principles may sometimes have been. Congregationalism has never held that Christian truth is the possession of a special order of men, or that it has been defined once for all in any creed or exposition of merely human composition. It has never believed that any man or council, since the days of the Apostles, has enjoyed infallible divine guidance; and if it has throughout most of its history yielded an unquestioning deference to the books of the Old and New Testaments, it is because of a conviction of their divine authorship. Congregationalism has always asserted that the God-given standard of its faith is open on equal terms to the investigation of laymen and of ministers; and that the occupant of the pew, if of equal learning, has no inferiority to the clergyman in the discovery of truth. That discovery, Congregationalism has maintained, is brought about by no mystical processes, or submissions to assertions of authority, but by the application to the divine principles of our faith, especially as revealed in the Bible, of the same reasoning faculties by which truth in any other realm of knowledge is attained. Hence, Congregationalism has been characteristically rationalistic, using that term in no opprobrious sense. As a result, also, New England has produced theologians of greater speculative originality than any other region of America. It is to one who was above all else a speculative theologian, who by severest logic carried the hints and the formulated principles of Edwards to positions which Edwards himself never reached, however latent they may have been in his system, who built on Edwards's foundation a distinct and original school of theologic thinking, that I wish to turn your thoughts to-day in speaking of the life and work of Samuel Hopkins.

Yet, in describing Hopkins as first of all a speculative theologian, the facts cannot be overlooked that he was also a forerunner in a great philanthropic reform and a hard-working pastor. It is to the honor of New England Christianity that its leaders — men as far apart in theological thinking as Edwards and Chauncy, Bellamy and Channing, Emmons and Bushnell — have been men of eminent piety of life and pastoral instincts prompting to the shepherding of souls. The speculative recluse, spinning his system apart from contact with his fellows, or the theologian of the intellect only, divorcing religious truth from personal conduct, have never found New England a congenial soil. But New England thinkers have differed much in the degree in which their presentations of truth have been the logically consistent outcome of principles clearly grasped by the intellect, and in the relentlessness with which they have allowed their premises to lead to the full sweep of the dialectic conclusions which those premises implied In that consistency which does not shrink from any conclusion that accepted principles seem to demand Hopkins was preëminent; and hence it may truly be said that the speculative theologian is the aspect under which he most characteristically presents himself.

The theme and the place alike remind me that it would be unjust to begin any lecture upon Hopkins in this classroom without some expression of appreciation of the admirable *Memoir*[1] in which his life was narrated and his work estimated by Professor Park nearly half a century ago—a memoir that renders the path of any later student of Hopkins comparatively easy, whether he agrees with all the judgments of the eminent biographer or not.

In an account of his life written in old age, Hopkins thus introduced himself:[2]

[1] By Edwards A. Park, forming the Preface to *The Works of Samuel Hopkins*, i., pp. iv.-264, Boston, 1852; also printed separately, Boston, 1854.

[2] Hopkins's quaintly expressed and interesting autobiography, begun

"I was born at Waterbury in Connecticut on the Lord's day, September 17, 1721. My parents were professors of religion; and I descended from christian ancestors, both by my father and my mother, as far back as I have been able to trace my descent. . . . As soon as I was capable of understanding, and attending to it, I was told that my father, when he was informed that he had a son born to him said, if the child should live, he would give him a public education, that he might be a minister or a sabbath-day-man, alluding to my being born on the sabbath."

The little town where Hopkins's father was a farmer, was, he records, a place " where a regard to religion and morality was common and prevalent";[1] to how great a degree may be imagined from his further statement:[2] " I do not recollect that I ever heard a prophane word from the children and youth, with whom I was conversant, while I lived with my parents, which was till I was in my fifteenth year."

Here the boy grew up, tall and heavily built, " of a sober and steady make," he said of himself, " not guilty of external irregularities, . . . disposed to be diligent and faithful in . . . business," so that he " gained the notice, esteem, and respect of the neighbourhood."[3] He had " sometimes, though rarely . . . some serious thoughts of God," and

"in the seventy-fifth year of my age," was published by Rev. Stephen West, of Stockbridge, in *Sketches of the Life of the Late Rev. Samuel Hopkins, D.D.*, etc., Hartford, 1805. The quotation is from pp. 23, 24.
[1] *Ibid.*, p. 24.
[2] *Ibid.*, p. 25.   [3] *Ibid.*

a dream in which his youthful fancy pictured himself as "sentenced to everlasting misery, and driven down to hell, with the rest of the wicked," made an impression on him that was vivid even to old age.

At fourteen, the serious-minded, reserved, and taciturn boy went from his father's home to the house of Rev. John Graham, the Scotch-born pastor at Southbury, ten miles from the Waterbury farm, to be fitted for college; and two years later, in 1737, he entered Yale. Of his course there he has recorded the following description:[1]

"While a member of the college, I believe, I had the character of a sober, studious youth, and of a better scholar than the bigger half of the members of that society; and had the approbation of the governours of the college. I avoided the intimacy and the company of the openly vicious; and indeed kept but little company, being attentive to my studies. In the eighteenth or nineteenth year of my age, I cannot now certainly determine which, I made a profession of religion, and joined the church to which my parents belonged in Waterbury. I was serious, and was thought to be a pious youth, and I had this thought and hope of myself. I was constant in reading the bible, and in attending on public and secret religion. And sometimes at night, in my retirement and devotion, when I thought of confessing the sins I had been guilty of that day, and asking pardon, I could not recollect that I had committed one sin that day. Thus ignorant was I of my own heart, and of the spirituality, strictness, and extent of the divine law."

[1] West, *Sketches*, pp. 27, 28.

But this degree of Christian experience, although equaling in depth that which many a theological student then or now could honestly claim, soon came to appear wholly inadequate to the young collegian. Whitefield preached his stirring discourses in New Haven just as Hopkins's Senior year was beginning; and Gilbert Tennent, fresh from his revival labors at Boston, delivered " seventeen sermons " in " about a week," " with a remarkable and mighty power," during the spring before Hopkins's graduation.[1]

Under Tennent's fiery discourses " many cried out with distress and horror of mind, under a conviction of God's anger, and . . . many professors of religion received conviction that they were not real christians. . . . The members of college appeared to be universally awakened." Several of Hopkins's fellow students, his classmates Samuel Buell and David Youngs, with David Brainerd of the then Sophomore class, " visited every room in college, and discoursed freely and with the greatest plainness with each one."[2]

Hopkins himself heartily approved these efforts and believed himself a Christian, till Brainerd, in the exercise of this student evangelism in which he was a leader, came to Hopkins for an account of that reticent scholar's religious state. Hopkins gave

[1] West, *Sketches*, pp. 30–32.
[2] *Ibid.*

no hint of his lack of such religious experiences as Brainerd thought were alone evidences of a regenerate condition; but, none the less, Brainerd's assertion that it was " impossible for a person to be converted and to be a real christian without feeling his heart, at sometimes at least, sensibly and greatly affected with the character of Christ," " struck conviction " through him. To the distressed and honest student it seemed, as it did to the aged minister, who thus recorded his youthful experiences, that he " was indeed no christian," but "a guilty, justly condemned creature," whose " condition appeared darker from day to day." Even a sudden and overwhelming " sense of the being and presence of God . . . and the character of Jesus Christ the mediator," which came to him one evening as he meditated and prayed alone, flooding his soul with a new consciousness of the blessedness of communion with God, while revealing his own unworthiness, did not dispel this feeling of lack of any saving change of nature; though the aged Hopkins, as he reviewed this experience, marveled that he did not then recognize in it his conversion.[1]

Hopkins was now twenty years of age. From his first listening to Tennent he had determined to seek him out and if possible live with that fervent evangelist as soon as college days were over; but a sermon by

[1] West, *Sketches*, pp. 33-37.

Jonathan Edwards on " the trial of the spirits," heard at New Haven just before graduation, turned Hopkins's preference to the Northampton minister, and he decided, if possible, to enjoy Edwards's personal instruction. It was characteristic of the shy and reserved young Senior that, though thus determined, he did not speak to the preacher who so powerfully moved him.[1]

Graduation saw Hopkins once more in his boyhood home, praying and fasting and " dejected and very gloomy in mind ";[2] yet he took some part in attempts " to promote religion among the young people in the town." But, by the December following the September commencement when he received his degree, Hopkins had reached the desired Northampton parsonage on horseback, unknown, and only to find that Edwards himself was absent on an extended evangelistic tour; yet welcomed and invited to spend the winter by Mrs. Edwards and her household.

Yet he could have been no cheerful visitor. " I was very gloomy and was most of the time retired in my chamber," he recorded, and though Mrs. Edwards offered spiritual comfort and declared to him her belief that " God intended yet to do great things " by him, " this conversation did not sensibly raise [his] spirits in the least degree." Nor did he admit a trembling hope that he might, after all, be one of the children of God,

[1] West, *Sketches*, pp. 37, 38.
[2] For the facts in this paragraph, see *Ibid.*, pp. 38–43.

till his classmate, Samuel Buell, had greatly stirred Northampton in January, 1742, and Mrs. Edwards had passed through her high-wrought experience in conscious submission to the divine will, even to a readiness to be with the lost forever.[1] And even when, after Edwards's return, the self-distrustful young man had related the reasons for his hesitatingly admitted belief to the Northampton pastor, it was with no expectation of receiving full assurance. Edwards " gave not his opinion expressly ; nor did I desire he should," Hopkins later recorded with transparent honesty, " for I was far from relying on any man's judgment in such a case. But I supposed he entertained a hope that I was a christian." Nor did Hopkins ever wholly rid himself of the fear that he had been self-deceived in the fundamental matter of his conversion. One of the most pathetic memorials of his experience is the concluding portion of his autobiographic sketches, in which the worn servant of God, then more than seventy-eight years of age, and able to look back on a ministry of fifty-six years' duration, sums up with hesitating judgment the evidences that point to the reality of his Christian life, and those which " sometimes are the ground of strong suspicion and doubt whether [he is] a real friend to Christ." [2]

Doubtless much of this self-distrust was temperamental in Hopkins; but much also was characteristic

[1] *Ante*, pp. 238-40.   [2] West, *Sketches*, pp. 113-131.

of the school of religious thought which he represented, viewing conversion, as it did, as involving the mightiest exercise of the sovereign and selective grace of God, and looking upon the human heart not only as infinite in its depth of wickedness, but wellnigh infinite, also, in its possibilities of self-deception.

Yet, though self-distrustful, a few weeks in Edwards's home had determined Hopkins to preach the Gospel. Accordingly, on April 29, 1742, less than eight months after graduating from Yale, he sought and received licensure from the Fairfield East Association of his native colony;[1] and, returning to Northampton, assisted Edwards in pastoral labors and preached in neighboring towns.[2] December brought an invitation to Simsbury, Conn., and a winter of preaching there was followed by a call to the Simsbury pastorate. But the fact that thirty votes were cast against the proposition induced Hopkins to decline, and he went back to the friendly household at Northampton for further study in theology. Northampton air did not agree with him, and the long horseback rides suggested as a remedy for his rheumatic ills led the young preacher, in July, 1743, to the frontier Berkshire village then known as Housatonick, but more familiar under its later name, Great Barrington. It was a discouraging little half-New

[1] F. B. Dexter, *Biog. Sketches of the Grad. of Yale College*, i., p. 671.
[2] West, *Sketches*, pp. 45-48.

England, half-Dutch parish of thirty families, of small worldly wealth, and of the lax religious and social habits which life on the verge of civilization always fosters. But the Great Barrington people gave a unanimous invitation to Hopkins to become their pastor, and here he was ordained, as he records, "on the 28th day of December, just at the end of the year 1743, when [he] was twenty-two years, three months, and eleven days old."

Here, at Great Barrington, four years after his ordination, Hopkins married a member of his congregation, Joanna Ingersoll,[1] whose twenty years of severe invalidism, ending in her death in 1793, added its burden of care and of sorrow to much of his ministry.[2] Here his five sons and three daughters were born. Here, too, he enjoyed for nearly seven years, from 1751 to 1758, the close companionship of his revered friend and teacher, Jonathan Edwards, whose call to the neighboring Stockbridge, only seven miles from his home, was procured by Hopkins's endeavors; and here also he enjoyed throughout his ministry the friendship of that other eminent disciple of Edwards, Joseph Bellamy, of Bethlehem, Conn. How influential this companionship with Edwards must have been for his younger admirer will readily be conjectured when it is remembered that Edwards's more

[1] West, *Sketches*, p. 54. Married January 13, 1748.
[2] *Ibid.*, pp. 82, 83. Died August 31, 1793.

important treatises were talked over with Hopkins and written during their author's Stockbridge pastorate, and that after Edwards's untimely death his manuscripts were confided to Hopkins's keeping. Nor was the friendship of the elder divine unrewarded by sacrifice on the part of the younger. It was Hopkins's refusal of the Stockbridge appointment, and of the handsóme increase in his income that it implied, in order that he might urge the selection of his friend, that opened the way for Edwards's settlement.[1]

Personally, the Great Barrington pastor was, and remained through his long life, a man of many peculiarities. "I have loved retirement,"[2] said Hopkins in his old age, "and have taken more pleasure *alone*, than in any company: And have often chosen to ride alone, when on a journey, rather than in the best company." Every Saturday he spent, when possible, "in retirement, and in fasting and prayer." His breakfast and his supper alike, on days not given to fasting, consisted of "bread and milk, from a bowl containing about three gills, never varying from that quantity, whether his appetite required more or not so much"—a diet which he changed during his later Newport years, as far as breakfast was concerned, for "a cup of coffee and a little Indian bread."[3]

[1] West, *Sketches*, p. 54.   [2] *Ibid.*, p. 86.
[3] William Patten, *Reminiscences of Late Rev. Samuel Hopkins*, 1843, quoted in Park, *Memoir*, pp. 52, 242.

Exercise he never took, save as his pastoral work brought it to him; but from fourteen to eighteen hours a day were spent in his study, beginning at four in the morning, or between four and five as a concession to winter's darkness and cold.[1] At nine every evening he ceased work, prayed with his family, and it is to be hoped conversed a little, for he could display much humor in talking with those who penetrated beyond his barrier of reserve.[2] At ten he was abed.

Though once at the beginning of his ministry, and in the excitement of the Whitefieldian revival, the congregation at Suffield had been so moved that he " could not be heard all over the meeting-house, by reason of the outcries of the people,"[3] Hopkins was esteemed a very dull preacher. " He was the very ideal of bad delivery,"[4] was Channing's comment on his pulpit manner; " such tones never came from any human voice within my hearing." And of these deficiencies Hopkins himself was painfully conscious. In his seventy-fifth year he wrote: " My preaching has always appeared to me as poor, low, and miserable, compared with what it ought to be. . . . I have felt often as if I must leave off, and never attempt any

---

[1] West, *Sketches*, p. 84.

[2] Park, *Memoir*, pp. 242, 243 ; and also W. E. Channing, *Works*, iv., pp. 347-354, Boston, 1849, a biographic note of very great value for Hopkins's appearance in his Newport old age.

[3] West, *Sketches*, p. 44.

[4] W. E. Channing, *Works*, iv., p. 348.

more."[1] Hopkins labored faithfully to overcome his defects. By diligent effort he freed himself from the fully written manuscript; but he never attained ease, animation, or effectiveness. Yet the matter of his discourses always won him friends, whose "satisfaction and approbation" he attributed with reason as well as with characteristic modesty " to their high relish for the truth," as he understood it, " however poor and defective the delivery and exhibition of it " might be. One of these satisfied hearers, who listened to a chance sermon from the aged Hopkins, delivered, at the invitation of Chauncy's Arian successor, John Clarke, in what had been Chauncy's very un-Hopkinsian Boston pulpit, presented him five or six hundred dollars as an expression of esteem at a time when Hopkins's stipend from his Newport congregation was not more than two hundred dollars a year.[2]

Hopkins always had a low estimate of himself. He walked very humbly with God, and with great devoutness of spirit and practice. His pecuniary generosity was far beyond that even of reputedly devoted ministers generally in that self-denying age,[3] and was given from a penury such as few ministers of that epoch had to endure. " I have taken care not to run in debt for the necessaries of life," wrote Hopkins in 1796,

[1] West, *Sketches*, pp. 88–92.
[2] Park, *Memoir*, pp. 233, 234.
[3] For instances, see Channing, *Works.* iv., p. 349; Park, *Memoir*, pp. 94, 95; West, *Sketches*, pp. xiv., xv.

"though frequently if a dollar extraordinary had been called for, it would have rendered me a bankrupt. I have endeavored to live as cheap and low as I could, and be comfortable, and answer the ends of living in my station and business."[1] His comforts were those of the mind rather than of the body; and being such he never impressed his acquaintances as a really poor man. "He was an illustration of the power of our spiritual nature," said Channing, speaking of Hopkins's old age.[2]

"In narrow circumstances, with few outward indulgences, in great seclusion, he yet found much to enjoy. He lived in a world of thought above all earthly passions. . . . It has been my privilege to meet with other examples of the same character, with men, who, amidst privation, under bodily infirmity, and with none of those materials of enjoyment which the multitude are striving for, live in a world of thought, and enjoy what affluence never dreamed of,— men having nothing, yet possessing all things; and the sight of such has done me more good, has spoken more to my head and heart, than many sermons and volumes."

But with all his humility, of one thing Hopkins was confident with a confidence that led him at times into arrogance toward or contempt for an opponent. "I had, from time to time, some opposers of the doctrines which I preached,"[3] wrote Hopkins, "but being

[1] West, *Sketches*, pp. 79, 80.
[2] Channing, *Works*, iv., pp. 352, 353.
[3] West, *Sketches*, p. 60.

persuaded, and *knowing* that they were the truths contained in divine revelation, this opposition, from whatever quarter, did not in the least deter or discourage me." He believed himself called of God to write his books,[1] and when asked, just at the end of his life, whether he would "make any alteration in the sentiments" expressed in his *System of Divinity*, he answered, " No: I am willing to rest my soul on them forever."[2] This confidence he imparted to those near to him. When the wife of his old age, who survived him, was approached with a suggestion that an abridged edition of his *System* would find a readier market than a full reprint, she answered: " If the public will not be at the expense of printing it *as it is*, let them do without it till the millennium; then it will be read and published with avidity."[3]

The mention of the second Mrs. Hopkins recalls the fact that she was almost as well read in theology as he, and that the intellectual bond was strong between the aged husband and the wife of his later days. On September 14, 1794, a twelvemonth after his first wife's release from her long years of distressing invalidism, Hopkins married Miss Elizabeth West, a member of his Newport congregation and a much esteemed teacher, who was already in her fifty-sixth year. Hopkins was then seventy-three. But much

[1] Diary, in Park, *Memoir*, p. 197.
[2] Park, *Memoir*, p. 232.   [3] *Ibid.*, p. 241.

more than an intellectual sympathy united them. Hopkins was always kindly and considerate in his household, and his affection went out toward his wife with a warmth which even the technically theological dress of its expression cannot conceal, as he wrote:[1]

"I . . . esteem it as one of the greatest favours of my life to have such a companion in my advanced years, in whose prudence, good family economy, friendship, and benevolent care I can confide; and who is to me the first object among creatures, of the love of esteem, benevolence, complacency, and gratitude."

In glancing thus at Hopkins's personal traits we have passed beyond the limits of his Great Barrington ministry. That pastorate was one of trial. The church, formed on the day of his ordination, began with only five members, to whom seventy-one were added by confession and forty-five by letter during his service of almost exactly a quarter of a century.[2] But the town was divided. Hopkins's sympathy with Edwards in opposition to the popular Stoddardeanism and to the Half-Way Covenant cost him the support of many, and aided in the establishment in 1760 of an Episcopal church in his parish ; while Hopkins's patriotism was equally distasteful to a large Tory element as the controversies preceding the Revolution ran their course.[3]

[1] West, *Sketches*, pp. 83, 84.
[2] Park, *Memoir*, pp. 35, 67.   [3] *Ibid.*, pp. 67-72.

But his theological views most of all made him enemies. Strenuous, like his teacher and friend Edwards, in asserting not merely the absolute sovereignty of God, but in representing every act of that sovereignty as a manifestation of a benevolence which had the good of the universe as its aim, Hopkins preached a sermon, in 1757, having as its theme, "The Lord Reigneth," which seemed to a parishioner to maintain " that nothing could possibly happen but what was right and ought to be rejoiced in, because all was exactly as *God would have it*, even events the most vile." To the parishioner's perplexed thought this seemed an assertion that " God and the devil are of one mind "; and the parishioner announced his intention of procuring, if possible, the dismission of a pastor who preached such doctrine.[1] This discussion led Hopkins to the publication, in 1759, of his first doctrinal treatise, under the caption:[2] *Sin, thro' Divine Interposition, an Advantage to the Universe; and yet, this no Excuse for Sin, or Encouragement to it;* a title, said Hopkins, writing thirty-seven years later, " so shocking to many that they would read no farther."[3]

In this treatise Hopkins maintained the following principles:

" The Holiness of God primarily consists in LOVE, or Benevolence to himself, and to the Creature; in the

[1] Park, *Memoir*, pp. 68, 69.
[2] Published at Boston.
[3] West, *Sketches*, p. 93.
[4] Ed. of 1759, pp. 45, 46.

Exercise of which, he seeks his own Glory, and the Happiness of the Creature; or, in one Word, he seeks the Good of the UNIVERSE, as comprehending both Creator and Creatures. And *this* God aimed at and sought in permitting Sin, as much as in any Act whatever; and therefore this was an Exercise of Holiness, even to permit Sin. For God permitted Sin, because he saw that this was the best way to promote this End, and accomplish the highest Good of the Universe. . . . The greatest Good of the *Whole*, may be inconsistent with the Good of every *Individual*. . . . God may be more glorified; yea, there may be more Happiness among Creatures, than if Sin had never taken Place. For tho Sin is the Means of the eternal Misery of many, yet it may be the Means of increasing the Happiness of others to so great a Degree, as that, upon the whole, there shall be more Happiness, than if there had been no Sin. . . . They who are made miserable by Sin, are *justly* miserable. Sin is their own Fault; and for it they deserve eternal Destruction; and therefore God does them no Wrong in casting them into Hell; they have but their Desert. . . . God exercises *Severity* towards some; but 't is a *just Severity;* 'T is *as just* as if no Good came to others by Means of Sin."

This was strong meat; though it involved little that was not implied in the thoughts of Edwards, or, indeed, that was not characteristic of the severer type of Calvinism generally. But it was speedily followed by a further application of Edwardean principles that brought Hopkins into sharp conflict with much of the Old, or " Moderate " Calvinism of his day. In a preceding lecture it has been pointed out that eighteenth-century New England Calvinism of the older school, as distinguished from the " New Divinity " of Edwards and his sympathizers, though asserting that salvation was wholly a work of the sovereign grace of God which man can in no way effect, nevertheless held that by the use of " means," such as attendance of public worship, reading the Scriptures, strenuous uprightness of conduct, and prayer, unregenerate men could put themselves in a position where God was more likely to save them. Such earnest and upright men, though guilty before God and needing a spiritual new birth for salvation, were not so guilty as if they lived in open contempt of God's ordinances.

This widely prevalent view, characteristic of eighteenth-century Old Calvinism, was pushed further by some. In 1744, the missionary to the Indians of Martha's Vineyard, Experience Mayhew, argued, in his *Grace Defended*, that " the best Actions of the Unregenerate are not properly called Sins, nor uncapable of being Conditions of the Covenant of Grace,"[1] his view being very similar to that of Samuel Phillips[2] of Andover, that a faithful use of the "means of grace" would fulfill the conditions on which God was pleased to bestow that special favor which alone brings salvation. These principles were carried yet further by those of the New England ministry who were not Calvinists. Thus Chauncy, for instance, declared in a passage already quoted from his volume of *Twelve Sermons*, pub-

[1] Page 148. [2] See *Ante*, p. 231.

lished in 1765, that God " no more ordinarily BEGINS, than carries on the work of faith, as it respects it's existence and operation in the hearts of sinners, without the concurring use of their powers and endeavours."[1]

But the immediate occasion of Hopkins's first controversial pamphlet on the means of grace was the publication, in 1761, of two sermons[2] by Experience Mayhew's un-Calvinistic and Arian son, Jonathan, the pastor of the West Church in Boston, in which he asserted that regeneration is conditioned on the earnest efforts of good men to obtain it. Four years later, Hopkins answered these sermons with *An Enquiry Concerning the Promises of the Gospel, whether any of them are made to the Exercises and Doings of persons in an Unregenerate State.*[3] To Hopkins's thinking,[4]

" the impenitent sinner, who continues obstinately to reject and oppose the salvation offered in the gospel, does in some respects, yea, on the whole, become, not less, but more vicious and guilty in God's sight, the more instruction and knowledge he gets in attendance on the means of grace."

Hence, in Hopkins's judgment, such preaching as that of Mayhew was radically wrong.[5]

" Instead of calling upon all to repent and believe the gospel, as the only condition of God's favor and eternal

[1] *Twelve Sermons*, p. 195.
[2] *Striving to Enter in at the strait Gate Explained and Inculcated; and the Connection of Salvation therewith Proved.* Boston, 1761.
[3] Boston, 1765.
[4] *Enquiry*, pp. 124, 125.   [5] *Ibid.*, pp. 99, 139, 140.

life, the most they [such preachers] do, with relation to unregenerate sinners, is to exhort and urge them to these doings which are short of repentance. . . . There is no difficulty in the sinner's complying with the offers of the gospel, but what lies in his want of an inclination and true desire to accept the salvation offered; and a strong and obstinate inclination to the contrary."

Means the sinner must use; for the means of grace give " speculative or doctrinal knowledge " of truth, and "there can be no discerning of the beauty of those objects, of which the mind has no speculative idea." But the use of means, without the full submission of the heart to God, only adds guilt. God has made " no promises of regenerating grace or salvation . . . to the exercises and doing of unregenerate men."[1] Sinners, while they remain sinners, have no share in any promise of the Gospel. Their prayers, their apprehensions of sin, their diligence in studying God's Word, and attendance upon God's worship are but aggravations of their guilt. They have the natural ability instantly to repent and serve God.

Hopkins's denial that there were any promises to the unregenerate led him to a negation which must have seemed to the thinking of his own age even more startling — a denial that there are " any promises in the bible to regeneration itself, or to the regenerate antecedent to any exercise of holiness, but only to those exercises which are the fruit and consequence of

[1] *Enquiry*, pp. 81, 123, 124.

regeneration."[1] This statement gives us a glimpse of another feature of the theology of Hopkins, based indeed on the Edwardean theories of will and of virtue, but much more definitely elaborated than by Edwards. In Hopkins's view, as set forth in the *Enquiry* under consideration, and even more fully in *Two Discourses*,[2] preached originally at Ipswich, Mass.,[3] and printed in 1768, praise and blame, sin and righteousness attach to acts, or "exercises of the mind." For the character of these acts man is responsible; but they root themselves back in a "biass,"[4] "heart," "taste, temper, or disposition," from which they flow. Yet of itself, and in its passive state, that bias gives no moral quality to its possessor; it is only to acts and "exercises" that moral values apply. What that "biass" may be in itself "antecedent to all thought," Hopkins declares difficult to conceive, though he drops a hint that shows an inclination toward the views later elaborated by Emmons, when he intimates that it "is wholly to be resolved into *divine constitution* or law of nature."[5] Now, in regeneration, this "biass" which results in acts

[1] *Enquiry*, p. 54.

[2] *Two Discourses—I. On the Necessity of the Knowledge of the Law of God, in Order to the Knowledge of Sin. II. A Particular and Critical Inquiry into the Cause, Nature, and Means of that Change in which Men are Born of God.* Boston, 1768.

[3] Letter to Bellamy, in Park, *Memoir*, pp. 199, 200. The sermons were preached in the summer of 1767. [4] *Enquiry*, pp. 77, 79.

[5] *Two Discourses*, p. 38; compare also Park, *Memoir*, pp. 191, 200.

of evil, is changed, " by the Spirit of God, immediately and instantaneously, and altogether imperceptibly to the person who is the subject of it," into " a new and opposite ' biass,' which is by our Saviour called an *honest and good heart*."[1] In this transaction " man, the subject, is wholly passive,"[2] but having this new " biass " his acts or " exercises " go out freely Godward in an active " conversion," and " all the promises of the gospel are made to these *exercises* of the mind "[3] which has thus been renewed by the Holy Spirit.

These may seem scholastic distinctions; but in reality they were concerned with matters of great practical importance, and, being so, they plunged their author into as heated a controversy as any that eighteenth-century New England witnessed. Let us put the problem in a more concrete form. Let us suppose the case, familiar in the experience of every New England congregation, of a man of high repute in the community, upright, a good citizen, a regular attendant upon and supporter of public worship, a reader of the Bible, habitual in prayer it may be, but not consciously or in public repute a Christian. You have most of you seen him oftentimes. Sedate, honest, reputable, very probably interested in philanthropic or moral reform, regularly in his pew, and his children regularly in the Sunday-school, he is very likely the main pillar in

[1] *Enquiry*, pp. 78, 79.
[2] *Two Discourses*, p. 38.
[3] *Enquiry*, p. 77.

the ecclesiastical society, and he is also apt to be the problem which most perplexes the minister in seasons of religious interest.

Now is such a man really better or worse than one who treats religion with open scorn? Hopkins answers that he is much worse. It is his " indispensable duty," his " highest interest immediately to repent. . . . Nothing can possibly be the least excuse for [his] neglecting it one minute";[1] and all exhortations to effort, all prayer, all knowledge of truth, if this primal duty is undone, are but aggravations of guilt; for " there is no difficulty in the sinner's complying with the offers of the gospel, but what lies in his want of inclination "[2] to do so.

Yet if such a man is perfectly free to accept or reject the Gospel if he *will*, is this then a haphazard world where God does not rule absolutely, and where He is uncertain or even undeterminating as to what His creatures shall do? Not at all, says Hopkins. Though the man is free, he is free only in the sense that he follows his inclinations. His acts are good or bad, and as such deserve praise or blame. But back of the acts lies a taste or propensity which in all natural men since Adam has made it certain that all their acts would, though free, be evil, till that bias is changed by the sovereign power of God. The man of our supposition may serve God if he will, he is infinitely guilty that he does

[1] *Two Discourses*, p. 65. [2] *Enquiry*, p. 99.

not do so; but, as a matter of fact, he will not serve God till he is born again, because till then he has no inclination to do so.

So fundamental is the divine control that not only is all virtue the product of the divine Spirit, but[1]

"there appears to be no rational or consistent medium, between admitting that God, according to the scriptures, has chosen and determined that all the moral evil which does, or ever will exist, should take place, and consequently is so far the origin and cause of it ; Or believing and asserting, that sin has taken place, in every view, and in all respects, contrary to his will, he having done all that he could to prevent the existence of it; but was not able; and is therefore not the infinitely happy, uncontrollable, supreme Governor of the world ; but is dependent, disappointed and miserable."

Hence the duty of a minister is to preach instant and complete repentance, and the guilt of all who do not exercise this grace, while recognizing that God will carry out His sovereign purpose in granting or withholding that " new heart " which alone makes repentance actual.

By the time that the *Two Discourses* that have just been considered were published, in 1768, Hopkins's own situation at Great Barrington was one of much difficulty. Opposition, partly from Tories and partly from doctrinal antagonists, made it very hard for him to gain even a meagre pecuniary support. Hopkins

[1] *System*, ed. 1811, i., p. 162.

himself felt that he had " had no great apparent success in the ministry."[1] And as a result of all these influences, on January 18, 1769, he was dismissed from his pastoral charge. The outlook was, indeed, gloomy from his point of view. Feeling between theological parties in New England was bitter, and Hopkins had won the hostility not only of the Liberals of the day, but of the Old Calvinists, a much more important factor in New England religious life. Moreover, he was determined not to settle over any church, the members of which did not appear to his strenuous judgment, " at least a good number of them, to be *real Christians*." And he recorded his opinion that " it was not probable that such a church could be found." It seemed to him that he would have to live as a farmer on the bit of land that he owned at Great Barrington.

But not even the personal trials just spoken of could keep Hopkins from writing in defense of the views which he believed to be the truth of God. His reply to Mayhew had drawn out an answer from the venerable and revivalistic minister at what is now Huntington, Conn., Rev. Jedidiah Mills,[2] in 1767;

[1] For the facts in this paragraph see Hopkins's autobiography, West, *Sketches*, pp. 49, 50, 60.

[2] *An Inquiry concerning the State of the Unregenerate under the Gospel; whether on every rising degree of internal Light, Conviction and Amendment of Life, they are (while unregenerate) undoubtedly, on the whole, more vile, odious and abominable (in God's sight) than they would have been had they continued secure and at ease, going on in their sins.* New Haven, 1767.

and also during the same year from the scholarly Old Calvinist, Moses Hemmenway, of Wells, Me.; the latter pamphlet bearing the suggestive title, *Seven Sermons on the Obligation and Encouragement of the Unregenerate to labour for the Meat which endureth to everlasting Life.*[1]

In the view of the first named of these able and worthy divines in particular, Hopkins's denial of any divine promise to "unregenerate doings" appeared not merely an erroneous but a dangerous perversion of the Gospel, to which the devil " puts his hearty Amen." To the task of answering Mills, Hopkins set himself immediately after his dismission, while still living at Great Barrington; and the result was a sturdy little volume, printed at New Haven in 1769, under the title, *The true State and Character of the Unregenerate, stripped of all Misrepresentation and Disguise*, in which Hopkins repeated, expanded, and reënforced the arguments of his previous *Enquiry*, in a tone of a good deal of arrogance and bitterness. That " severity," as he later described it, some of his friends deprecated, since in their judgment, as well as that of Hopkins himself, Mills " was a good man, and had done much good," and in his old age Hopkins came to believe that his friends were right, although he declared that he had " had no perception " of personal animus when writing.[2] One is not surprised to find that Hopkins

[1] Boston, 1767.   [2] West, *Sketches*, p. 96.

seemed to a liberal theologian like Chauncy " a troublesome, conceited, obstinate man ";[1] or that Chauncy, in Hopkins's view, was the standard of "all the uncircumcised in and about Boston."[2] Neither was correct in his estimate of the other; but these mutually condemnatory judgments show the theological animosities of the time.

Hopkins's writings roused strenuous opposition. An evidence of this hostility appeared in the severe criticism of his views put forth in 1769 by one of the most respected and talented men in the Connecticut ministry of that day, the vigorous Old Calvinist, Rev. William Hart of Saybrook, under the title, *Brief Remarks on a number of False Propositions, and Dangerous Errors, which are spreading in the Country ; Collected out of sundry Discourses lately publish'd, wrote by Dr. Whitaker and Mr. Hopkins.*[3] And, not content with this attack, Hart stirred Hopkins by an anonymous satirical pamphlet of the same year, purporting to be *A Sermon of a New Kind, Never preached ; nor ever will be ; Containing a Collection of Doctrines, belonging to the Hopkintonian Scheme of Orthodoxy; or the Marrow of the Most Modern Divinity. And an Address to the Unregenerate, agreeable to the Doctrines.*[4]

[1] Letter to Stiles of November 14, 1769, in the possession of Yale University.
[2] Letter to Bellamy of July 23, 1767, quoted in Park, *Memoir*, p. 133.
[3] New London, 1769.
[4] New Haven, 1769.

The satire just mentioned was published in December, 1769, at an interesting juncture in Hopkins's history. During the spring and summer of that year he had sought a new settlement.[1] The Old South congregation at Boston had shown him some favor, but a strong opposition made a call impossible. Hopkins's own disinclination had prevented a settlement at Topsham, Me.; but six weeks of preaching at Newport, R. I., had led to an invitation to the pastorate of the First Church of that thriving seaport by a vote of seven to three. Hopkins decided to accept the call, divided though it was; but when he had reached this conclusion, after some weeks of thought, he found that Hart's pamphlets had roused such opposition that the committee requested delay, urging that he supply the pulpit till the minds of the people could be more united. So Hopkins labored on, till, by March, 1770, it was evident that the majority was against him. Convinced that his usefulness at Newport was at an end, he asked leave to preach a farewell sermon,—a discourse which, wholly unintentionally on the part of the preacher, so moved the congregation in his favor that within a few days, and under the leadership of some of his chief opponents, the church gave him, well-nigh unanimously, the long doubtful call to its pastorate. On April 11, 1770, the

[1] For some of the facts in this paragraph see West, *Sketches*, pp. 61–74.

formal relationship was instituted which was to continue till his death on December 20, 1803.

That pastorate was, however, destined to be a time of severe pecuniary trial. The Revolutionary War broke down the trade of Newport, while the British and afterward the French occupation of the town brought in all the distractions and distresses of military control. Hopkins's intense Americanism compelled him to fly for safety from the British invaders in December, 1776, and to be absent till the spring of 1780 —a time which he spent in pastoral labors at Newburyport, Canterbury, and Stamford. His homecoming found his congregation scattered, the parsonage destroyed, and the meeting-house rendered unfit for use. For a year the congregation could pay him nothing, while an attractive call to Middleboro promised a comfortable support for his invalid wife and considerable family.[1] But Hopkins was not a man easily discouraged regarding what he deemed a duty, however distrustful of his own spiritual life, and he elected to remain at Newport without fixed salary and dependent on weekly contributions which are said not to have exceeded two hundred dollars a year in their usual aggregate.[2] Nor was the spiritual fruitage of his pastoral labors at all encouraging. His church at the comparatively flourishing period of his settlement had only seventy members, and he added but

[1] West, *Sketches*, pp. 77–79. [2] Park, *Memoir*, p. 243.

fifty-nine by profession and by commendation from other churches in the thirty-three years of his Newport ministry.[1]

At the time of Hopkins's Newport settlement we saw that he was smarting under Hart's criticisms, which he believed were not only an attack on the truth in general but a special cause of difficulty in his Newport congregation. To a man of his temperament a speedy answer to Hart was inevitable, and before 1770 had run its course Hopkins's *Animadversions on Mr. Hart's late Dialogue*[2] had been given to the public. In this pamphlet he charged Hart with failure to read his own publications thoroughly, with a denial of total depravity, and with standing "on the arminian side, so far as he is on any side, or attempts to reason at all." Hopkins, moreover, urged Hart's attention to Edwards's posthumous, but extremely influential, essay on the *Nature of True Virtue*, which Hopkins had published in 1765, calling on Hart to attempt its confutation.[3] The effort to which the Saybrook minister was thus dared, he undertook with a good deal of acumen in 1771;[4] and, in 1772, his fellow Old

[1] Park, *Memoir*, pp. 84, 85.   [2] Published at New London.

[3] *Animadversions*, pp. 17, 29; Professor Park, *Memoir*, p. 195, has fallen into error in saying, regarding Hart's anonymous satire entitled *A Sermon of a New Kind*, etc., that "Mr. Hopkins took no notice of this pamphlet." He did, and very positively, see *Animadversions*, pp. 29–31.

[4] *Remarks on President Edwards's Dissertations concerning the Nature of True Virtue: Showing that he has given a Wrong Idea and Definition of Virtue*, etc. New Haven, 1771.

Calvinist, Moses Hemmenway of Wells,[1] Me., like Moses Mather of Darien, Conn., two years earlier,[2] took up the cudgels against what Hart had styled " New Divinity " and the " Hopkintonian " scheme.[3] To all these Hopkins replied in 1773 in his strongest controversial treatise, *An Inquiry into the Nature of true Holiness.*[4]

In presenting his view Hopkins claims no more than an amplification of Edwards's theory of virtue.[5] Holiness, to his thinking, is love.[6] It is " universal, disinterested good-will, considered in all its genuine exercises and fruits, and acted out in all its branches towards God and our neighbour." It is "essentially, in nature and kind, the same thing in all beings that are capable of it." It is " the greatest good in the universe " and that " union of heart, by which the intelligent system becomes one." The opposite of holiness is any form of self-love which puts self before the good of the universe as a whole. A man may truly and disinterestedly estimate himself at the value he has in the universe as a whole; but love for self, as self, has nothing disinterested in it, and is the essence

[1] *Vindication of the Power, Obligation . . . of the Unregenerate to attend the Means of Grace*, etc. Boston, 1772.

[2] *The Visible Church, in Covenant, with God: Further Illustrated.* New Haven, 1770.

[3] The latter epithet was first employed in Hart's *Sermon of a New Kind*, see West, *Sketches*, p. 97.

[4] Published at Newport.   [5] Hopkins, *True Holiness*, pp. iv., v.

[6] For the statements and quotations in this paragraph, see *Ibid.*, pp. 2, 3, 7-9, 19-31, 41, 74.

of sin. Nor can any man be sure that he has that disinterested benevolence wherein holiness consists till he is ready for whatever disposition of himself the wise Ruler of the universe may see is for the largest good of all. He must be able to say " with Moses, ' Blot me, I pray thee, out of thy book.' If God may not be God, and order all things for his own glory, and the greatest good of his kingdom; and if my salvation is inconsistent with this, I give all up, I have no interest of my own to seek or desire." True, says Hopkins, " when he comes to know that he is thus devoted to God, he may be sure of his own eternal salvation. But let it be observed, he must *first* have such exercises of disinterested affection as these, before he can have any evidence that he shall be saved."

The passages last quoted bring to our attention one of the most famous peculiarities of Hopkins's theology, his doctrine of " willingness to be damned," as it is generally phrased, or, more truly, of willingness to be disposed as seems best to divine wisdom, whatever that disposal may be. It is a doctrine that appears constantly in his writings, but is nowhere more drastically set forth than in a *Dialogue between a Calvinist and a Semi-Calvinist*, written in Hopkins's old age and published after his death.[1] " If any one,"[2] says he, " thinks he loves God, and shall be saved; if

[1] West, *Sketches*, pp. 141–167. [2] *Ibid.*, p. 150.

he finds that his love to God does not imply a willingness to be damned, if this were most for his [*i. e.*, God's] glory, he has reason to conclude that he is deceived, and that what he calls love to God is really enmity against him." Yet this, to most Christians, utterly repellent demand was not original with Hopkins. Edwards had, indeed, rejected the doctrine;[1] but, to say nothing of thinkers in other branches of the Church, Thomas Hooker and Thomas Shepard had forcibly maintained it in the early days of New England.[2]

From this strenuous doctrine, however, Hopkins drew hope rather than despair.[3] And, however discouraged about the religious condition of his own times, he was far from taking gloomy views of the history of mankind as a whole. The universe, he believed, is made for happiness. An all-wise and all-powerful God has allowed no more sin and misery than he sees necessary for the largest happiness of the whole. And Hopkins felt convinced that, taking into view the millennial years which his fancy loved to picture, there is " no reason to conclude that but few of mankind will be saved, in comparison with those who shall perish; but see ground to believe that the number of the former will far exceed that of the

[1] See *ante*, p. 239.

[2] For this subject and references to the literature, see G. L. Walker, *Some Aspects of the Religious Life of New England*, pp. 27, 28.

[3] West, *Sketches*, pp. 165-167.

latter."[1] He held, also, contrary to an impression that has sometimes been given of him, that no infants were in hell.[2] Indeed, this doctrine of infant damnation, maintained by some of the divines of seventeenth-century New England, as a corollary of election and reprobation, had almost completely died out of Christian thought in New England by the time that Hopkins published his first controversial tractates.

The discussion that ended, as far as Hopkins was concerned, with the publication of his *Nature of true Holiness*, in 1773, was his great controversy; in it most of the peculiarities of his religious opinions were expressed, and he felt that the victory had been his in the debate. But Hopkins's pen was busy with other writings, at which we can simply glance. Thus, in 1768, he published a sermon, preached in the Old South Church, Boston, which warmly defended the full divinity of Christ, then beginning to be doubted or denied by some in eastern Massachusetts.[3] Again, in 1783, moved by the spread of Universalist opinions, Hopkins published an able and extremely uncompromising defense of the doctrine of eternal punishment, in which he ventured to affirm that:[4]

---

[1] *System*, i., p. 308, ed. 1811.

[2] William Patten, quoted in Park, *Memoir*, p. 103.

[3] *The Importance and Necessity of Christians considering Jesus Christ in the Extent of his high and glorious Character.* Boston, 1768.

[4] *An Inquiry concerning the future State of those who die in their Sins.* Newport, 1783. The quotation is from pp. 154, 155.

"eternal punishment reflects such light on the Divine character, government and works, especially the work of redemption; and makes such a bright display of the worthiness and grandeur of the Redeemer, and of divine love and grace to the redeemed; and is the occasion of so much happiness in heaven; and so necessary, in order to the highest glory, and greatest increasing felicity of God's everlasting kingdom; that, should it cease, and this fire could be extinguished, it would, in a great measure, obscure the light of heaven."

But all Hopkins's wealth of imagination and of hope,—and he had both in abundance,—was poured into his treatise on the *Millennium*,[1] which was published with his *System* in 1793. The prophecies of Daniel and Revelation were searched for guidance to the nature, time, and duration of that blessed dispensation which Hopkins concluded would be ushered in "not far from the end of the twentieth century,"[2] and for which his soul longed.

Hopkins's feeling that the universe was made for the largest happiness, and that it is the duty of all disinterestedly to seek that happiness, made him one of the pioneers in a great philanthropic reform—that of the abolition of slavery. Like his friends, Edwards and Bellamy, Hopkins, in his early ministry, was a slaveholder.[3] But by the time of his settlement at Newport he had become convinced of the enormity of the traffic in human flesh. Hopkins was not a man

---

[1] *A Treatise on the Millennium*, bound with his *System*. Boston, 1793.
[2] *Ibid.*, ii., p. 488, ed. 1811.   [3] Park, *Memoir*, pp. 114, 118.

to conceal his convictions. Newport was the centre of the slave trade in New England; Newport fortunes were largely made in slave ships; men in his own congregation were interested in the trade; but by 1770 or 1771, first of the Congregational ministry of New England, Hopkins was vigorously denouncing slavery from his pulpit, and appealing for its abandonment.[1] By personal solicitation, and even by contribution from his scanty means, he secured the freedom of quite a number of slaves owned by his Newport neighbors or his ministerial friends.

But his thought went out beyond the freeing of a few; and at his own suggestion and persuasion, he and his ministerial neighbor, Ezra Stiles, later to be president of Yale, sent out an appeal, in 1773, for means to train colored missionaries for labor in Africa.[2] For this purpose a society was organized by Hopkins and Stiles at Newport the same year, that was able to report gifts of £102 1s. 4¾d. by 1776.[3] Of this amount, one hundred dollars was the contribution of Hopkins himself as a kind of reparation to the African race—it being the sum for which he had, long before, sold his slave.[4] By this society and other friends raised up by Hopkins's efforts, two young men in Hopkins's

---

[1] Park, *Memoir*, pp. 116, 118, 160. Judge Samuel Sewall had written against slavery in his *Selling of Joseph* in 1700.

[2] *Ibid.*, pp. 129–132. Circular letter of August 31, 1773.

[3] Stiles's and Hopkins's circular letter of April 10, 1776, p. 4.

[4] Park, *Memoir*, p. 138.

congregation were so fitted at Princeton and elsewhere as to be ready to go to Africa in 1776, had not the Revolutionary War prevented. Successive hindrances, for which Hopkins was in no way responsible, robbed the missionary project of success during his lifetime, as it did the plan for African colonization which he formed before 1784; but the seed he sowed did not die.[1]

These efforts Hopkins accompanied by frequent publication and by letters to men of influence. Much of this address to the public was through the newspapers;[2] but two appeals were in more permanent form. A *Dialogue concerning the Slavery of the Africans; shewing it to be the Duty and Interest of the American States to emancipate all their African Slaves* was put forth in 1776,[3] with a dedication to the Continental Congress, and was republished in a large edition by the New York Manumission Society in 1785. A less important tract was *A Discourse upon the Slave-Trade, and the Slavery of the Africans*, delivered in 1793.[4] Moreover, Hopkins succeeded in having his own church pass votes discouraging the owning of slaves by its members; and the number of colored hearers in his congregation and of colored subscribers to his *System* testified to his unfailing kindness to those of the oppressed race in his own town, and to their appreciation of his labors in their behalf.[5]

[1] Park, *Memoir*, pp. 138-156.   [2] *Ibid.*, p. 119.
[3] Published at Norwich.   [4] Published at Providence.
[5] Park, *Memoir*, pp. 157, 166.

Hopkins's prominence as a citizen of Rhode Island led to the bestowal upon him of the degree of Doctor of Divinity by Brown University in 1790. At that time he had been for eight years engaged on his chief work, his *System of Doctrines, Contained in divine Revelation, explained and defended*, which was to employ him for two years more and to be published in 1793.[1] This rock-ribbed exposition of divinity had a sale of over twelve hundred copies, and, to the surprise of the author, brought him in nine hundred dollars—a sum, wrote Hopkins, " without which I know not how I should have subsisted." " I consider [it]," said he, " the greatest public service that I have ever done. It has met with more general and better acceptation by far than I expected, both in America and Europe; and no one has undertaken to answer it."[2]

The expiring hour precludes the possibility of any consideration of this monument of indefatigable labor, and fortunately none is needed, since the chief peculiarities of Hopkins's thought have already passed before us. Without the genius of Edwards, Hopkins's iron and relentless logic, his exaltation of the divine sovereignty, his reduction of righteousness and of evil to single principles, and his strong conviction that the universe moves toward a single goal, that of the greatest possible happiness of the whole, and

---

[1] Published at Boston and reprinted there in 1811 ; and again in *Works*, i. and ii., Boston, 1852. [2] West, *Sketches*, pp. 101, 102.

moves by steps of absolute divine appointment, give to his system the power that comes from unity, consistency, and intellectual transparency. While built on the Edwardean foundations, boldness, freedom, and fearlessness are the prime characteristics of Hopkins's thinking. It dared attack accepted truths and question their rightfulness to be. It had no shrinking from any consequences that the logic of the premises demanded. It was as strenuous and as able a critique of current beliefs as New England has ever seen. And its influence was great. Seven years before his death Hopkins wrote:[1]

"About forty years ago[2] there were but few, perhaps not more than four or five who espoused the sentiments, which have since been called *Edwardean*, and *new divinity*, and since, after some improvement was made upon them, *Hopkintonian*, or *Hopkinsian* sentiments. But these sentiments have so spread since that time among ministers, especially those who have since come on the stage, that there are now more than one hundred in the ministry who espouse the same sentiments, in the United States of America. And the number appears to be fast increasing, and these sentiments appear to be coming more and more into credit, and are better understood, and the odium which was cast on them and those who preached them, is greatly subsided."

Could Hopkins have looked forward with prophetic eye, he would have seen the opinions which he cherished remain a powerful influence in American

[1] West, *Sketches*, pp. 102, 103.
[2] *I. e.*, about the time of Edwards's death.

religious thought till the time of the Civil War. As the influence of these views widened after his death, however, the peculiar intensities of his presentation constantly diminished.

I said, in speaking of Edwards in a previous lecture, that as a controversialist and a theologian he seems remote, when viewed from the standpoint of the present age. I presume most of us have that feeling in a higher degree regarding Hopkins. The problems that busied him are not those to which the theologians of our day most readily turn. The conceptions of the Gospel that his peculiarities involved are not those which find large support in current religious thought. Whether men regret or rejoice that it is so, the presentation of Christian truth that he made is largely of the past. But, if I may borrow a somewhat overworked current phrase, I query whether more of " life " ever flowed through the work of any religious leaders of New England than through that of the Edwardean school of which Hopkins was the most strenuous, and on the whole the most influential, representative.

The Master said, when He gave His disciples a test of the value of claimants to their regard, " by their fruits ye shall know them." Hopkinsianism presented a view of the religious life which called for an instant and unreserved consecration to the service of God. Hopkinsianism was the chief human instrumentality in bringing about the series of revivals that, between 1791 and 1858, revolutionized the spiritual life of our New England churches; its leader was the pioneer of our Congregational ministry in attempting to remove the curse of slavery, and in endeavoring to send missionaries to Africa; its representatives, more than any other party in our churches, checked the Unitarian defection; it contributed at least as largely as any other force to the reforms in theological education inaugurated by the foundation of Andover Seminary; and its influence, beyond that of any other religious party in New England, led to the establishment of home missions, and to the formation of the American Board. If these are not good fruits, then the religious history of New England has none to show.

Hopkins himself survived the publication of his *System* ten years. For him they were years of trial and of increasing feebleness due to old age. His congregation was small and composed mostly of those advanced in life. His church membership included few men. His sermons were reputed " dry and abstract " by the young people of his flock, who wandered to other churches.[1] His unanimated delivery became less attractive with years; and his bodily weakness was greatly augmented by a paralytic stroke which he suffered in January, 1799.[2] Still he

[1] Sprague, *Annals of the American Pulpit*, i., p. 433, ii., p. 472, 473.
[2] West, *Sketches*, p. 105.

continued to preach till October, 1803, though with feebler voice, and needing the assistance of his colored protégé, the sexton, Newport Gardner, to enter the pulpit and sometimes even to rise to deliver the sermon.[1]

It was not much that he could do; and perhaps it was a consciousness of his limitations in public speech that induced him to make a list of his congregation and pray for each in his study daily by name. "We have this treasure in earthen vessels, that the excellency of the power may be of God, and not of us," said an Apostle who resembled Hopkins in this at least, that his written argument was considered more effective than his spoken discourse. Hopkins saw the fruit of his prayers before he died. On the coming of Rev. Caleb J. Tenney as a candidate for settlement as Hopkins's colleague, in July, 1803, the revival for which the old pastor had so long vainly waited began, and more than thirty owned themselves the subjects of a regenerative change.[2] Hopkins lived to witness and feebly to take part in the work; but on December 20, 1803, he died. As one of his brother ministers[3] sat by his side just before his departure, the sufferer groaned from excess of physical distress. "Doctor, why do you groan?" said his would-be comforter; "you know you have taught us

[1] Park, *Memoir*, p. 252.
[2] Sprague, *Annals*, ii., p. 472; Park, *Memoir*, p. 259.
[3] Rev. Joshua Bradley, of the Newport Baptist Church.

that we must be willing even to be eternally lost." The dying theologian, thus reminded of a cardinal article of his faith, replied, " It is only my body; all is right in my soul." [1]

[1] Bradley's letter, in Sprague, *Annals*, i., p. 435.

LEONARD WOODS

IX.

LEONARD WOODS

IN our consideration of the life and work of Samuel Hopkins it was made evident that his theological battles were even more largely with those of Calvinistic faith than with the anti-Calvinist and Liberal divines of his day. Though he directed his attack upon the Liberals when he maintained the full divinity of Christ against the Arian innovators about Boston, and criticised Mayhew's wellnigh Arminian conceptions of the share of man in conversion, his heaviest shots were sent against the Old Calvinists, Mills, Hart, Hemmenway, and Mather, who held none of the distinctively "Liberal" doctrines. Not that Hopkins had any sympathy with the tendencies of such men as Chauncy and Mayhew. Far from it. He wholly rejected their views, and undoubtedly esteemed the Old Calvinists as much more worthy of approval. But to Hopkins the Calvinism of the Old Calvinists appeared defective. He and his friends were the "Consistent Calvinists," as they often styled themselves, who carried their principles to a logical completeness. In Hopkins's judgment much of the preaching of the

Calvinism which had never come under the renovating Edwardean touch was wellnigh fatally misleading, and, as such, deserved strenuous opposition.

It was remarked also in the last lecture that Hopkins rejoiced in his old age that " more than a hundred in the ministry " had adopted his views, and that the number appeared to him " to be fast increasing." [1] This conviction was no delusion. If all shades of Edwardeanism are taken into view,—the comparative moderation of the younger Edwards, the much greater moderation of Timothy Dwight, as well as the strenuousness of Hopkins,—it may truly be said that, by the year 1800, Edwardeanism had obtained a decided numerical superiority over Old Calvinism in Connecticut and western Massachusetts, and had gained possession, though in its most moderate form, of the chief educational center of western New England, Yale College. By the same year, Edwardeanism, especially in its more radical Hopkinsian presentation, was beginning to press into eastern Massachusetts with power, where it had not heretofore been largely represented.

It was this incoming of the Edwardean type of Calvinism in general, and of Hopkinsianism in particular, with its eager and confident polemics, its positive assertions of divine sovereignty, of total depravity, of the prime need of a radical regeneration,

[1] See *ante*, p. 353.

of the duty of instant repentance and submission, and of the spiritual worthlessness of all that fell short of such self-surrender, that made evident the departure from the historic conceptions of Christianity which Liberalism had silently, and largely unconsciously, brought about in eastern Massachusetts. Easy-going Old Calvinism had dwelt side by side with the new Liberalism, and neither had distinctly perceived the cleft between them. The new Edwardeanism came in its aggressive Hopkinsian form and precipitated the Unitarian separation.

But at the beginning of the nineteenth century it seemed as if Hopkinsianism was about as much opposed to Old Calvinism as to Liberalism; and it appeared probable that the effect of the incoming of Hopkinsianism into eastern Massachusetts would be to split the historic Congregational body of that region into three mutually jealous denominations. This triple schism was avoided, and the conservative forces of Old Calvinism and New Divinity were so welded together in opposition to the Liberalism which soon became Unitarianism, that the fact that they once stood in danger of cleavage has faded out of the knowledge of all save historical students. No event in the development of modern Congregationalism was more important than this union. Doubtless many causes contributed to effect it; but as far as it was due to any person, the Congregational churches of eastern

Massachusetts owe this service most of all to the subject of the present lecture—Leonard Woods.

The parents of Leonard Woods [1] lived at Princeton, Mass., where his father was a farmer. Both the father and the mother were of marked character and warm religious faith; the father, in particular, being of much more than usual mental gifts, and a considerable reader of philosophy, theology, and English literature. The little town gave more than usual opportunity for some acquaintance with these themes, since a large portion of the extensive library collected by Rev. Thomas Prince of the Old South Church, Boston, had been taken thither by Prince's son-in-law, Moses Gill, afterward Lieutenant-Governor of the State, and placed at the service of his neighbors who cared to read. Here, under the shadow of Mount Wachusett, Leonard was born on June 19, 1774, almost exactly a year before the battle of Bunker Hill. Here he grew up on the farm, his parents expecting to make a farmer of him, till his own strong desires to become a minister, his evident abilities of mind, and an illness which impaired his physical

[1] The chief sources of biographical information regarding Leonard Woods are three brief sketches of his life : (a) in Sprague, *Annals of the American Pulpit*, ii., pp. 438-441, based on facts furnished by Woods himself ; (b) in the funeral sermon preached by Prof. E. A. Lawrence in memory of his father-in-law, *A Discourse Delivered at the Funeral of Rev. Leonard Woods, D.D., in the Chapel of the Theological Seminary, Andover, August 28, 1854*, Boston, 1854 ; (c) and in an enlargement of the sketch contained in this sermon published by Professor Lawrence in the *Congregational Quarterly* for April, 1859, i., pp. 105-124.

strength led his mother to encourage, and his father to consent to, his entering on preparation for college under the supervision of the pastor of the Princeton church, Rev. Thomas Crafts. The pecuniary resources of a farmer's family in the time of financial reaction that followed the Revolutionary War were meager at best, and scanty aid could be given the boy in his preparation; so that, save for three months at Leicester Academy, and a little guidance from his minister, he was self-taught till he entered Harvard in the autumn of 1792. It gives a glimpse of the home affection which followed the young student, and of the simplicity of a hundred years ago, to learn that his mother spun and wove all the clothing that he wore during his college course.[1]

The Harvard of the closing years of the eighteenth century had altered much from the college of Increase Mather's day, at which we glanced,[2] but was very unlike the great institution of the present. Its faculty included a president and seven professors, three of whom were attached to the then newly created medical department. Four tutors also carried much of the burden of instruction. The classics— that is to say, Horace, Sallust, Cicero, Livy, Xenophon, and Homer—still constituted the chief employment of the first three years.[3] Freshmen also studied

[1] Lawrence, funeral *Discourse*, p. 10.   [2] See *ante*, p. 178.
[3] Quincy, *History of Harvard University*, ii., pp. 265, 274, 277-279, 350, 499, 539, 540.

Arithmetic, Sophomores Algebra, and Juniors Doddridge's *Lectures on Divinity* and the Greek Testament. Senior year was the special province of Logic, Metaphysics, and Ethics, while declamation was practiced and a modicum of History instilled all through the course. Hebrew was passing away as an undergraduate study; those students whose parents furnished them with a written request so to do being allowed to substitute French; and the change from the emphasis once laid upon themes of specific value for technical ministerial preparation was further recognized by the recent addition of instruction in English to the duties of the Hebrew professorship.

From a modern standpoint the course of study was not exacting, nor was the discipline very thorough. Many ancient customs were then passing away. The Freshman was beginning to wear his hat when on the campus, and ceasing to be at the beck and call of upper classmen when his superiors wished errands done. The college was struggling to keep its classes clothed in distinctive uniforms, and fines were still the punishment for many infractions of college discipline. Religiously, Harvard, like Yale, was carefully observant of worship and of doctrinal instruction, as far as its officers could make it so. Just twenty years before Woods entered Harvard students had been relieved from repeating publicly the heads of the sermons they had recently heard; and for eight years they had been excused from attending the more technical of the two courses of instruction given by the Hollis Professor of Divinity unless they intended to enter the ministry.[1] But some theological instruction was still given to every student.

Yet the period of Woods's residence at Cambridge was about the ebb-tide of religion among the students of American colleges. The French alliance in the Revolutionary struggle and sympathy for France in her own revolution had popularized the French contempt of religion; and able and in many ways most devoted and patriotic Americans, like Franklin, Paine, and Jefferson, by their example or their writings, had spread wide among the students, the young lawyers, the physicians, and the politicians of the period a state of indifference or of hostility to revealed religion. While Woods was at Harvard, there was at one time only one professed Christian among the undergraduates.[2] Harvard was no exception in this matter; the first labor of President Timothy Dwight, when he became president of Yale, just as Woods was entering on his Senior year at Harvard, was to combat the all but universal infidelity of the students of his new charge. Indeed, so far had the matter gone at New Haven that many of the Senior class "had assumed the names of the principal English and French

[1] Quincy, *History of Harvard University*, ii., pp. 259, 260, 274.
[2] Lawrence, in *Congregational Quarterly*, i., p. 106.

infidels," and were generally known by these nicknames throughout the college.¹

Plunged into such a student atmosphere on coming from a religious home to college, Woods naturally experienced some mental trials in that painful process through which many a young collegian has to pass when a faith received from parental instruction is being developed into a personal conviction. Steady and upright in personal conduct he remained; but the philosophy of the eminent English Unitarian minister and chemist, Joseph Priestley, greatly attracted him; and, for a time, he made Priestley's material and mechanical explanations of the visible world his own.² In scholarship Woods easily led his class of thirty-three members, delivering an oration, entitled *Envy Wishes, then Believes*, at his graduation in 1796.³

The young graduate returned from college to his parents' home inclined to pursue a general course of philosophic, historical, and literary reading, for which the Prince library gave unusual opportunity. But a fresh influence now came into his life. A new pastor, Rev. Joseph Russel, son of Rev. Noadiah Russel, of Thompson, Conn., had just been settled over the Princeton church and was preaching a strenuous Edwardean type of theology. Naturally, the two young

¹ *Life of Pres. Dwight* (by his sons), prefaced to his *Theology*, i., pp. 20, 22, 23.
² Sprague, *Annals*, ii., p. 439.
³ Lawrence, in *Cong. Quart.*, i., p. 107.

men talked on the themes suggested by the sermons,[1] and the interest thus aroused in the young graduate was deepened by a visit to Cambridge and a conversation with his intimate friend of the class below his own, John Hubbard Church,[2] who had recently declared himself a Christian. Church persuaded his friend to read Doddridge's *Life*, and *Rise and Progress*: while, at Russel's suggestion, Woods studied Romans, Galatians, and Ephesians. He had now become a teacher at Medford, and as he thought on the themes suggested by his reading his perturbation of soul rapidly deepened. As he himself wrote to his friend, Church:[3]

"Terror, amazement, cold chills of body and mind, sometimes a flood of sorrow, hard thoughts of God, dreadful conceptions of his character,—I have no words to express my state for about a week. I felt my health declining. I wandered about. I tried to run from myself. I awoke in the morning and read my sentence for having committed the unpardonable sin."

But light and peace came at last; and with it a desire to confess Christ which led him to unite with the church at Medford in 1797, and to determine to devote his life to the ministry.[4]

Woods had already come under moderate Hopkins-

[1] Russel's statement, quoted by Lawrence, *ibid.*, pp. 107, 108.
[2] For his biography, see Sprague, *Annals*, ii., pp. 445-449.
[3] Lawrence, in *Cong. Quart.*, i., p. 109.
[4] Sprague, *Annals*, ii., p. 439.

ian influences at Princeton, and though he debated whether he should not put himself under the theological instruction of the Old Calvinist Hollis Professor of Divinity at Harvard, David Tappan, the advice of the Princeton pastor, Russel, and the wishes of his Edwardeanly inclined parents, led him to decide in favor of a more strenuous type of theology.[1] The autumn of 1797 saw Woods on his way, with his friend Church, to the home of Rev. Dr. Charles Backus,[2] at Somers, Conn., then one of the most noted of the household theological schools of the Edwardean type. The arrival of the two students found Somers enjoying one of the earlier of the great transforming series of revivals which, beginning in 1791, were repeated at intervals till 1858.

Backus was no believer in multiplied meetings. As Woods said later of him: "He wished those who were impressed with the importance of religion to have time for retirement, for reading the Scriptures and other books, and for prayer."[3] A man of great self-control himself, he would allow no expressions of religious self-conceit, whether of former wickedness or of present grace, in others. In theological opinions he sympathized with the more moderate Edwardeanism rather than with all of Hopkins's peculiarities; rejecting, for instance, Hopkins's test of disinterested

---
[1] Lawrence, in *Cong. Quart.*, i., p. 111.
[2] Biography in Sprague, *Annals*, ii., pp. 61–68.
[3] Letter of August 19, 1849, in Sprague, *Annals*, ii., p. 63.

benevolence, the " willingness to be damned." But he was enough of Hopkins's way of thinking to commend his *System* as a whole to the approval of his students. Personally Backus was marked by a profound sense of sin, and of the greatness of a salvation which could rescue men from its control.

Such an experience as Woods now enjoyed was the best possible for a young convert coming from the chill religious atmosphere of college. Entering thus into the thought and work of an active, sensible, acute-minded pastor, his own spiritual life deepened as his doctrinal thought quickened and clarified. But his residence at Somers was only for three months, his studies thus initiated being continued through the winter of 1797-98 at his Princeton home. So, fitted by less than a year of special theological training, he was licensed by the Cambridge Association in the spring of 1798; and in the summer following was called to the Second Church in what is now West Newbury, from which the Old Calvinist David Tappan had gone to the Hollis Professorship of Divinity at Harvard in 1792.[1] The terms offered by the parish were five hundred dollars for a " settlement,"—that is, to enable the young minister to establish a home in the community, —the " use of the parsonage land," a salary of four hundred dollars and eight cords of firewood annually, " with the liberty of going to see his parents for two

[1] See Sprague, *Annals*, ii., p. 439.

Sabbaths every year."[1] Woods's ordination to the pastorate thus offered occurred on December 5, 1798. On October 8, 1799, Woods followed the establishment of these ecclesiastical relations by his marriage to Miss Abigail Wheeler, a daughter of Joseph Wheeler, long Register of Probate for Worcester County. Mrs. Woods was a woman of rare devoutness of spirit, Christian confidence, and great patience during the long invalidism that preceded her death in 1846.[2] Ten sons and daughters were born into their household.

Like many a young minister since, the new pastor at West Newbury speedily induced his congregation to adopt a revised Confession of Faith; and in Woods's draft several Edwardean peculiarities distinctly appear. Thus, with Hopkins and the later Edwardeans generally, the new creed asserted the doctrine of general atonement. In consonance with Edwardean opinion it, tacitly at least, denied the imputation of Adam's sin to his descendants, while affirming that " by the wise and holy constitution of God, the character and state of his posterity depended on his conduct." And a forecast of controversies speedily to come is seen in the declaration " that Jesus Christ is a true God and true man, united in one mysterious person."[3]

---

[1] *Contributions to the Ecclesiastical History of Essex County*, p. 106. Boston, 1865.

[2] A biographical sketch by her husband was appended to Stuart' *A Sermon Preached at the Funeral of Mrs. Abby Woods*. Andover, 1846.

[3] *Contributions*, pp. 382, 383.

Personally the young minister was tall, slender, and dignified; and he was marked also by a ready ease of manner and kindliness of spirit that won for him the good-will of those he met, whether children or men and women of age and learning.[1] As a pastor, Woods was greatly beloved; though, if judged by that almost valueless basis of estimate, numerical success, his ministry was inconspicuous. Probably it was largely owing to his exalted conception of the requirements of a Christian profession that only fourteen were admitted to the church during his ten years' pastorate. Forty-nine had professed their faith during the eighteen years of his predecessor, Tappan; and fifty-one were to join the church in the eight and a half years included in the pastorates of the three ministers who came after him.[2]

Woods, however, soon came to be a man of public influence outside his parish. At the Harvard Commencement next following his ordination, July 17, 1799, he delivered a master's oration that attracted considerable attention, his theme being *A Contrast between the Effects of Religion and the Effects of Atheism*,[3] in which he argued " that the disbelief of GOD presupposes the depravation of moral principle," and found a " picture of the genuine spirit and fruits of Atheism . . . in the character and conduct of the

[1] Lawrence, in Sprague, *Annals*, ii., p. 441.
[2] *Contributions*, pp. 383-385.   [3] Published at Boston, 1799.

FRENCH "[1] black enough to have satisfied the most exacting Federalist. In his own association, as well as in his church, he earnestly advocated the abandonment of the Half-Way Covenant, which Edwardeans generally opposed.[2] This opposition won the hearty approval of the chief Hopkinsian and, on the whole, the leading minister of the region, Rev. Dr. Samuel Spring, who, since 1777, had been pastor of the North Church, Newburyport, and was related by marriage to the most noted Hopkinsian then in New England, Rev. Dr. Nathaniel Emmons of Franklin, Mass.[3] From the beginning of his West Newbury ministry his friendship for the strenuous Newburyport divine strengthened and deepened till the death of Dr. Spring in March, 1819.[4] So great was Spring's regard for his theological opinions that, when the strongly Hopkinsian *Massachusetts Missionary Magazine* was begun in 1803, Spring asked him to become one of the contributors.[5] And, on the whole, without advocating several of the Hopkinsian peculiarities, Woods was reckoned as belonging in sympathy at this time to the Hopkinsian side.[6]

[1] Pp. 7, 11.
[2] Lawrence, *Cong. Quart.*, i., p. 115 ; see also Spring's letter of June, 1805, in Woods, *History of the Andover Theo. Seminary*, p. 451.
[3] Mrs. Emmons and Mrs. Spring were half-sisters.
[4] See Woods's own account of his intimate relations with Spring, in Sprague, *Annals*, ii., p. 87.
[5] Lawrence, *Cong. Quart.*, i., p. 115.
[6] Woods reports Jedidiah Morse as saying of him, in 1807, that "he

But the young West Newbury minister no less warmly attracted men of Old Calvinist sympathies. David Tappan and Eliphalet Pearson had become his friends when he was their pupil at Harvard; and an even more influential and extremely moderate Edwardean, who was regarded as essentially Old Calvinist, Rev. Dr. Jedidiah Morse of Charlestown, father of the inventor of the electric telegraph, so valued his friendship and support that he asked Woods to join in the editorship of the broadly Calvinist magazine, the *Panoplist*, which Morse was chiefly instrumental in founding in 1805, to offset the Liberal *Monthly Anthology* that had been established in 1803.[1] The help which Woods contributed to the *Panoplist* led to an earnest exhortation to the young minister from the vigorous Hopkinsian, Rev. Dr. Samuel Austin of Worcester, not to " secede from the Hopkinsian doctrine."[2]

Such a mind as that of Woods is difficult for extremists in times of excitement rightly to value. Constitutionally cautious in the expression of opinion, moderate in his judgments of men and of theories, he valued union more than the maintenance of what seemed to him distinctions of secondary moment. In the great controversy with the Liberal party that

knew that in a moderate sense I was a Hopkinsian." Woods, *History of the Andover Theological Seminary*, p. 106. Boston, 1885.

[1] *Ibid.*, pp. 42, 43, 70, 106, 426.   [2] Letter, *ibid.*, p. 453.

was soon to be forced to take the name Unitarian, Woods saw that the union of all those who supported the main doctrines in which Old and New Calvinists were agreed was of more importance than the furtherance of any "improvements" in theology at the expense of increased division. But, though the personal friendship of a Hopkinsian neighbor like Dr. Spring might thoroughly comprehend a position like that of Woods, one cannot wonder that a Hopkinsian extremist like Emmons looked upon his moderation as in a measure disloyalty to Hopkinsian truth, and gave scant sympathy to a man whose discrimination between the two schools of current Calvinism was so held subservient to a desire for their association.

This largely conciliatory and irenic quality of Woods's mind in what he regarded as comparatively minor matters was coupled, however, with much positiveness of conviction and expression on what he deemed fundamentals of the faith; and the combination of the two fitted him admirably for the work involved in the foundation and early maintenance of Andover Seminary.

It would be as impossible in the time at my disposal as it should be unnecessary in this lecture-room, to recount at length the involved story of the establishment of this oldest of American institutions specifically devoted to ministerial education; but so much of the facts, however familiar, as may be necessary for an understanding of the share of Woods in the undertaking may rapidly be passed in review.

Liberalism, as was pointed out in our consideration of Chauncy, had so far invaded eastern Massachusetts by the time of his death in 1787, that the doctrine of the Trinity was largely questioned, the total depravity of man was discredited, and the everlasting suffering of the wicked denied. In the year of Chauncy's death, King's Chapel, the oldest Episcopal congregation in Boston, ordained the anti-Trinitarian James Freeman at the hands of its own membership as its rector, and became the first distinctly recognized Unitarian congregation in New England.

No Congregational church immediately adopted an avowedly anti-Trinitarian position. But Liberal views steadily and rapidly advanced, pressed into definition by the spread of Edwardeanism into eastern Massachusetts, and by October, 1801, the old Mayflower Church at Plymouth had led the schism by dividing on the issue. The Hopkinsians had established the Massachusetts Missionary Society in 1799, and its *Missionary Magazine* in 1803; the Old Calvinists and moderate Edwardeans had organized the Massachusetts General Association in the year last named, and had sent forth the *Panoplist* in 1805. The Liberals had begun the *Monthly Anthology* in 1803, and Boston had witnessed the opening of Channing's notable pastorate the same year. Parties were ranged for conflict, and the lines were tightening month by month; so that when the death of Professor Tappan, in August, 1803, left vacant the Hollis Professorship of Divinity at Harvard, it was recognized on all sides that the character of his successor would reveal the forces to be dominant in this ancient seat of learning. The election of Henry Ware, on February 5, 1805, was the visible token of the passing of Harvard into the control of the anti-Trinitarians.

The manifest loss of the oldest New England college to the Evangelical cause quickened into action a desire that had been growing for some years previous for a more thorough system of ministerial education. Harvard and Yale had been founded primarily to supply the churches with an educated ministry. Their courses of study had been originally framed with this purpose in view; and, on the whole, they had met the requirements of the early colonial ministry. But the youth of the students and the elementary character of the curricula rendered the training of the ordinary college graduate of the eighteenth century inadequate to the advancing claims of the ministerial office; and, to afford a better preparation, the Hollis Professorship of Divinity was founded at Harvard in 1721, and a professor of theology appointed at Yale in 1755.

Yet more efficient and popular than these professorships was the habit that grew throughout the eighteenth century of taking a few months of theological study with some leading pastor between the candidate's graduation from college and his entrance on ministerial labor. Many of the New England clergy thus received students into their households, but the Edwardean leaders most of all. Edwards, Bellamy, Smalley, Backus, Emmons, and others of this party were notably active in making their own homes theological seminaries. The training thus afforded was by no means inconsiderable. It familiarized the student with problems of parish administration. It propagated most effectively the theological opinions of the instructor. But it is almost needless to point out that this system of education gave no broad view of church history, no careful study of linguistics or exegesis, and no extensive acquaintance with the development of Christian doctrine as a whole. A busy New England pastor of the eighteenth century had neither the time nor the books nor the technical education to give instruction along such lines.[1]

By the beginning of the nineteenth century the desire for yet better facilities for theological education was strongly felt, and with the defection of Harvard, in 1805, this desire was crystallized into action. In 1806, leaders of the Old Calvinists and of the Hopkinsians in eastern Massachusetts were planning, each

[1] In this paragraph I have borrowed from my *History of the Cong. Churches*, pp. 346, 347.

party at first without knowledge of the purpose of the other, for the establishment of a theological seminary.[1]

The Old Calvinist effort centered at Andover, where Samuel and John Phillips had founded their Academy in 1778, and had impressed upon the remarkable institution that then had its birth a strongly religious character. Their thought seems to have included the possible establishment in this institution of a professorship of divinity like those of Harvard and Yale; and John Phillips had intrusted funds to the trustees of the Academy, in 1795, for the express purpose of aiding students in theological branches " under the direction of some eminent Calvinistic minister."[2] By the help of this fund some twelve students of theology were educated at Andover under the tuition of Rev. Jonathan French of the South Church, between 1797 and the opening of the Seminary in 1808.[3] When, therefore, Professor Eliphalet Pearson, who had been from 1778 to 1786 the principal of Phillips Academy, resigned his chair of Hebrew at Harvard in 1806, convinced that the passage of that institution to the Liberals demanded a new and conservative seat of theological instruction, it was natural that he and his friends, Rev. Dr. Jedidiah Morse of Charlestown and

[1] Woods, *History of the Andover Theological Seminary*, p. 47. The best account of the founding of the Seminary is in the work just cited.

[2] *Report of Committee on Deeds of Gift and Donations*, p. 42. Andover, 1856.

[3] Woods, *History*, p. 49.

Samuel Farrar, Esq., of Andover, should view Andover as the town with which to associate the enterprise that they had at heart. In consultation with them the "Founders," as they were technically called,—Samuel Abbot, Madame Phœbe Phillips and her son John Phillips, Jr., of Andover,—were ultimately led to provide the means for such an undertaking; and as early as July, 1806, Pearson, Morse, Farrar, Abbot, and other members of a "Voluntary Association" were laying definite plans for the establishment of a theological seminary at Andover. A constitution for the proposed seminary was soon after prepared; and in June, 1807, the Massachusetts legislature authorized the trustees of Phillips Academy to to hold funds for its use.[1]

Meanwhile that strict Calvinist of the Hopkinsian type, Rev. Dr. Samuel Spring of Newburyport, in ignorance of the Old Calvinist enterprise at Andover, was planning a theological school. He had suggested the thought of such an undertaking to his young friend, Leonard Woods, as early as 1801;[2] and by the close of the year 1806, he had interested in the enterprise three laymen of wealth and religious character, though none of them were at this time church members. These three, William Bartlett and Moses Brown of Newburyport, and John Norris of Salem, were those afterward known as the "Associate Founders" of

[1] *Report of Committee*, pp. 67–69. [2] Woods, *History*, p. 72.

Andover Seminary. Yet at first they had no thought of anything but an institution exclusively of their own creation, and they suggested that their seminary might be at West Newbury, with Woods as its instructor.[1] For this purpose they proposed to give thirty thousand dollars.

The day following this eventful decision at Newburyport brought Woods to Morse's house in Charlestown on business connected with the *Panoplist*.[2] Of course, the younger minister told his older friend what had been done by Dr. Spring and his associates; and heard in return from his astonished editorial colleague the plans of the Old Calvinists at Andover. Morse at once presented the advantages that would flow from a union of the two enterprises, and Woods agreed with him, though hesitating at first to put himself forward in advocacy of combination on account of his youth and almost filial relations to Rev. Dr. Spring. Professor Pearson, and the Andover Old Calvinists generally, favored the union; but Dr. Spring believed it fraught with too serious doctrinal peril, and long opposed all compromise so strenuously that, in March, 1807, Woods consented to accept a professorship in the proposed West Newbury institution. But no sooner had Woods come to this decision than he repented it under the strong conviction that rival seminaries would be a great misfortune, and, throwing

[1] Woods, *History*, p. 75.   [2] *Ibid.*, p. 76.

off all hesitation, began to labor most assiduously to bring about the consolidation of the enterprises.[1]

At first, however, it looked as if union were unattainable, and during the early summer of 1807, Spring drafted, with some assistance from Woods, a broadly Edwardean creed for the proposed Hopkinsian seminary;[2] while the Andover Old Calvinists committed their foundation to the care of the trustees of Phillips Academy in August and September of the same year, stipulating that the doctrinal test required of instructors should be conformity to the Westminster Shorter Catechism.[3] But Pearson and Woods still labored for union, and chiefly through their persistence it was ultimately brought about. A hopeful sign was the appointment of Woods to the Professorship of Christian Theology in the proposed Old Calvinist institution at Andover by the " Founder," Samuel Abbot, in October, 1807,—an appointment which Woods did not accept till just before the union became an accomplished fact in May, 1808.[4] The joint institution thus laboriously brought into being was placed under the care of the trustees of Phillips Academy; but to guard their own rights the Hopkinsian " Associate Founders " procured the establishment of a " Board of Visitors " with supervisory powers. And the

[1] Woods, *History*, pp. 80, 87.   [2] *Ibid.*, pp. 98–103.
[3] *Report of Committee on Deeds of Gift and Donations*, pp. 69–85, particularly pp. 75, 76.
[4] Woods, *History*, pp. 108, 128, 129.

"Associate Founders" and "Founders" agreed, by a further compromise, that each professor of their appointment should assent to the creed which Spring had prepared for the proposed West Newbury seminary, as a statement in which those doctrines are "more particularly expressed" which are summarily expressed in the Westminster Shorter Catechism.[1]

The accomplishment of this union of Hopkinsian and Old Calvinist interests at Andover led immediately to more cordial relations between the parties elsewhere. In June following the agreement of the "Founders" and "Associate Founders," the *Panoplist* and the *Missionary Magazine* were consolidated; and the Massachusetts General Association, heretofore looked upon askance by Hopkinsians, received in much larger degree the support of all the Evangelical forces of the State.

It must have been evident, from the story just narrated in outline, that no small share of the success that ultimately crowned these complicated endeavors was due to the labors, and even more to the personality of Woods. His efforts for union were positive and influential; but even more influential was the fact that he was a man on whom both parties could heartily unite. The same qualities that had made him equally welcome to the constituents of the *Missionary Magazine* and of the *Panoplist* rendered him an acceptable

[1] *Report of Committee on Deeds of Gift and Donations*, pp. 113, 114.

professor of theology to the Hopkinsians of Newburyport and to the moderate Edwardeans and Old Calvinists of Andover. To a few, indeed, this union and the man who symbolized it were not satisfactory. To Emmons the union always seemed too great a concession to Old Calvinistic laxity and error; to Pearson, who perhaps labored more than any other in the negotiations which brought it about, it appeared ultimately too complete a Hopkinsian victory.[1] But, looking backward over the ninety years that have passed since these events, it is manifest, I think, that no work of greater importance to our New England churches was accomplished in the opening decades of the nineteenth century than the junction of the two Evangelical streams — that flowing out from Edwards's work and teachings, and that having its source in the older Calvinism. It consolidated the apparently divided conservative forces of eastern Massachusetts, it set a higher standard for our ministerial education, it put a barrier to the Unitarian advance. And, on the whole, no man contributed so materially to this union as Leonard Woods.

Woods's acceptance of the Andover call was followed, in June, 1808, by his resignation of the West Newbury pastorate, his removal to Andover Hill, and

[1] Professor Park, in *A Memorial of the Semi-Centennial Celebration of the Founding of the Theological Seminary at Andover*, p. 236, Andover, 1859; Woods, *History*, p. 134.

his inauguration, together with that of Pearson, as professors in the Seminary, at its opening, September 28, 1808. On the next day he began his teaching in the parlor of his house, for Seminary buildings were yet to be.[1] The teacher was thirty-four years of age.

If any justification of the new foundation was needed, the Seminary received it amply in the immediate response of the churches to its work. Dr. Spring had hoped that, " in due time," there might be " twelve or fifteen students in the Seminary at once;" the first year saw an attendance of thirty-six, and before Woods resigned his professorship, in 1846, after thirty-eight years of service, he could say that he had taught " more than fifteen hundred students," of whom nearly a thousand had " finished the regular course of study."[2] Before that resignation, also, nearly thirty theological schools had been founded by the Protestant religious bodies of the United States. By Congregationalists Bangor had been opened in 1816; Yale Divinity School in 1822; Hartford, then at East Windsor Hill, in 1834; and Oberlin in 1835. The Presbyterian body had closely paralleled this development, opening Princeton Seminary in 1812; Auburn in

[1] Lawrence, Funeral *Discourse*, pp. 16, 17; Woods, *History*, pp. 130-133; an account of the services of September 28, 1808, which included the ordination of Dr. Pearson, a sermon, on Matt. xiii. 52, by President Timothy Dwight, and the inaugural address of Professor Woods *On the Glory and Excellency of the Gospel*, may be found in the *Panoplist*, New Series, vol. i., p. 191.

[2] Woods, *History*, p. 137.

1821; Western, at Allegheny, in 1827; Lane in 1832; and Union in 1836. The Baptists had begun instruction at Hamilton in 1819, and at Newton in 1825; and Episcopalians, Lutherans, the Reformed, and Unitarians all established strong seminaries early in this period.

But the attendance of numbers, or imitation by other groups of Christians, was not the only, or the best, result of the new foundation, and of the union of heretofore jealous forces on which it was based. The rising tide of religious feeling in our churches here overflowed in missionary consecration. Andover Seminary did not, indeed, originate American foreign missions. That movement had many roots. Chief of all it was due to the new baptism of our churches which came with the revivals whose first manifestation was in 1791. The Home Missionary endeavors of Connecticut and Massachusetts in the last decade of the eighteenth century stimulated it. The *Connecticut Evangelical Magazine*, founded in 1800, and the *Massachusetts Missionary Magazine* of 1803, spread before the public the stories of English missionary endeavor, —for foreign missions had begun with power in England with the work of William Carey in 1792. It was from the missionary household of one of the editors of the *Connecticut Evangelical Magazine*, at Torringford, Conn., that Samuel J. Mills went to Williams College, determined to give his life to missionary service, in 1806. Missions were in the air; and when, in 1807, Mills opened his heart, under the shelter of the Williamstown haystack, to Gordon Hall and James Richards, he found that the Spirit of God had anticipated his words, and the path was ready for the organization of the Williams College Society of Inquiry in the spring of 1808.[1]

Yet, if Andover Seminary did not see the beginning of the foreign missionary movement of New England, it gave such a focus to that movement as made its speedy success possible. Here Judson, Hall, Mills, Newell, Nott, Richards, and Rice stimulated one another's consecration to the missionary cause. Here they found sympathetic counselors in the faculty and in Dr. Spring of Newburyport and Dr. Samuel Worcester of Salem. Here on June 25, 1810, in consultation with Professors Woods and Stuart, and Rev. Drs. Spring and Worcester, the historic application to the Massachusetts General Association, which was to meet two days later at Bradford, was determined upon, and signed by Judson, Nott, Mills, and Newell. From this consultation Spring and Worcester, on Tuesday, June 26th, made their memorable journey by chaise to Bradford—a journey in which the American Board, as established by the Association at Bradford on the Friday following, was planned.[2] It

[1] Tracy, *History of the American Board*, pp. 21-24. New York, 1842.
[2] *Ibid.*, pp. 25-27; Lawrence, Funeral *Discourse*, p. 17.

must have been with a sense of large participation in an enterprise of far-reaching significance that Woods preached the sermon on February 6, 1812, at Salem, when Newell, Judson, Nott, Hall, and Rice were ordained " as missionaries to the heathen in Asia." [1]

The advancement of missions through the American Board, on the Prudential Committee of which he served from 1819 to 1844, was by no means the only form of their novel Christian service that interested Woods. The American Tract Society originated at Andover, through efforts begun in 1813; the Education Society of 1815 claimed much of Woods's labor; and his share in the origin of the American Temperance Society of 1826 was conspicuous.[2]

All these services to the causes of religion or of reform, important as they might be, were subordinate to Woods's main work at Andover, that of instruction in systematic theology. It was in the classroom that his best labor was accomplished; yet he had not all the qualities that bring fame to an instructor. His mind seldom flashed forth the brilliant, epigrammatic shafts that make some lecture-rooms scintillate like the meteor-shot sky of a November night. In the circle of his friends he could display a considerable degree of quiet humor, yet he rarely revealed this

[1] Published at Boston, 1812. The text was the Sixty-seventh Psalm.
[2] Woods, *History*, p. 199; Lawrence, Funeral *Discourse*, p. 18.

gift in the classroom.[1] His cast of mind was naturally cautious; on the sharper distinctions between the shades of Calvinism of his day he sometimes seemed indefinite; he lacked, in a measure, that power which comes in the classroom from having a full, definite, promptly expressed, and dogmatically asserted opinion on every question that student inquirers may present. But he had many of the most salient gifts of a great teacher. If his instruction was seldom brilliant, it was solid, well thought out, and thoroughly buttressed with argument. His patience was remarkable, his manner uniformly courteous, his skill in drawing out and directing the thought of his pupils by questions conspicuous. The story is told that an embarrassed student of Andover, thrown into perplexity by the unexpected intricacies developed in an examination for licensure, cried out to his ministerial judges, " Now, gentlemen, if Dr. Woods could only ask me one or two questions, the whole thing would be cleared up."[2] His spoken words and his written page had the beauty of simplicity, clearness, and ready comprehensibility. And he had that perhaps most effective of all qualities in a teacher, a hearty personal interest in the students under his charge that led him to labor not merely for their individual intellectual advancement, but for the deepening in them of the

[1] Compare the remarks of his son-in-law, Funeral *Discourse*, pp. 20, 21.
[2] *Ibid.*, pp. 23, 24.

personal spiritual life which is worth more in the progress of the Kingdom of God than any mental attainment, however great.

To give any adequate idea of his doctrinal system in a single lecture is, of course, impossible; partly because it so agreed in its main outline with the historic faith of the moderate Edwardean school to which he more and more inclined that any adequate characterization of his peculiarities would carry us into the minutiæ of doctrinal discussion, and partly because its range of thought covered the whole field, from the divine existence down to the particularities of church government. The age in which a man lives largely determines by its discussions and its needs the themes about which his thought will center. With Woods the salient topics of his argument were the absolute authority of Scripture, the Trinity and the nature of Christ's person, the divine purposes as revealed in the methods by which God has ordered and governs the animate and inanimate creation, moral agency as illustrated in man's present powers, responsibilities, abilities, and inabilities, man's total depravity, and the nature of the atoning work by which sin is forgiven and he is reconciled to God. Such an enumeration signifies little, and I prefer, therefore, instead of attempting any enlargement of these topics, to give you a hint alike of Woods's doctrinal emphases and of his literary style, by a quotation from the " Dedicatory

Address" to his pupils prefixed to his lectures n his collected *Works :* [1]

"As to matters of doctrine, I entreat you to keep at the greatest distance from all unscriptural speculations, and to repose unlimited confidence in the word of God. The minds of men at the present day are, to a fearful extent, in an unsettled state, and are reaching after something to satisfy a vain and restless curiosity. . . . There is, in my view, no ground of safety but a serious, unquestioning belief, resulting from thorough examination and Christian experience, that all Scripture is divinely inspired—that the whole Bible was written under the special guidance of the Holy Spirit, and is consequently clothed with divine authority, and is infallible in all its teachings. Hold fast to this principle, and you are safe. If you either reject or doubt it — if you consider the whole or particular parts of the Bible, as written without any special direction of the Holy Spirit, or if you regard the inspiration of the sacred writers as of a similar nature with the inspiration of poets and orators — I say, if thoughts like these are suffered to lodge in your minds, you are standing on slippery places, and there is reason to fear that your feet will quickly slide.

"A disbelief of the plenary inspiration of the Scriptures is generally found in those who are inclined to dissent from the common creed ; and though it may sometimes arise from other motives, it is often adopted as an expedient to get rid of unpalatable doctrines. Beware then of that state of moral feeling which would render any of the teachings of revelation unpalatable. See to it that you have that renewed, spiritual mind, which discerns and loves the truth — which specially recognizes the doctrine that we are by nature the children of wrath; that in our fallen state we

[1] i., pp. xii., xiii. Boston, 1849.

are not sufficient of ourselves to obtain salvation or to do anything acceptable to God, and that, unless we are regenerated by the Holy Spirit, we cannot see the kingdom of heaven — the doctrine that Christ, who is both God and man, died for our sins in our stead, and that his atoning blood secures to believers the forgiveness of sin and the blessedness of the world above. Shun every theological scheme, which gives an unscriptural prominence to the agency of man, and comparatively overlooks the agency of the divine Spirit. . . . On the other hand, I would, with equal earnestness, warn you against any such views of our dependence on God, as would interfere in the least with our free, accountable agency, or with our complete obligation to obey the law and the gospel. . . . Avoid all unscriptural views, and unscriptural representations, and maintain those doctrines of religion, which the experience of ages has shown to be best adapted to bring men to believe in the all-sufficient Saviour, and which, through the divine blessing, have had the greatest influence in promoting personal holiness, and genuine revivals of religion.

" And here let me suggest a very necessary caution. It is a fact, that the greatest difficulties, and those which human reason is least able to obviate, exist in regard to doctrines which are of the greatest value, and which are supported by the most satisfactory evidence. I might instance in the eternal, uncaused existence of God, the Scripture doctrine of the Trinity, the atonement, and the endless punishment of the impenitent. Now, if you should adopt the principle, that this or that doctrine is not to be believed because it is attended with insolvable difficulties, what would be the consequence ? Evidently, that you would reject from your creed the most certain and the most important truths, and in the end be plunged in downright skepticism. I caution you to guard against whatever would lead to so fatal a result, and particularly against the habit of looking off from the truths of religion, and from the clear evidence of those truths, and occupying your thoughts and your time with efforts to remove objections and cavils, which is frequently a hopeless undertaking.''

During his years of instruction at Andover, Woods was constantly busy with his pen. It has already been pointed out that when a young minister at West Newbury he was asked to have a part in the two Evangelical periodicals of that day. The custom of writing for current publications, thus early begun, Woods kept up through life. He was, moreover, in constant demand as a preacher of ordination sermons, of discourses commemorative of the older ministers or laymen with whom he had been associated in the founding of Andover Seminary or in the early history of the American Board, or as a speaker on special occasions; and many of these felicitous and appropriate addresses were printed. But his chief publications, during his active teaching at Andover, were either semi-controversial expositions of the truth as he understood it, or full-panoplied polemics against what he deemed the chief errors of the day. Many of these publications grew directly out of his classroom lectures. Thus, in 1825, he put forth a series of *Lectures on Infant Baptism*, and followed them, a year later, by *Lectures on the Inspiration of the Scriptures*. In 1832, he published in the *Spirit of the Pilgrims* several *Letters* to *Young Ministers.* In 1835, his *Essay on Native Depravity* was put forth. The year 1843 witnessed his vindication of Congregationalism and criticism of Episcopal claims, the *Lectures on Church-Government;* and this was followed, in 1846, by his *Lectures on Swedenborgianism.* Five years after his retirement from active duties, in 1851, he issued his defense of the older New England divinity and criticism of what he deemed current errors, the *Theology of the Puritans.*

While all these discussions had some degree of importance in their own day, three controversies, yet to be mentioned, are of greater significance, not so much because Woods showed higher skill in them than in the arguments just enumerated, but because they had to do with movements of larger moment in American religious thought. These more noteworthy controversial efforts were his *Letters to Unitarians* of 1820, his *Reply to Ware* of 1821, and his *Remarks on Ware's Answer* of 1822, which may be grouped together as a single discussion; his *Letters to Taylor* of 1830; and his *Examination of the Doctrine of Perfection as held by Rev. Asa Mahan, President of the Oberlin Collegiate Institute* of 1841. Woods was not by nature a controversialist. He did not go out of his way to encounter theological quarrels; but he did not avoid such discussions when they came to him as a consequence of his office or of his teachings; and his public position as professor of theology in the leading

Evangelical seminary of New England during those years of heated controversy made theological polemics unavoidable. Yet, when he is compared with the theological disputants of the eighteenth century, and with many in his own day, one is struck with the courtesy with which Woods argued with an opponent. His own true feeling of Christian charity for those he deemed in error he well expressed when he said:[1]

"I cannot avoid the persuasion that I should commit a less offence against the Christian religion by bad reasoning than by a *bad spirit*, and therefore that I am bound to take as much pains at least to cherish *right feeling* as to frame right arguments."

At an earlier point in this lecture we glanced at the triumph of the Liberal party in the contest for supremacy over the theological teaching of Harvard, and saw the decisive effect of that victory in determining the foundation of Andover Seminary. The Liberal movement had thenceforward intensified, and growing opposition to it had drawn the lines more and more sharply between the two parties. Park Street Church had been organized as an Evangelical outwork in Boston in 1809; from about that time onward conservative ministers, under the lead of Rev. John Codman of Dorchester, had begun to refuse to exchange pulpits with their Liberal associates; in 1815, Jedidiah Morse had published the much-discussed pamphlet on

[1] Lawrence, Funeral *Discourse*, p. 26.

American Unitarianism which ultimately fixed that designation on the Liberal party and led to its general recognition as a separate religious body; and, in 1819, Channing had outlined the theology of the new denomination in his famous sermon delivered at Baltimore on the occasion of the ordination of Jared Sparks.

In all this contention Woods had, of course, interested himself deeply; and, as his published lectures show,[1] he had elaborately discussed with his students the most loudly controverted point in debate, the nature of Christ. It is probably true, as has been said of late, that neither side in this warfare comprehended the doctrine of the Trinity in its historic Athanasian sense; yet the Evangelical champions defended with vigor and success not merely the full and eternal divinity of our Lord, but His full and complete humanity as well, against the crude Arian hypotheses of the earlier American Unitarians, who removed Christ from entire partnership in humanity, while denying Him a true participation in deity.[2]

But it was not this side of the debate between American Evangelicals and Liberals, so fully set forth in Woods's lectures, that he discussed in the *Letters to Unitarians* which Channing's sermon drew forth. The

[1] *Works*, i., p. 243-455.
[2] Compare Chadwick, *Old and New Unitarian Belief*, pp. 147, 148. Boston, 1894.

public defense of the person of Christ against the interpretations of Channing he left, in 1820, to his gifted colleague, Prof. Moses Stuart, while he applied himself to those questions which, though not so fundamental when viewed from the standpoint of universal Christian truth as is that of the person of Christ, yet were, even more than that, the topics of deepest interest and widest divergence in the debates of the first two decades of the nineteenth century. What is the nature of man? Is it full of vast possibilities of good, and in need only of a salvation by education through which character may be improved and developed, as the Unitarians claimed; or is it profoundly sinful and depraved, needing the special elective application of a divine transforming grace to work in it the regeneration that it requires, as Woods contended? This was the point at issue. Woods's *Letters* were elaborately answered by Prof. Henry Ware of Harvard,[1] to whom Woods replied in 1821, only to have Ware fire a second shot, which Woods answered in 1822; but little was added to the arguments already advanced.

Woods's discussion with Taylor grew out of a controversy, now almost forgotten, but which profoundly convulsed Connecticut in the third and fourth decades of the nineteenth century, and even affected to some degree the Presbyterian Church. Nathaniel W. Taylor had passed from the pastorate of the First Church

[1] *Letters addressed to Trinitarians and Calvinists.* Cambridge, 1820.

in New Haven to the Professorship of Theology in Yale Divinity School, when that department of what is now Yale University was opened in 1822. A favorite pupil of President Timothy Dwight, he carried further than any had thus far done the moderate and conciliatory type of Edwardeanism which Dwight had represented, till he seemed to all Hopkinsians and to many Edwardeans to be radically astray from Edwardean principles. Man's acts, Taylor asserted, are not necessitated by an unqualified law of cause and effect. God knows, indeed, what man's choices will be, for He perceives and determines or permits the antecedent conditions of soul and of man's situation from which those choices flow. Yet man has the power of contrary choice at all times. Man is free; but this " certainty with power to the contrary," allows God to be sovereign and man dependent. Man has natural ability to choose aright, and this ability can be aroused to action by an appeal to self-love—a self-love, indeed, wholly consistent with that benevolence which has the best good of the universe as its aim. Yet while man has entire natural power to change his character so as to love God supremely, it is certain that he will not so change his ruling purposes unless the Divine Spirit so moves upon his feelings as to induce his will to act, yet to act without coercion. Moreover, contrary to the opinion of the older Edwardeans and of all Hopkinsians, sin is not necessarily the means of the greatest good to the universe as a whole. Possibly God could not have excluded sin from a system permitting free action by His creatures. Yet, though God may not be able to prevent sin in such a system of freedom, man can, by resisting temptation; and such resistance would be preferable to any yielding to sin, not only for the interests of the individual but for those of the universe as a whole.

To the older type of Edwardeans this seemed subversive enough. That self-love, which Edwards and Hopkins had declared the essence of sin, could be a motive to holiness, the more conservative disciples of Edwards could not believe. Doubtless they did not use the word in the sense in which Taylor did; but to use it at all was enough to cause alarm. To affirm that God possibly could not have prevented sin in any system was, to many, to deny His sovereignty. The conflict waxed so bitter that, in 1834, the opponents of Taylorism in Connecticut founded a new theological seminary, under the charge of Rev. Dr. Bennet Tyler, at East Windsor, Conn., which is now located at Hartford and is known by the name of its present domicile.

It was in the earlier stages of this controversy, in 1830, that Woods wrote his *Letters to Taylor*. Courteous and cautious in tone, yet positive and severe in his criticisms, Woods directed his attention to Taylor's treatment of the divine relationship to sin, charging him with holding "that sin is *not* the necessary means of the greatest good," and " that, in a moral system, God could *not* have prevented all sin, nor the present degree of it."[1] Over against this denial Woods strove to vindicate the common Edwardean position that " God did not prevent all sin nor the present degree of it, because it seemed good in his sight not to prevent it." To Woods, it seemed that in asserting the possibility that God could not have excluded the invasion of sin among free moral agents, while man could have prevented sin by not sinning, Taylor had attributed to creatures a power which he had denied to the Creator. And, after a fashion characteristic of theological controversy in all ages, Woods proceeded to draw inferences from Taylor's supposed principles, finding in them a denial that God can accomplish the good that He desires, or be completely happy, or has adopted that system in the government of the universe which He knows to be best, or that God's control over the world is more than a limited rule; and deducing from them the conclusion that, on Taylor's premises, a Christian cannot be justly happy or truly humble, or confident that God is able to grant the requests he offers in prayer, however much God may wish to do so. It is almost needless

[1] *Letters to Rev. Nathaniel W. Taylor*, pp. 22, 54, 94-97. A good contemporary account of this discussion may be found in Crocker, *The Catastrophe of the Presbyterian Church in 1837*, pp. 157-173. New Haven, 1838.

to say that Taylor replied with a denial that Woods had correctly stated his principles, and a rejection of Woods's inferences from, and supposed logical consequences of, those principles.[1]

Of Woods's discussion with Mahan it will not be necessary to speak at length. Among the evidences of the abounding spiritual life of this period none was more individual than the foundation, in 1833, of Oberlin College — an institution designed to foster a warmly spiritual type of piety, to give education to men and women at a most moderate cost, and to be the center of a consecrated, self-denying, reform-seeking religious community. In large measure the aims of the founders of Oberlin have been realized; but the founders and early leaders of the college were men of individuality which bordered in some things on eccentricity, and led to a good many social and doctrinal innovations. The presidency of Oberlin was held from 1835 to 1850 by one of Woods's pupils, a graduate of Andover Seminary, Asa Mahan; while the professorship of theology in Oberlin Seminary was occupied during the same period and long after by Charles G. Finney. Standing in general on the basis of the later Edwardeanism, Mahan drew from the obligation of all men to obey the law of God and from the promises of the Gospel the conclusions that " we

[1] *Christian Spectator* for September, 1830; Crocker, *Catastrophe*, pp. 165-171.

may now, during the progress of the present life, attain to entire perfection in holiness," and that "the sacred writers assert the fact that some of the ancient saints did, in this life, attain to a state of entire sanctification."[1] These views Mahan first advanced in his *Scripture Doctrine of Christian Perfection*,[2] and they were substantially adopted by his colleagues at Oberlin. They were looked upon by Presbyterians and Congregationalists in general with great suspicion, and in consequence of them Oberlin long lay under accusation of doubtful orthodoxy.

To these views of Mahan, Woods replied with a wealth of argument in 1841,[3] maintaining that " we ought to pray God to sanctify us wholly, and to do it with the expectation that he will, at no distant period, bestow the very blessing we ask. But as to expecting the blessing to be fully granted in the *present life*, we differ from the advocates of perfection." Moreover, Woods affirmed that, instead of attaining holiness in this life, the truth was that even " the most advanced saints have always been *conscious* of the imperfection of their holiness."

In September, 1846, five years after the publication of the argument just noted, Woods resigned the pro-

[1] Mahan, in *American Biblical Repository*, pp. 409, 419, for October, 1840.

[2] Boston, 1839.

[3] *American Biblical Repository* for January and April, 1841, pp. 166-189, 406-438. The quotations are from pp. 409, 427.

fessorship he had held for thirty-eight years and which was growing to be too heavy a burden for a man of seventy-two. For almost eight years more, till August 24, 1854, he lived at Andover, till death came to him at the age of eighty. The surrender of work which one has long performed faithfully and well to younger hands and altered methods is perhaps the hardest trial that comes to old age. Woods felt its burden. But his sunset years were a season of considerable physical strength and mental fruitage. The hand of time rested kindly on him. He gathered and arranged his lectures, with such essays and sermons as he wished to preserve, and published them in five substantial volumes during 1849 and 1850. At the close of his life he had nearly finished a *History of Andover Seminary*, narrating at length the story of its foundation in which he had had so large a share — a *History* that, by a curious fate, was not published till 1885.

Under the impressive influence of the death of this venerable and useful teacher of Christian truth, the preacher of the *Discourse* at Woods's funeral declared of his published lectures: "They will constitute a monument more enduring than Parian or Pentelic marble."[1] Unhappily, it is given to few theological instructors to write much that after generations care to read. New presentations of old truths, new discussions of altered problems, cast a veil over the old. To build

[1] Lawrence, Funeral *Discourse*, p. 20.

one's life and thought into the progress of one's own generation in some greater or smaller measure is the highest service granted to most teachers or ministers. Excellent, in many respects, as Woods's lectures are, they are not his chief claim to remembrance. His monument is to be found, rather, in a union of the Evangelical forces of New England so complete that they have wellnigh forgotten that they were ever in danger of schism by debates between Hopkinsians and Old Calvinists, in the junction of these forces at a critical moment in New England history, in the establishment of an advanced system of theological education, and in the moderate and judicious, yet earnest, spiritual and positive type of Edwardean Calvinism that he made part of the mental equipment of a large proportion of the early graduates of Andover Seminary.

LEONARD BACON

X.

LEONARD BACON

OF the eminent Congregationalists whose lives and work we have thus far considered, only one can have been personally known to any who have followed this course of lectures. Professor Woods is remembered by a few of those who have kindly listened to these biographies; but the subject of to-day's address is doubtless clearly pictured in the recollection of many of the older of those who are here assembled as I speak the name Leonard Bacon. It was the lecturer's good fortune to sit, in young boyhood, Sunday after Sunday, in the pew directly in front of the pulpit in which Dr. Bacon, then virtually *pastor emeritus*, habitually took his place beside his younger colleague. And no figure was more distinctly impressed on the speaker's boyhood memory than that of the slight, erect, active, nervous frame, wearing the coat which fashion has since relegated to evening dress, but which was then the ordinary pulpit garb; the forceful figure crowned with a noble head, beautiful in the whiteness of its abundant hair and beard, and in the quick, incisive expression, to which the piercing blue-gray eyes that age had hardly dimmed and the firm yet mobile mouth gave perpetual play and change. The boy who then sat before him well remembers, too, the sweetness of his voice as he would often rise to pray when the sermon by his colleague and successor in the active work of the parish had concluded; and even childish years could appreciate something of the tenderness, felicity, and strength of the words in which he would lift the petitions of the congregation along the pathway of the thoughts to which it had listened in the discourse just concluded. To the boy below, the figure in the pulpit seemed the type of what an aged minister ought to be in look, in word, in dignity; and even the boy knew in some childish way that it was a great man that sat before him, and felt the power of that greatness, though it was beyond his abilities then to define wherein that greatness lay.

It was in a cabin in the then frontier fur-trading town of Detroit that Leonard Bacon was born on February 19, 1802. His father, David Bacon,[1] by birth of Woodstock, Conn., had married Alice Parks of Lebanon, in December, 1800, and on December 31st of that year had been ordained at Hartford by the Trustees of the Missionary Society of Connecticut " as an Evangelist among the Indian tribes of North

[1] The story of the pathetic life-struggle of David Bacon was most sympathetically told by Leonard Bacon himself in the successive numbers of the *Congregational Quarterly* for 1876; the facts of this and the following paragraphs are principally gleaned from that source.

America."[1] The ordination of the young missionary —the husband being twenty-nine and the wife seventeen—had been followed by the weary journey by sleigh and on horseback or afoot to Detroit,—a journey requiring from February 11th to May 9th of the year 1801 for its accomplishment.

At Detroit, when his eldest child, Leonard, was born, the baffled but courageous missionary was planning to transfer his labors to the banks of the Maumee, near the present city of Toledo, as affording a better opportunity for reaching the Indians; and the same hope led the missionary parents to go to Mackinaw when Leonard was four months old. But the work, though self-denying and difficult to a degree without example at present in home missionary labor in the United States, had little promise of success. The Indians proved practically inaccessible; and, in the autumn of 1804, the missionary family reached the village of Cleveland, O., destitute and burdened with the debts which the unexpected expenses of frontier life, in spite of rigid economy, had forced upon them. The missionary left his anxious young wife and little family at Hudson, O., while he made an arduous winter journey to Hartford and back to explain matters to the Trustees of the Missionary Society of Connecticut, who had intimated their desire to see him in terms

[1] *American Mercury*, quoted *ibid.*, p. 19. See *Connecticut Courant* of January 5, 1801.

which he deemed far more savoring of censure than they intended. On his return, he settled in the raw village of Hudson as part missionary and part pastor.

But the thought of establishing a Christian town that might leaven the Western Reserve with the best elements of New England life took strong hold on his enthusiastic spirit; and, from 1805 to 1812, David Bacon was engaged in an attempt to create in the township soon to be known as Tallmadge,[1] a community resembling in some features of its religious basis that later organized at Oberlin. To Tallmadge he removed his family in July, 1807, and took possession of "the new log house" that then constituted the only sign of civilized life in the forest by which the township was covered. At Tallmadge David Bacon aided in the organization of a church in January, 1810; and there, amid the sights and experiences of a frontier settlement, Leonard Bacon grew from his sixth to his eleventh year. At a school exhibition in the neighboring town of Hudson the little Leonard and his schoolmate, John Brown, later to write his name indelibly on American annals at Harper's Ferry, took the parts of William Penn and Hernando Cortés in a dialogue as to the proper treatment of the Indians, drawn from the *Columbian Orator*.[2]

[1] Some facts regarding this enterprise may be found in L. W. Bacon, *A Discourse delivered in the Memorial Presb. Church, Detroit . . . Dec. 24, 1882*, pp. 3, 4, 14, 15; see also the *Congregationalist*, Feb. 2, 1899.

[2] L. W. Bacon, *ibid.*, etc., p. 14.

But, though advantageous for the larger interests of northern Ohio, the Tallmadge enterprise brought only anxiety and grievous financial burden to its projector; and at last, in May, June, and July, 1812, the disappointed pioneer and his household journeyed back to Connecticut. David Bacon's remaining years were few. Hardship and disappointment had laid their hands upon his physical frame, though they could not dampen his Christian faith and courage, and he died on August 29, 1817, at Hartford, not quite forty-six years of age, leaving seven children, of whom Leonard, the eldest, was fifteen.

The boy thus early left fatherless had found a helper, on his coming to Hartford, in 1812, in his father's older brother, Leonard Bacon, whose name he bore, and who was a leading physician of the little city. Through his aid the younger Leonard had received the training of what was then known as "the Hartford Grammar School," the excellent institution for preparatory education that traces its history from 1638 to the Hartford Public High School of the present. Thus equipped, the boy entered the Sophomore class of Yale College, in the autumn of 1817, within a month of his father's death.

The purpose already formed within him was to devote his life to the ministry,[1] and his Christian character as manifested in college was decided. But

[1] See the Commemorative Volume issued by his congregation, entitled *Leonard Bacon, Pastor of the First Church in New Haven*, p. 254, 1882.

though he engaged actively in the discussions of the literary societies, read English literature extensively, and maintained a good scholastic standing, the boy of eighteen who was graduated in 1820, had not yet awakened to the full possibilities and responsibilities of his intellectual life, so that he impressed his friends as not sufficiently strenuous a student for his own best development, and as " in danger of hurting himself by superficial habits of reading."[1] Two of these friends had the kindness to tell him their judgment, and their words had effect. The theological course which he began at Andover in the autumn subsequent to his graduation was marked by a thorough application that had its reward in his appointment to deliver the principal address at the Seminary commencement of 1823.[2] Graduation at Andover was followed by a fourth year at that Seminary as a resident licentiate and to some extent as an assistant to Professor Ebenezer Porter in the department of Sacred Rhetoric.[3] But the missionary spirit of Bacon's father attracted him to the Western frontier, and with the thought of this labor in view he was ordained as an evangelist by the Hartford North Consociation, assembled at Windsor, Conn., on September 28, 1824.[4]

[1] President Woolsey, in the Commemorative Volume, pp. 226, 227.
[2] *Ibid.*, pp. 227, 228.
[3] *Leonard Bacon, Two Sermons Preached on the Fortieth Anniversary of his Settlement*, published in the Commemorative Volume above cited, p. 77. [4] *Ibid.*, p. 77.

Yet the next day brought the young man who had just been set apart to the ministerial office a letter that altered his entire later life. The ecclesiastical society representing the business interests of the venerable First Church in New Haven, moved thereto by the suggestion of a former pastor, then the honored Professor Moses Stuart of Andover, asked Bacon to preach for them; and on October 3rd, 1824, he delivered his first sermon in the pulpit that was to be his own for the next fifty-seven years.[1] Thirteen more discourses so largely united the congregation in his favor, that on December 15th, the society, by a vote of sixty-eight to twenty, invited him to become its minister and requested the church to join in the call. Four days later the church expressed its approval by formal vote,[2] passed with "uncommon unanimity."[3] The salary offered was a thousand dollars. On January 17, 1825, Bacon wrote from Andover, accepting the invitation.

On March 8th following, a council of representatives of six churches convened at New Haven, after "a day of fasting and prayer" had been kept by the New Haven congregation.[4] The candidate was examined at length; to quote his own description, forty years later, " Many questions were asked, of which I could

---

[1] Commemorative Volume, pp. 77, 78.
[2] Documents in the Commemorative Volume, just cited, pp. 13-19.
[3] Leonard Bacon, *Letter of Acceptance, ibid.*, p. 18.
[4] Commemorative Volume, pp. 20, 21, 79.

not then see the bearing, and which I answered without suspecting their relation to theological parties and controversies soon to break forth;"[1] but all resulted in his approval. The next day, March 9th, he was installed over the church of his lifelong ministry, Rev. Joel Hawes of the First Church in Hartford preaching the sermon. The new pastor was twenty-three years of age.

Yet some things besides youth made the beginning of the pastorate a time of great trial and difficulty for the young minister. The pulpit was one of the two popularly ranked as the most conspicuous in Connecticut, and much was to be expected of its occupant. Bacon's immediate predecessors had been among the princes of the New England pulpit. From March, 1806, to his dismissal to the professorship at Andover which was to be the scene of his most conspicuous service to the churches, the New Haven pastorate had been fulfilled by Moses Stuart, and the time had been one of constant spiritual quickening. From April, 1812, till December, 1822, Nathaniel W. Taylor, who left the First Church for the chair of Theology in Yale Divinity School, had set forth in sermons of attractive eloquence and searching power the doctrines which were to lead to such heated controversy when expounded in his classroom. The young pastor was conscious of the difficulty of standing in the place of

[1] Commemorative Volume, pp. 79, 80.

men of such talents and repute. Addressing his congregation forty years later, he said with characteristic truthfulness, "I think I understand myself; and I know it is not an affectation of modesty to say that I never had any such power in the pulpit as they had in their best days."[1]

The end of the first year left the new pastor "with the desponding expectation that [his] ministry would be a failure."[2] But courage, patience, and strength were characteristic of the young man; and when he was visited by several prominent members of the society, headed by James Hillhouse, treasurer of Yale, Senator of the United States, and New Haven's leading citizen, with a suggestion that his sermons were not what the congregation had heard from Stuart and Taylor, the young pastor simply answered: "Gentlemen, they shall be made worthy;" and in due time they were. Always grave, dignified, and thoughtful in the pulpit, he was soon heard with entire acceptance; and if not usually manifesting great oratorical powers in what may be called the more ordinary ministrations of the house of God, when the question was one of spiritual interest, moral significance, or public concern, he speedily showed the possession of an eloquence, force, and cogency of argument that marked him as a born leader of men. By the

[1] Commemorative Volume, p. 82; compare also President Woolsey, *ibid.*, p. 228. [2] *Ibid.*, p. 83.

close of the third year of his pastorate Bacon was able to see the visible fruit of his preaching in a revival movement that added forty-eight members to the church, and from then onward, if not before, his position was fully secure, not only in the affection of his congregation, but in his own confidence of the divine blessing on his work.[1]

As a pastor, Leonard Bacon grew deeper into the love of his people year by year. Proud of his church, the history of which he did so much to expound, recognized as a leader in the community, then in the State, and ultimately in national affairs, the church grew proud of him; and he endeared himself to its members by his ready and genuine sympathies with their joys and sorrows, and his own deepening and expanding spiritual life. His pastorate was one which witnessed a strengthening bond between pastor and people to the end.

Dr. Bacon's personal experiences of joy and sorrow were such as to fit him to sympathize with and minister to the happiness and burdens of the common lot. Four months after his ordination, in July, 1825, he married Miss Lucy Johnson, of Johnstown, N. Y. Nineteen years later, in November, 1844, she was taken from him by death. In June, 1847, he married Miss Catherine Elizabeth Terry, of Hartford, Conn., who survived her husband for a few months. Of his

[1] Commemorative Volume, pp. 83, 84.

fourteen children, five were called from the father's household before his own summons came. But he had the satisfaction of seeing four sons enter the Congregational ministry, and a daughter devote herself to the elevation of the race whose release from slavery he had so vigorously advocated. In household joys and sorrows alike he felt that the providence of God was teaching his soul, and fitting him the better for the Master's service.[1]

Dr. Bacon's long pastorate was broken by only one considerable absence. In July, 1850, when the pastor had been a quarter of a century in service, the society granted such a vacation as he might desire to enable him to visit Europe and the Mediterranean Orient. The journey is chiefly important for our story as affording Dr. Bacon, when taken captive by Kurds between Mosul and Ooroomiah, and in imminent danger of death, an opportunity to display a physical courage akin to the moral fearlessness always characteristic of him.[2]

Useful and successful as Dr. Bacon was as a minister in his own congregation, his largest service was beyond the bounds of his parish. For this wider ministry he had some remarkable natural talents. His disposition was sanguine, with a genuine belief in the triumph of

[1] See his biographic *Half-Century Sermon*, in *ibid.*, pp. 119-135, especially pp. 132, 133.

[2] An interesting account of this experience, from his own pen, is given, *ibid.*, pp. 29-38.

righteousness. His sympathies with efforts for reform were broad; and he was ready to take a part in any contest which had as its aim the advancement of a moral principle. He did not shun controversy. In a measure, he joyed in the battle with the confidence of one who trusts alike in the justice of his cause and the adequacy of his powers. But his polemics were under the control of a sound judgment as to when and what to strike. From the beginning of his pastorate Dr. Bacon was recognized as a debater of power in the local ecclesiastical gatherings of Connecticut; for the last thirty years of his life he was regarded as without an equal among contemporary American Congregationalists in skill and effectiveness of argument; and so ready and well furnished was his mind that it often seemed to his associates that he spoke most effectively when drawn unexpectedly into discussion.

To this parliamentary skilfulness Dr. Bacon added a literary style of remarkable felicity. His writings were not merely transparent: they sparkled with wit, glowed with feeling, and expressed his thought with a precision, appropriateness, and freshness that showed him a master in the use of language, and made it a pleasure to read that which he wrote. He could be largely oblivious to external distractions in writing, and his thoughts were transferred to the written page with a quickness and an apparent ease [1] that was a constant source of

[1] See the remarks of Rev. Dr. R. S. Storrs, *ibid.*, pp. 197, 198.

surprise to his associates. An evident appreciation of these gifts is to be seen in his election, in 1839, to a professorship of Rhetoric and Oratory in Yale College, an election which he declined.

One minor evidence of Dr. Bacon's versatility of mind, not, indeed, as marked as the qualities just mentioned, was his poetic strain. He was not conspicuously a poet,—he does not even rank among our foremost hymn writers,—yet no hymn promises to be more permanently acceptable to the sons and daughters of New England than his noble psalm of 1833:—

> " O God, beneath Thy guiding hand,
> Our exiled fathers crossed the sea."

The mention of this stirring hymn of thanksgiving for Pilgrim and Puritan achievements reminds us that one of the greatest of Dr. Bacon's services to Congregationalism was his illumination of its history. In that story he took an intense and personal delight. As far as any beginning may be assigned to the studies which bore fruit till the close of his life, they had their origin in his reading during those trying years of his early ministry,[1]—reading which, among other results, led him to put forth, as a stimulus to the spiritual life " of private Christians, and of Christian families,"

[1] Dr. Bacon, in a debate in the Boston Council of 1865, assigned weight in the development of his interest in Congregationalism to an article published by Rev. Joshua Leavitt, in 1830, in the *Quarterly Christian Spectator* ; see *Debates and Proceedings of the National Council . . . held at Boston, June 14-24, 1865,* pp. 445, 446.

his first important publication, the *Select Practical Writings of Richard Baxter*, in 1831.[1] To this selection he prefixed an elaborate biographical sketch of Baxter, the preparation of which gave him a thorough initiation into the story of the Puritan movement.

The same pastoral zeal which led Dr. Bacon to the publication of Baxter's edificatory writings, prompted him to preach a series of " Sunday evening lectures " which were gathered up in a useful little volume in 1833, under the title, *A Manual for Young Church Members*.[2] In this treatise the author's interest in and love for Congregationalism are clearly outspoken. " I cannot but think," he remarks, " that if the Congregational organization should be extensively adopted by evangelical Christians everywhere, the result would be not only a vast extension of the principles and of the life of rational liberty, but a great development of the spirit of christian purity and fidelity, and of the energy of christian zeal."[3]

Such enthusiasm was needed, for Congregationalists were then generally in the depths of their denominational self-distrust. The Unitarian defection seemed to many to be due to a lack of " a strong government," such as Presbyterianism then prided itself on possessing. The ascription of Unitarianism to this cause was indeed an error; but our pulpits and our

[1] Published at New Haven in two volumes of six hundred pages each.
[2] Published at New Haven.   [3] *Manual*, pp. 7, 8.

theological chairs with rare exceptions made little of the distinctive principles of Congregationalism; the majority of our ministers regarded polity, at least between Congregationalists and Presbyterians, as a question of geography to be determined by one's position to the eastward or to the westward of the Hudson River. And, in Connecticut, Consociationism had so modified the feelings as well as the usages of our churches that at the time when Dr. Bacon published his *Manual* their popular designation was " Presbyterian." To no man was the reëntrance of our churches upon their heritage more due than to Dr. Bacon.

The historic bent of Dr. Bacon's mind was revealed by these early studies, so that when the years 1838 and 1839 brought the two hundredth anniversaries of the planting of New Haven colony and of the foundation of the church of which Dr. Bacon was pastor, it was to be expected that the events should receive some historic treatment from his pen. But the volume of *Thirteen Historical Discourses*[1] in which he commemorated these occurrences was a work of more than a passing significance. It was the first attempt for more than a generation to tell the religious story of Connecticut; and the story is so admirably combined and correlated with the local history of his own church that ever since its publication it has served as a pattern for our better church histories. Its clearness of historic insight,

[1] Published at New Haven, 1839.

breadth of treatment, and charm of presentation won immediate repute for its author as a historian. He had already, in 1838, been made a corresponding member of the Massachusetts Historical Society. He now, in the year of the publication of his *Thirteen Historical Discourses*, was elected to the Historical Societies of Connecticut, New York, and Georgia. And doubtless this volume had much to do with the bestowal upon the still rather youthful pastor of the degree of Doctor of Divinity by Hamilton College in 1842.

This repute as an interesting interpreter of history led to frequent calls on Dr. Bacon for commemorative occasions. Thus, on Thanksgiving Day, 1840, he spoke in his own pulpit on *The Goodly Heritage of Connecticut*,[1] and, in May, 1843, at Hartford, before the Connecticut Historical Society, on the *Early Constitutional History of Connecticut*.[2] As the best equipped of the graduates of Andover, it fell to him to deliver the *Commemorative Discourse*[3] at the celebration in August, 1858, of the fiftieth anniversary of the founding of the Seminary; and a similar sense of preëminent fitness induced the Connecticut General Association to call upon Dr. Bacon for a *Historical Discourse*,[4] in June, 1859, on the completion of a cent-

---

[1] Published at New Haven, 1840.   [2] Published at Hartford, 1843.

[3] *A Memorial of the Semi-Centennial Celebration of the Founding of the Theological Seminary at Andover*, pp. 70–113. Andover, 1859.

[4] *Contributions to the Ecclesiastical History of Connecticut*, pp. 1–72. New Haven, 1861.

ury and a half of its existence. So, once more, when the Connecticut General Conference celebrated the centennial of American national life, in 1876, Dr. Bacon gave the address on *The Relations of the Congregational Churches of Connecticut to Civil Government, and to Popular Education and Social Reforms*, during the period antecedent to the Declaration of Independence.[1]

Naturally Dr. Bacon was interested in local history. A charter member of the New Haven Historical Society and a director from its organization in 1862, he presented before it, in 1863, the results of his studies regarding the development of *Civil Government in New Haven Colony*.[2] On repeated occasions in his own pulpit, as on the fortieth anniversary of his settlement, in March, 1865,[3] and on the completion of his fiftieth year of connection with the church of his ministry,[4] he gave sermons of rare felicity of expression and of much historic and autobiographic interest. The centennial of American independence drew from Dr. Bacon an address on *New Haven One Hundred Years Ago;*[5] and in 1879 he published *Three Civic*

[1] *Centennial Papers Published by Order of the General Conference of the Congregational Churches of Connecticut*, pp. 145-170. Hartford, 1877.

[2] *Papers of the New Haven Historical Society*, i., pp. 11-27.

[3] In *Four Commemorative Discourses*, New Haven, 1866; see also the Commemorative Volume, entitled *Leonard Bacon*, etc., pp. 75-104.

[4] *Half-Century Sermon*, New Haven, 1875; also in the Commemorative Volume, pp. 119-135.   [5] Published at New Haven, 1876.

Orations for New Haven, in which he further served the city of his pastorate.

The most important as well as the most extensive of Dr. Bacon's later contributions to history was, however, his volume of 1874, entitled *The Genesis of the New England Churches*,[1] in which he narrated with filial and graphic pen the story of Congregationalism from its beginnings to its full establishment on New England soil by the addition to the Separatist colony of Plymouth of the Puritan settlement of Salem — the forerunner of the Puritan emigration which made New England strong. Perhaps this proportioning of the story indicates, what was the fact, that Dr. Bacon's sympathies were more with the independent aspects of Congregationalism than with its centralizing tendencies.

Dr. Bacon's interest in the history of New England was manifested to the close of his life; two of his latest publications being an address on *The Providential Selection and Training of the Pilgrim Pioneers of New England*,[2] in 1880; and a paper on *Old Times in Connecticut*,[3] printed in 1882, after his death.

Such interest in the history of Congregationalism was naturally accompanied by an acquaintance with the details of its polity and a desire to extend its influence. Dr. Bacon's first essay in the practical application of Congregational principles — the *Manual for Young*

[1] Published at New York.   [2] Hartford, 1880.
[3] New Haven, 1882, reprinted from the *New Englander*, xli., pp. 1-31.

Church Members, of 1833 — has already been mentioned. His next exposition of Congregational usages was a careful *Digest of the Rules and Usages in the Consociations and Associations of Connecticut* [1] — a compilation and condensation as clear, as technical, as accurate, as valuable for reference, and as uninteresting for general reading as a code of criminal law. This task was performed as a member of a committee appointed by the General Association of Connecticut of which Dr. Bacon was chairman.

Dr. Bacon's most ambitious draft of a system of church polity was made more than twenty years later than his *Digest*. The Conference of Committees which prepared the way for the National Council of our Congregational churches that assembled at Boston in June, 1865, appointed Dr. Bacon, Rev. Dr. A. H. Quint, and Rev. Dr. Henry M. Storrs a committee to prepare a statement of polity for submission to the Council. Such a statement Dr. Bacon drafted, on the model of the Cambridge Platform, and it was duly laid before the Council, which referred it, after a spirited debate in which Dr. Bacon bore large part, to a numerous committee.[2] By this committee it was somewhat amended, and at length, in 1872, was reported to the churches.[3]

[1] *Congregational Order*, pp. 289-322. Middletown, 1843.
[2] *Debates and Proceedings of the National Council of the Congregational Churches, held at Boston, Mass., June 14-24, 1865*, pp. 9, 10, 101-115, 117-129, 427-464. Boston, 1866.
[3] *Ecclesiastical Polity. The Government and Communion Practised*

This document, generally known as the " Boston Platform," was the fruit of great labor, and deserved a better fate than the oblivion which immediately overtook it; but extended platforms of polity are doubtless as little acceptable to the Congregational churches of the present as the minute statements of faith in which the seventeenth century delighted.

Such a man as Dr. Bacon, of active temperament and ready willingness to bear his part in public efforts for the advancement of the kingdom of Christ, was naturally largely interested in organized Christian work. Thus, from 1825 to 1829, he was the Secretary of the Domestic Missionary Society of Connecticut, and one of its directors from 1832 to 1869. In 1837 he became a director of the American Bible Society, and, in 1845, of the American Tract Society. From 1842 till his death, he was a corporate member of the American Board; from 1841 till 1862, he served as a director of what is now the Congregational Home Missionary Society, a position which he exchanged in the latter year for the vice-presidency of the corporation; and from 1844 to the close of his life he had an official part in promoting Christian education in the newer sections of the country, at first as a director of the Society for Promoting Collegiate and Theological Education at the West, and then of the

by the Congregational Churches in the United States of America. Boston, 1872.

American College and Education Society into which the longer-named organization was merged in 1874.

His connection with the two associations last mentioned may well remind us that Dr. Bacon never forgot that he was the son of a western missionary; and that recollection, coupled with his sturdy belief in Congregationalism as a polity suited to all parts of our land, fitted him to do a great work for Congregational advancement in connection with the Albany Convention of 1852, and the movements that flowed from that significant assembly. It has already been pointed out in this lecture that, at the time of Dr. Bacon's settlement in New Haven, Congregationalism had about reached its lowest depth of self-distrust, and that a large proportion of Congregationalists emigrating beyond the Hudson joined or organized Presbyterian churches. This transformation was made all the easier by the " Plan of Union," formed, in 1801, by the Presbyterian General Assembly and the Connecticut General Association, and designed to adjust in a perfectly equitable manner the question of the harmonious working together of Presbyterian and Congregational ministers and church members in frontier communities. In practice, the " Plan " aided Presbyterianism and proved one of several causes which gathered the Congregational settlers of New York, Ohio, Michigan, and Illinois largely into the Presbyterian fold. Yet some Congregational churches were organized in what was then known as the West; but they were looked at askance by their Presbyterian neighbors, and to some extent by the people of New England, as under a cloud of doctrinal or governmental suspicion,—an erroneous view, which the local eccentricities displayed by early Oberlin tended to foster rather than to dispel.

It was to secure a better understanding in both East and West and to plan effectively for Congregational advancement that agitation was begun in Michigan by Rev. L. Smith Hobart as early as 1845, and furthered by the General Association of New York, led by Rev. Dr. Joseph P. Thompson. This discussion resulted in the meeting at Albany, in October, 1852, of a Convention representative of any Congregational church that chose to send its pastor and a delegate, and including a large proportion of those in our body[1] conspicuous for leadership.

By the unanimous vote of this Convention the "Plan of Union" was abrogated; a greater intercourse between the Congregationalists of the East and West was urged; "insinuations and charges of heresy in doctrine and disorder in practice" were discountenanced ; an unanimous declaration was adopted that the missionary societies should support

[1] It included four hundred and sixty-three pastors and delegates from seventeen States. For its work, see *Proceedings of the General Convention of Congregational Ministers and Delegates in the United States*, New York, 1852.

only such ministers in slave States as would "so preach the Gospel . . . that, with the blessing of God, it shall have its full effect in awakening and enlightening the moral sense in regard to slavery, and in bringing to pass the speedy abolition of that stupendous wrong."[1] A call was issued for $50,000—that proved to be nearly $62,000 when the response came—to assist struggling churches to procure meeting-houses in Ohio, Michigan, Wisconsin, Iowa, Indiana, Illinois, Missouri, and Minnesota. In all this significant work Dr. Bacon was the foremost figure, not only as chairman of the Business Committee, to which, in the first instance, action on these matters was due, but as the ablest and most convincing of all the keen-minded debaters who led the Convention's deliberations. And in the more permanent organization that sprang from the Convention and crystallized its work Dr. Bacon was eminent in service. When the American Congregational Union — now much more appropriately known as the Church Building Society—was formed in May, 1853, " to collect, preserve, and publish authentic information concerning the history, condition, and continual progress of the Congregational churches " and " to promote—by tracts and books, by devising and recommending to the public plans of coöperation in building meeting-houses and parsonages— . . . the progress and

[1] *Ibid.*, p. 21.

well-working of the Congregational polity," Dr. Bacon was chosen the first president of the new society, and continued to hold this office until 1871.

Of his prominence in the next National Council of Congregationalism—that held at Boston in 1865—there has already been occasion to speak in describing the Platform of Church Polity which he then presented. The first of our modern series of triennial Councils, at Oberlin, in 1871, had Dr. Bacon for its preacher. The second he welcomed to his church edifice in New Haven, in 1874; and he was heard gladly and influentially in both. Yet it is but just to remark that Dr. Bacon was so much of an Independent in his type of Congregationalism that he did not approve the creation of a representative National Council, meeting at stated intervals, lest it interfere at length with the freedom of the churches,[1] and he therefore looked with some degree of disfavor on an effort to unite the wisdom and suggest the policy of our widely scattered churches, which to most has seemed to contain nothing but good.

The first thirty years of Dr. Bacon's pastorate were a time of heated controversies in the Congregational and Presbyterian communions, and the New Haven pastor had his full share in them. Yet his participation was, in general, other in intention and effect from that which the nickname, " the fighting parson," often

[1] Pres. Woolsey, in Commemorative Volume, p. 232.

applied to him in those days, would lead one to suppose.[1] His influence was, as a whole, irenic and conciliatory, because his sympathies within the lines of evangelical truth, though largely " new school," were also broadly catholic. Dr. Bacon's efforts were rather to prevent than to foster ecclesiastical division, and in his own State certainly they had a marked effect.

Dr. Bacon's earliest participation in an ecclesiastical discussion of the first magnitude, as such controversies then appeared, came almost by chance. So intimate were the relations of Congregationalists and Presbyterians at the beginning of the nineteenth century, that, from 1794 onward to the rupture of the Presbyterian body in 1837, the Connecticut General Association and the Presbyterian General Assembly each sent delegates who enjoyed full powers of voting in the sessions of the other body—an exchange which was afterwards shared by the General Associations of Massachusetts and New Hampshire, the General Convention of Vermont, and the Evangelical Consociation of Rhode Island.

Yet within the Presbyterian Church itself two parties were rapidly drawing into antagonism as the first four decades of the nineteenth century advanced. Of these parties, that soon known as the " Old School " represented in large measure the Scotch-Irish and less inclusive element in the Church, strict

[1] Compare the remarks of G. L. Walker, *ibid.*, pp. 178, 179.

in its adhesion to the older Calvinism, a party in doctrinal position substantially identical with the Old Calvinists of eighteenth-century New England, but more intense in feeling. The opposite, or "New School" party, was composed largely of men of New England antecedents, who sympathized generally with the Edwardeanism that, by 1830, had become almost universally prevalent in New England. This Edwardean theology had, as we have seen, many shades; but its general points of contrast to the Old Calvinism, both of earlier New England and of existent Presbyterianism were well stated by Dr. Bacon as follows:[1]

"Of these views, one was the doctrine of general atonement, or that Christ's expiatory death was for all men, and not exclusively for an elected portion of mankind. Another was the rejection of the theory of imputation, in the sense of a transfer of personal qualities, or of responsibilities. A third was the opinion, strongly maintained, that there is in man as fallen, no physical impotency to obey God's requirements; that the inability which hinders men from coming to Christ till they are drawn by Almighty grace, is an inability not of the constitutional faculties, but only of the voluntary moral disposition."

The alarm felt by the "Old School" party over the spread in Presbyterian ranks of such common Edwardean views as have just been noted was greatly intensified from 1830 onward by the rise of that modification of Edwardeanism known as "New Haven

[1] *Views and Reviews*, i., pp. 52, 53. New Haven, 1840.

Theology," of which Professor Nathaniel W. Taylor was the champion. And the contest in Presbyterian ranks between those who were willing to tolerate and those who opposed New England presentations of doctrine was brought to a head by the dispute occasioned by the settlement of Albert Barnes over the First Presbyterian Church in Philadelphia.

It so happened that the young New Haven pastor, as a delegate from Connecticut, was a member of the General Assembly of 1831, before which first came the question of the orthodoxy of the sermon in which Albert Barnes had expressed Edwardean views. Dr. Bacon was appointed upon the committee to which the case was referred.[1] Naturally, his sympathies were with the comparatively catholic and largely New-England-born wing which was soon to become the excluded "New School" party, rather than with their "Old School" opponents; but his youth, his self-control, and his position as a representative of another body prevented him from taking any leading part in the discussion.[2]

Contemporary with these disruptive debates in the Presbyterian Church, and to some extent contributing to them, ran the heated Taylor and Tyler controversy in Connecticut, at which we glanced in the last lecture.

[1] *Minutes of the General Assembly of the Presbyterian Church*, vii., pp. 176, 180, 181.
[2] Dr. Bacon gave a full account of this session in the *New Englander*, xxviii., pp. 173–180.

As Dr. Taylor's personal friend and successor in the New Haven pastorate, from which Taylor had gone to the theological chair at Yale, Dr. Bacon warmly sympathized with the " New Haven Theology;" but the feature of this controversy which seems most to have excited his concern was the possible division of the Connecticut churches into two warring denominations as a consequence of the foundation of a new theological seminary — now Hartford Seminary — at East Windsor Hill, by Dr. Tyler and his sympathizers in 1834. This is the ground note of Dr. Bacon's *Seven Letters to the Rev. George A. Calhoun* [of Coventry] *concerning the Pastoral Union of Connecticut*, originally published in the *New Haven Record*, and reprinted as a pamphlet in 1840; and of the sequel to these letters, the *Appeal to the Congregational Ministers of Connecticut against a Division*, of the same year.[1] In these tracts, which constitute Dr. Bacon's chief contribution to the dispute then disturbing Connecticut, the writer defended the orthodoxy of the New Haven divines with ardor, and attacked their opponents with vigor and some personal severity; but the most characteristic passage is that in which he pointed out the substantial agreement of both parties on twenty-six important articles of the Christian faith, and urged that though " there are differences in the present case, differences of no slight moment in respect

[1] Published at New Haven in 1840 as *Views and Reviews*, Nos. 1 and 2.

to the illustration and defense of that evangelical system which both parties agree in holding," "there may," nevertheless, " be differences, of great importance to the science of theology, among brethren who have yet no occasion to exscind or renounce each other."[1]

Fierce as was the controversy aroused in Connecticut by what Dr. Bacon regarded " as a great work " done by the New Haven divines " for the liberation of New England Calvinism from certain traditional encumbrances "[2] — a work which certain other good men in the State estimated in very different fashion — it was largely forgotten, as the century was passing its middle point, in the debates occasioned by the publications of Horace Bushnell. Dr. Bushnell's theology was a departure from the Edwardeanism which had dominated Connecticut for more than half a century and which was represented alike by the theologians of East Windsor Hill and of New Haven. In his first important publication, that on *Christian Nurture*, in 1847, Dr. Bushnell went back from the Edwardean emphasis on a conscious conversion as the ordinary means of entrance into the kingdom of God, to the pre-Edwardean New England view of the covenant consequences of membership in a Christian family, though he presented his thoughts in a very modern way. In his opinion, a child in a Christian household should

[1] *Views and Reviews*, No. 2, pp. 36-43.
[2] *New Englander*, xxxviii., p. 702.

438   LEONARD BACON

" grow up a Christian," and never know himself as being otherwise; and that, for such a child, a great change of experience is not necessary.[1]

This argument, so foreign to the prevailing conceptions of New England at the middle of the nineteenth century, made much commotion; but the stir was greatly increased when, in 1849, Bushnell put forth his volume entitled *God in Christ*. Affirming that the Trinity is a truth of Christian experience, he held, in this work, that the Godhead is " instrumentally three —three simply as related to our finite apprehension, and the communication of God's incommunicable nature."[2] In the same volume, Bushnell advanced a view of the atonement which denied to the great sacrifice any penally satisfactory or governmental significance, and held that in estimating the work of Christ we must regard " everything done by him as done for expression before us, and thus for effect in us."[3]

Dr. Bushnell's views were at once attacked; but the Hartford Central Association, of which he was a member, decided, after full discussion, not to proceed against him, and proved his bulwark in all·the succeeding controversy.[4] Yet in this the Association was quite out of harmony with the feeling of probably a

---

[1] *Christian Nurture*, pp. 6, 7. Boston, 1847.

[2] *God in Christ*, p. 177.

[3] *Ibid.*, p. 237.

[4] See Rev. Dr. E. P. Parker, *The Hartford Central Association and the Bushnell Controversy*. Hartford, 1896.

majority of the ministers of Connecticut; and, by June, 1850, the Fairfield West Association laid the case before the General Association of the State. The struggle that followed in successive meetings of the General Association was strenuous, and threatened to become divisive. A positive decision in favor of either party would have resulted in two denominations. That this greater evil was avoided was due more, possibly, than to any other influence, to the ability and statesmanlike temper of Dr. Bacon, notably at the meeting of the General Association in 1853. Dr. Bacon, though a personal friend of Dr. Bushnell, was far from sympathizing with all his opinions;[1] but he deprecated division, and when a petition signed by fifty-one Connecticut ministers was laid before the General Association, calling upon that body to exclude from its fellowship the Hartford Central Association of which Dr. Bushnell was a member, Dr. Bacon secured the passage of a resolution by the General Association, the point of which, like that of many similar important decisions, was in what it did not say, but which made hopeless the attempts to coerce Dr. Bushnell and his supporters. This resolution affirmed[2]

that "the opinions imputed to Dr. Bushnell by the complainants, and the imputation of which is no doubt warranted, if the constructions are just which they conscientiously

[1] *New Englander*, xxxviii., p. 702.
[2] *Minutes of the General Association of Conn.*, p. 9, 1853.

give to certain quotations from his published books, are opinions with which the ministers in the churches of Connecticut, as represented in this General Association, have no fellowship, and the profession of which on the part of candidates for the ministry, ought to prevent their receiving the license or approbation of any of our Associations."

It did not affirm, however, and it was intended not to affirm, that the opinions complained of were in reality justly chargeable on Dr. Bushnell, and it left the question as to whether or not he really held censurable views a matter of individual opinion.

It will be seen, from the story as thus far narrated, that Dr. Bacon's sympathies were with the more liberal movements of his day in the evangelical churches of New England, but that, in the main, his efforts were irenic. This catholic tendency of his mind increased with years, and was never more marked than in his old age. At the same time, it should be remarked that partly by reason of his opposition to the coercive use of the ecclesiastical system of Connecticut, partly by reason of his own native inclination to a type of Congregationalism which emphasized the independence of our churches, he contributed powerfully to the breakdown of the peculiar consociational organization of the State of his ministry, and its practical assimilation into what may be called the normal present type of American Congregationalism.

Dr. Bacon's interests, or rather his conceptions of his ministerial privileges and duties, were much wider than the bounds of his parish or the ecclesiastical discussions of his State. On the first Thanksgiving after his settlement, it is instructive to note, he made the theme of his discourse the betterment of the public schools, then in sore need of reformation and development.[1] The topic thus chosen by the youthful pastor was illustrative of his wide interest in the practical questions of his time and his readiness to enter into their debate. And in the discussion of such themes Dr. Bacon had the instincts and the ready pen of a born journalist, so that not a little of his most useful work was as an editor.

His editorial labors began early. In 1826, a year after his settlement in New Haven, he became editor of the *Christian Spectator*, a monthly that later became a quarterly, published in the city of his ministry, and sympathetic, in a general way, with the rising " New Haven Theology." But Dr. Bacon's editorial zeal was not strongly enlisted in purely theologic controversy. As his lifelong friend, President Noah Porter, has remarked of his connection with this magazine, " His contributions were chiefly literary, and ethical, and reformatory, rather than theological."[2] The reformer was always stronger within him than the

[1] Leonard Bacon, in Commemorative Volume, p. 90.
[2] *Ibid.*, p. 220.

theologic partisan. Dr. Bacon's service on the *Spectator* continued till 1838.

The year 1843 witnessed the next step in his editorial career in the foundation, chiefly through his initiative and labors, of the *New Englander*, a magazine designed to be, as he declared in the first issue, " on the side of order, of freedom, of simple and spiritual Christianity, and of the Bible as the infallible, sufficient, and only authority in religion,"[1] rather than the organ of any of the theological parties into which New England was divided. Dr. Bacon remained on the editorial committee of the *New Englander* for over a score of years, nor did he cease his contributions to its pages while he lived. A list drawn up nineteen years after the magazine was founded credited sixty-two titles to his authorship, and probably over a hundred articles in all were from his pen. It is instructive to note some of the topics discussed in these witty, discriminating, and earnest papers, as illustrative of the breadth of Dr. Bacon's interests. The first of the long series was in advocacy of the reduction of the rate of postage and the improvement of the postal service, then exorbitant in price and inefficient in delivery.[2] Ministerial education and public libraries were topics on which he had something to say;[3] capital punishment he deemed worthy of discussion;[4] the

[1] *New Englander*, i., p. 8.
[2] *Ibid.*, i., p. 9; iii., p. 536.
[3] *Ibid.*, i., pp. 126, 307. [4] *Ibid.*, iv., p. 563.

conduct of public worship and the development of music as one of its elements were to him congenial themes.[1] Some articles were critiques of Episcopal pretensions,[2] others expositions and defenses of Congregational history,[3] yet others biographic studies;[4] and all along ran a series of trenchant criticisms on the politics of the years which saw the growth of the pretensions of the slave power, from the war with Mexico to the attack on Fort Sumter.

Of Dr. Bacon's third, and on the whole most important, editorial labor, his participation in founding the *Independent*, in 1848, and of his service as one of its editors till 1863, there will be speedy occasion to speak in another connection.

Two of Dr. Bacon's reformatory efforts deserve special attention; and both were labors which cost him the friendship of some of his congregation and of many outside. When he was installed in his New Haven pastorate the temperance reform was just beginning to be felt. But the conservatism characteristic of Connecticut led the New Haven Ecclesiastical Society to provide a generous entertainment for the installing council, which included, to quote Dr. Bacon's

[1] *New Englander*, vii., p. 350 ; xiii., p. 450.
[2] *Ibid.*, i., pp. 545, 586 ; ii., pp. 175, 309, 440 ; iii., p. 284 ; vii., p. 143, etc.
[3] *Ibid.*, i., p. 250 ; iv., p. 288 ; xi., p. 136 ; xviii., pp. 711, 1020 ; xix., p. 437, etc.
[4] *Ibid.*, vi., p. 603 ; viii., p. 388 ; x., pp. 42, 488.

own words used forty years later in describing the event, " an ample supply not only of wine but also of more perilous stuff."[1] The tone of the community was such—and New Haven did not differ materially from the rest of New England in this respect—that, to quote Dr. Bacon again, " none could abstain from the personal use of those liquors without incurring the reproach of eccentricity and perhaps of moroseness."[2] But a reform movement was just beginning; and, though it meant running counter to the prejudices of many of his congregation, the young pastor threw himself into it with characteristic energy. In 1829 he published a pamphlet urging *Total Abstinence from Ardent Spirits*. Again, in 1838, he printed a very plain-spoken sermon on the theme, directed especially against the saloon where liquor is sold by the glass;[3] and later he enforced in repeated sermons the same reform.[4] And he had the satisfaction of being able to record, in the discourses commemorative of the completion of forty years of his pastorate, the change wrought by these and associated efforts:[5]

[1] Commemorative Volume, p. 92.

[2] *Ibid.*, p. 91.

[3] *A Discourse on the Traffic in Spirituous Liquors, Delivered in the Centre Church, New Haven, Feb. 6, 1838.* New Haven, 1838.

[4] *Sermon before the Washington Temperance Society of New Haven*, New Haven, 1843. *The Christian Basis of the Temperance Reformation*, in the *American Temperance Preacher*, January, 1848.

[5] Commemorative Volume, p. 92.

"In a little while the tyrannical fashion had lost its power. Every man was at liberty to practice personal abstinence, either for his own safety or for the sake of saving others; and there was no law of hospitality requiring any man to tempt his guests by inviting them to drink with him."

The most important of Dr. Bacon's reformatory efforts, the greatest single work of his life, was his opposition to slavery. His ministry began just as the question of slavery was passing from the status of a moral reform earnestly desired by good men both in the North and in the South—though without any very definite views as to how the reform was to be effected where the institution was intrenched—to the position of a political question on which parties were gradually to range for an inevitable conflict. The Missouri Compromise, effected in Congress when Leonard Bacon was half-way through his Senior year at Yale, marks the beginning of this new stage of the question — the struggle for the extension of slavery into the new Territories of the West. At Andover the young graduate found a warm anti-slavery spirit. The topic was one of frequent debate before the Seminary "Society of Inquiry;" and the first of Dr. Bacon's writings to have extensive circulation was a *Report* to that Society on African colonization, condemning slavery in most positive terms.[1] This *Report*,

[1] L. W. Bacon, *Irenics and Polemics*, pp. 183, 184, New York, 1895. The *Report* was published in 1823.

prepared in the Senior year of its author's Seminary course, was given wide publicity by his fellow-students.

Leonard Bacon carried this reformatory spirit with him to his pastorate, and speedily organized in his new home a young men's club called the Anti-Slavery Association, from which grew the African Improvement Society of New Haven, designed for the spiritual, mental, and physical elevation of the local colored population.[1] On the Fourth of July, 1825, the newly settled pastor gave, as his oration, *A Plea for Africa;* and a year later, on the same anniversary of freedom, he declared that:[2]

"Public opinion throughout the free States must hold a different course on the subject of slavery from that which it now holds. Instead of exhausting itself fruitlessly and worse than fruitlessly upon the *operation* of the system, it must be directed towards the *principle* on which the system rests."

These views Dr. Bacon persistently advocated in every channel open to him, notably in the *Christian Spectator*, of which mention has already been made.

But a new force came into the field with the publication of the *Liberator* by William Lloyd Garrison, from 1831 onward, and the foundation of the American Anti-Slavery Society by that vigorous agitator in 1832. In the thought of Garrison and his associates not only was slavery a wrong for which immediate abolition was

[1] L. W. Bacon, *Irenics and Polemics*, pp. 184, 185.   [2] *Ibid.*, p. 186.

the only cure, but "slaveholders are the enemies of God and man; their garments are red with the blood of souls; their guilt is aggravated beyond the power of language to describe."[1] To Dr. Bacon's thinking, such indiscriminating condemnation of all slaveholders was not merely prejudicial to a good cause, it was unjustifiable. As Dr. Bacon declared in 1846, in words which Abraham Lincoln recoined into a famous phrase:[2]

"If that form of government, that system of social order is not wrong,—if those laws of the southern states, by virtue of which slavery exists there, and is what it is, are not wrong—nothing is wrong."

But he added:[3]

"The wrongfulness of that entire body of laws, opinions, and practices is one thing; and the criminality of the individual master, who tries to do right, is another thing."

To declare the master who had received slaves by inheritance, and was trying to do them good, as of practically equal guilt with the master who treated his slaves as cattle and sold their offspring for gain, seemed to Dr. Bacon a confusion of moral distinctions. And so he fought his battle with ever-increasing success, but with much opposition even in his own home, against slavery on the one hand and against what he deemed the damaging methods of the extremer

[1] Garrison, *Thoughts on African Colonization*, p. 67. Boston, 1832.
[2] *Slavery Discussed in Occasional Essays*, x. New York, 1846.
[3] *Ibid.*

abolitionists on the other. As he told the Albany Convention in 1852:[1]

"I have always found myself in a state of 'betweenity in relation to parties on questions connected with slavery, so that, as Baxter said of himself in regard to the controversies of his day, where other men have had one adversary I have had two."

But this "state of betweenity" was no state of uncertainty, either in his own mind or that of others, as to his estimate of the moral turpitude of the slave system, and the duty of all good men to do what they could to overthrow it. To no leadership did the sober judgment of New England, and especially of his own State, more positively respond than to his.

Just what measures besides moral opposition to this evil were possible was a question which Dr. Bacon, like most of the early seekers for its reform, found puzzling. For a long time he supported the colonization plan, which had been a favorite among his friends at Andover. But time showed the hopelessness of that solution; and the course of political events, leading, through the annexation of Texas, to the conquest of vast territories from Mexico — a conquest accompanied and followed by demands that they be thrown open to slavery — pointed out the straight path of definite resistance to a definite aggression. It was primarily as a step forward in this struggle for freedom

[1] *Proceedings of the General Convention . . . held at Albany*, p. 84.

that Dr. Bacon took the editorial leadership, with Rev. Drs. Joseph P. Thompson, Richard Salter Storrs, and Joshua Leavitt as fellow-laborers, and with financial support furnished by Messrs. Henry C. Bowen, Theodore McNamee, and others, in founding the *Independent*, in December, 1848,[1] under the declaration, " We take our stand for free soil."

The successive aggressions of the slave power led Dr. Bacon, in his Thanksgiving Sermon for 1851, to support the view which William H. Seward had made famous on the floor of Congress, that the public domain was dedicated to liberty, not only by the Constitution but by a " higher law " than the Constitution —a law which must not be disobeyed. The Kansas-Nebraska act moved him to advocate forcible resistance to the introduction of slavery into the Territories involved. And when the war began there was no more strenuous advocate of freedom and patriotism in the New England pulpit than he.

These labors cost Dr. Bacon much opposition, and often from those whose friendship he esteemed; but when it was nearly over and slavery was close to its end he could say to his own congregation:[2]

" You know how I have been blamed and even execrated, in these later years, for declaring, here and elsewhere,

[1] See Dr. Storrs's account, *Independent*, December 8, 1898.
[2] *Two Sermons Preached on the Fortieth Anniversary of his Settlement* (March 12, 1865), Commemorative Volume, p. 95.

the wickedness of buying and selling human beings, or of violating in any way those human rights which are inseparable from human nature. I make no complaint in making this allusion; all reproaches, all insults endured in the conflict with so gigantic a wickedness against God and man, are to be received and remembered not as injuries but as honors."

And Dr. Bacon was given a special and peculiar gratification in the recollection of those years of controversy, besides the larger satisfaction of a conspicuous share in the most momentous work of his generation. In the heat of the struggle, in 1846, he had published at New York a small, black-bound volume, made up of various contributions to the great debate, under the title *Slavery Discussed in Occasional Essays from 1833 to 1846*. The volume never had much of a circulation, but one copy reached the office table of Abraham Lincoln, then a comparatively unknown lawyer in his Illinois home. The story of its reception may be told in the modest words in which Dr. Bacon related it in 1865. Speaking of a visit paid to the great emancipating President, Dr. Bacon said:[1]

"Less than four years ago, not knowing that he had ever heard of me, I had the privilege of an interview with him; and his first word, after our introduction to each other, was a reference to that volume, with a frank approval of its principles. Since then I have heard of his mention-

[1] *Two Sermons Preached on the Fortieth Anniversary of his Settlement* (March 12, 1865), Commemorative Volume, p. 96.

ing the same book to a friend of mine in terms which showed that it had made an impression on his earnest and thoughtful soul."

Dr. Bacon might, without exaggeration, have said much more.[1]

Dr. Bacon's work was complete, to a degree vouchsafed to few men, before he reached old age. The end of the struggle over slavery terminated the contest to which he had given his largest effort. The contests over the "New Haven Theology" and over the views of Dr. Bushnell had died away before the Civil War. And, in a peculiar degree, his old age was a time of growing ripeness and sweetness of Christian life as the golden sunset drew near. It was a life of activity and usefulness to the end.

Dr. Bacon intimated, in a sermon preached on the completion of his fortieth year of service, his desire to be relieved of active pastoral responsibilities, and on September 9, 1866, the partial separation was accomplished on terms alike honorable to pastor and to people.[2] His resignation was accepted, but he was never dismissed by council, and he continued to render aid to his successors and minister to his people as strength and opportunity offered, being till the day of his death the *pastor emeritus* of his church. Few men

[1] L. W. Bacon, *Irenics and Polemics*, p. 198 ; *Century Magazine*, xxv., p. 658.

[2] Commemorative Volume, pp. 39–49, 104.

have ever borne themselves as generously in the often trying situation of a retired minister, compelled to see the work in which he had been so long a leader pass into younger hands, as did Dr. Bacon. His immediate successor in the active work of the pastorate thus bore witness to him:[1]

"He was the most magnanimous man I ever knew. Had I been his son after the flesh he could not have been more coöperative or kind. Always ready to help when asked, he never volunteered even advice; he never in any instance or slightest particular gave me reason to wish he had said or done anything otherwise. Apparently incapable of jealousy—even had there been vastly more opportunity for it than there was—he was to the pastor who followed him a supporter and a comfort always."

Dr. Bacon's old age was a time of honor in the churches and in the community at large. He ranked in public repute as the representative American Congregationalist. Harvard gave him the degree of Doctor of Laws in 1870. The two Brooklyn Councils, of 1874 and 1876, the most talked-of Congregational advisory bodies of the last half-century, chose him as their Moderator. And his years of retirement from the pastorate proved a time of unexpected but conspicuous labor in a new field also. As soon as his purpose to resign the pastoral office became known, the corporation of Yale sought his services for the vacant theological chair in the Divinity School; and

[1] G. L. Walker, *Memorial Sermon, ibid.*, p. 184.

as a consequence of this invitation he taught as Acting Professor of Revealed Theology in Yale Seminary from 1866 to 1871, when he became Lecturer on Church Polity and American Church History, a post that he occupied as long as he lived. He threw himself into the new work with characteristic energy, and it was during the period of his professorship that the present buildings occupied by the Divinity School were erected—a material gain for the school of his service in which his wide acquaintance and influence made him conspicuously helpful.

So he passed onward to the close of his useful life, beloved and reverenced by the community in which he had labored, and honored by the churches of which he had been so long a leader. His old age was a peaceful and fruitful autumn, and he went from among men on December 24, 1881, without having been seriously laid aside from active life till the summons came.

At his funeral, just before his six sons bore his body from the church where he had ministered for fifty-six years, the mourning congregation sang his serene hymn — a hymn no less appropriate in its suggestion of the character of Dr. Bacon's ripening years than expressive of his Christian hope:

> " Hail, tranquil hour of closing day!
> Begone, disturbing care!
> And look, my soul, from earth away,
> To him who heareth prayer.

" How sweet the tear of penitence,
   Before his throne of grace,
 While to the contrite spirit's sense,
   He shows his smiling face.

" How sweet, through long-remembered years,
   His mercies to recall ;
 And, pressed with wants, and griefs, and fears,
   To trust his love for all.

" How sweet to look, in thoughtful hope,
   Beyond this fading sky,
 And hear him call his children up
   To his fair home on high.

" Calmly the day forsakes our heaven
   To dawn beyond the west ;
 So let my soul, in life's last even,
   Retire to glorious rest."

We have followed the lives of ten eminent Congregationalists as we have met together for these successive hours. The biographies have been those of men diverse indeed in the circumstances of their history, in the times in which their work was done, in the interests that were the uppermost topics of discussion among those with whom their lot was cast, in their methods of Christian activity, in their own interpretations of aspects of Christian truth. From the exile for his faith, leading a pioneer community in its efforts to strike root in the somber forest wilderness, to the opponent of slavery, preaching for more than half a century from an historic pulpit, and spending his last days as a theological instructor in a venerable university, is indeed a far cry, if the flight of time and alteration of external circumstances alone are considered. But a unity greater than any seeming diversity characterized these men. To them all God was the veriest of realities; to them all his service was the highest earthly privilege; to them all his Word was the sufficient guide of life. No one of them but walked close with God. No one of them but lived " as seeing the invisible." And they were one, also, in their thought of the Church as finding its highest and truest expression, not in a priesthood divinely appointed to dispense sacraments necessary for salvation to a laity divinely committed to its control, but in self-governing and mutually responsible fellowships of Christian men and women, knit by a common covenant to one another and to the living Lord whose name they bear, and enjoying an Apostolic freedom in His worship and service. They were every one of them in the truest sense ministers in the household of God.

One they were, too, in their conception of the Christian life as one of consecration, drawing its strength from the divine Spirit to whom it owes its birth, and manifesting in its fruits the presence of the transforming power of God. It is an honorable succession. Not one of them but made New England stronger, better, freer, by reason of his work.

INDEX.

A

Abbot, Samuel, 381, 383.
Abrams, Margaret, 98.
Adams, Charles Francis, *cited*, 29, 30, 75, 80, 81.
Ainsworth, Henry, the Separatist, 22, 120, 121.
Albany Convention, The, 429-432, 448.
Allen, Prof. A. V. G., *cited*, 220, 228, 259.
Allerton, Isaac, 25.
Allin, Rev. John, 158.
American Bible Society, The, 428.
American Board, The, 388, 389, 394, 428.
American Congregational Union The, 431.
American Temperance Society, The, 389.
American Tract Society, The, 389, 428.
Amsterdam, The Separatists in, 21, 22, 45.
Andover Theological Seminary, why founded, 376-379; circumstances of foundation, 379-385; Woods's services to, 381-386; early growth, 385, 386; interest in missions, 387-389; Bacon at, 414, 424; *mentioned*, 389, 390, 394, 396, 402-405, 416.
Andros, Sir Edmund, 196.
Anglican Party, its aims, 51, 52.
Antinomianism, Controversy regarding, 75-81.
Apthorpe, Rev. East, 293.

Arber, Prof. Edward, *cited*, 15, 18, 21, 22, 31, 39.
Arianism, in eighteenth-century New England, 293, 297-299, 308-310, 326, 348, 361.
Armada, The Spanish, 6, 12.
Armine, Lady, 159.
Arminianism, 51, 231, 233, 252, 254, 268, 297, 298, 344, 361.
Aspinwall, Edwin, 102.
Atonement, Doctrine of the, 305, 306, 372, 438.
Auburn Theological Seminary, 386.
Austerfield, Bradford's early home at, 6-20, 49, 55.
Awakening, The Great, 237, 240, 246, 270, 275-287.

B

Babworth, 15, 20.
Backus, Rev. Dr. Charles, 370, 371, 379.
Backus, Rev. Isaac, *cited*, 211.
Bacon, Rev. David, 410-413.
Bacon, Francis, 7.
Bacon, Dr. Leonard, of Hartford, 413.
Bacon, Rev. Dr. Leonard, early life, 410-413; education, 413, 414; ordination, 414; settlement at New Haven, 415, 416; early pastorate, 416-418; household experiences, 418, 419; in the Orient, 419; as a religious leader, 419, 420; literary gifts, 420; poetic strain, 421; services as a historian, 421-426; his *Thirteen*

Bacon—*Continued.*
Discourses, 424 ; doctorate of divinity, 424 ; his Andover *Discourse,* 424 ; his *Historical Discourse,* 424 ; his *Genesis of the New England Churches,* 426 ; services to Congregational polity, 426-428; his *Manual* and *Digest,* 426, 427 ; the " Boston Platform," 427, 428, 432 ; services to missionary societies, etc., 428-432 ; at the Albany Convention, 429 ; in theologic controversies, 432-440 ; the Taylor and Tyler division, 435-437 ; the Bushnell controversy, 437-440 ; his editorial services, 441-443, 449 ; the *New Englander,* 442 ; the *Independent,* 443, 449 ; temperance reform, 443-445 ; anti-slavery efforts, 445-451 ; President Lincoln's opinion, 450, 451 ; retirement from the pastorate, 451, 452 ; services to Yale, 452, 453 ; his last days, 453, 454.
Bacon, Rev. Dr. Leonard W., *cited*, 412, 445, 446, 451.
Bacon, Oliver N., *cited*, 169.
Baillie, Prof. Robert, 81, 88, 93.
Ball, Rev. John, 87.
Bancroft, Archbishop Richard, 51.
Bangor Theological Seminary, 386.
Barlow, Bishop William, 59.
Barnes, Rev. Dr. Albert, 435.
Baron, Dr. Peter, 62.
Bartlett, William, 381.
Baxter, Rev. Richard, 164, 202, 422, 448.
Bay Psalm Book, The, 120-122, 148.
Bayly, Bishop Lewis, 164.
Bawtry, 6, 8, 10.
Bellamy, Rev. Dr. Joseph, 238, 249, 258, 280, 314, 323, 335, 341, 349, 379.
Benevolence, Disinterested, 255-257, 330, 331, 345-347, 399, 400 ; *see also* Willingness to be Damned.

Berkeley, Bishop George, 220.
Bernard, Rev. Richard, 117.
Bernhard, Saint, 240.
Bible, English translation of the, 9, 13.
Blyth, Monastery of, 8, 10.
Boston, England, Bradford's imprisonment at, 21; Cotton's work at, 59-68.
Boston, Mass., settled, 53 ; Cotton settled in, 69 ; the Antinomian controversy in, 75-81 ; Roger Williams declines settlement in, 83 ; Eliot invited to, 142 ; Increase Mather settled at, 183 ; the " Thursday Lecture," 187, 275 ; great fires in, 190 ; Liberal movement in, 203-207 ; first half of eighteenth century, 273-275 ; Whitefield's characterization of, 275 ; the Revolutionary War, 296, 297 ; early Unitarianism in, 299, 377, 378.
Boston, churches of, — First Church, Cotton settled, 69 ; divided, 132 ; Chauncy's settlement, 270 ; Foxcroft's pastorate, 270; Whitefield's preaching,277: —Second Church, 183, 194, 195: —Old South Church, 133, 207, 278, 342, 348, 364 :— Brattle Church, 203 - 207 : — King's Chapel, 377 : — New North Church, 279 :—West Church, 293, 333:— Park Street Church, 396.
Boston Platform, The, 428, 432.
Bourne, Rev. Richard, 165.
Bowen, Henry C., 449.
Bradford, Alden, *cited*, 291-293.
Bradford, Rev. Dr. Amory H., 3.
Bradford, John, 38.
Bradford, Gov. William, early life, 6-11, 54 ; religious training, 15-18 ; reasons for leaving England, 19, 20, 50 ; goes to Holland, 20, 21 ; learns a trade, 21, 22 ; marriage, 22 ; at Leyden, 21-24 ; emigration to America,

Bradford—*Continued.*
23-25 ; governor, 25, 26 ; second marriage, 27 ; services to colony in peril of famine, 26-29 ; in peril from hostile countrymen, 29-32 ; secures financial freedom for Plymouth, 32-35 ; welcomes Salem church, 35-37 ; his *History*, 37-39 ; his minor writings, 39, 40 ; his style, 40 ; his character, 41, 42 ; last days, 42-44 , his faith, 45 ; on luxury, 147 ; *mentioned*, 5, 56.
Bradford, Deputy-Gov. William, 38.
Bradley, Rev. Joshua, 356.
Brainerd, Rev. David, 242, 243, 318, 319.
Branford, Indian missions at, 166.
Brattle Church, *see* Boston churches.
Brattle, Thomas, 205, 206.
Brattle, Rev. William, tutor at Harvard, 195, 202 ; in liberal movement, 204-207 ; pastor at Cambridge, 205, 206.
Brewster, Ruling Elder William, at Scrooby, 15-18, 49 ; at Leyden, 23, 25 ; at Plymouth, 42, 44.
Briant, Rev. Lemuel, 298, 299.
Bridge, Rev. William, 91.
Brown, Rev. Dr. John, of Bedford, *cited*, 15.
Brown, Rev. John, of Cohassett, 299.
Brown, John, of Harper's Ferry fame, 412.
Brown, Moses, 381.
Browne, Robert, the Separatist, 14, 82.
Buell, Rev. Samuel, 318, 321.
Builli, John de, 8.
Burial Hill Declaration, The, 194.
Burr, Pres. Aaron, 260, 261.
Burr, Rev. Jonathan, 112, 113.
Burroughs, Rev. Jeremiah, 91.
Bushnell, Rev. Dr. Horace, 314, 437-440

C

Calef, Robert, 202.
Calhoun, Rev. George A., 436.
Callender, Rev. Elisha, 211.
Calvin, John, Cotton's love for, 72 ; *mentioned*, 223.
Calvinism, "Consistent," 361.
Calvinism, "Old" or "Moderate," 331, 332, 339, 341, 344, 345, 361-363, 375-377, 379-385, 405, 434.
Calvinism, Stages of, 229-231.
Cambridge Platform, The, 91, 93, 124-126, 427.
Cambridge Synod, *see* Synod.
Cambridge University, student life in, 55, 56 ; colleges of, — Emmanuel, 56, 57, 139, 140 ; Jesus, 139 ; Peter House, 58 ; St. John's, 58 ; Trinity, 8, 55, 56, 268.
Canonicus, Indian chief, 29.
Canterbury, Archbishop of (Thomas Secker), 293.
Carey, Rev. William, the missionary, 138, 163, 387.
Carpenter, Alice, 27.
Cartwright, Thomas, Puritan leader, 13.
Carver, Gov. John, 25.
Chaderton, Laurence, Puritan leader, 57.
Chadwick, Rev. Dr. J. W., *cited*, 397.
Chamberlain, Dr. Mellen, *cited*, 292.
Chandler, Rev. Dr. T. B., 294.
Chandler, William, 145.
Channing, Rev. Dr. W. E., 314, 325-327, 377, 397, 398.
Charles I., of England, 52, 53, 159.
Chauncy, Pres. Charles, 131, 178 268, 269.
Chauncy, Charles, merchant, 269.
Chauncy, Rev. Dr. Charles, ancestry and early life, 268, 269 ; settlement at Boston, 270 ; sermon on Foxcroft, 271 ; his

460 INDEX

Chauncy—*Continued.*
personal traits, 269-273, 287; opposes the Whitefieldian revival, 282-288; his course criticised, 283; on conversion, 283, 303, 304; his *Seasonable Thoughts*, 286; health affected, 287; doctorate received, 288; opposes legislature, 288, 289; controversy regarding Episcopacy, 289-297; reply to the Bishop of Landaff, 293, 294; *Answer* to Chandler, 294; his *View of Episcopacy*, 295; his patriotism, 296; his "Liberal" theology, 297-310; his moderation, 299; on Original Sin, 258, 301, 302; his *Twelve Sermons*, 301-304; views on Saving Faith, 302, 303, 309, 332, 333; his *Benevolence of the Deity*, 304; view of the Atonement, 305, 306; his *Salvation of All Men*, 306-308; his Arianism, 308-310; unfavorable opinion of Hopkins, 341; his death, 310; *mentioned*, 314, 326, 377.
Chauncy, Rev. Isaac, 269.
Christian Spectator, The, 441, 446.
Church Building Society, The, 431.
Church, Rev. John H., 369, 370.
Chutchamaquin, Indian chief, 155.
Clark, Rev. Peter, 301.
Clark, Prof. William, *cited*, 10.
Clarke, Rev. John, 326; *cited*, 269, 272.
Clarke, Rev. Dr. Samuel, 298, 300.
Clement of Alexandria, 295.
Clement of Rome, 295.
Clyfton, Rev. Richard, Separatist, 15, 18, 19, 49.
Coddington, William, 66.
Codman, Rev. Dr. John, 396.
Cole, Nathan, quoted, 276.
College and Education Society, The, 428, 429.
Collins, Anthony, the Deist, 254.
Colman, Rev. Benjamin, 205, 206, 281.

Columba, Saint, 138.
Confession, The Savoy, 193; — of 1680, 193, 194; — The Westminster, 193.
Congregational Home Missionary Society, The, 428.
Connecticut Evangelical Magazine, The, 387.
Conversion, a difficult process, 102, 181, 318, 319, 369; under declining Calvinism, 229-232; Increase Mather's view of, 189; Edwards's experience and theory of, 222-225, 233-235; Chauncy's view of, 283, 303, 304; Hopkins's view of, 317-322, 333-338.
Cooper, Thompson, *cited*, 18.
Corbitant, Indian chief, 29.
Cortés, Hernando, 412.
Cotton, Rev. John, parentage, 54; education, 55, 56; religious awakening, 57-59; settlement at Boston, Eng., 59; marriages, 59, 60; his activity, 60-63, 105; his defense of Calvinism, 62; his nonconformity, 63-65; consequent difficulties and flight, 66-68; letter to his wife, 67; his child's baptism, 68, 69; settles at Boston, Mass., 69, 70; appearance and preaching, 70-72; habits and influence, 72-75; opinion of Democracy, 74; his draft of laws, 75; in the Antinomian controversy, 75-81; his controversy with Roger Williams, 81-86; views on persecution, 85, 86; his answer to Ball, 87; his Catechism, 87; on church-music, 87, 88; on infant baptism, 88; on church membership, 88; his treatises on Congregationalism, 89-93, 115; the *Way*, 90; the *Keyes*, 90-92; the *Way Cleared*, 93; invited to the Westminster Assembly, 91; the *Cambridge Platform*, 93, 124, 170; moderator in 1643, 119; possible letter

Cotton—*Continued.*
  to Richard Mather, 108 ; death and character, 94 ; *mentioned*, 107, 109, 115, 117-119, 134, 142, 151, 166, 175, 180, 225.
Cotton, Rev. John, Jr., of Plymouth, 165, 166.
Cotton, Rev. John, of Hampton, 184.
Cotton, Roland, 54.
Cotton, Rev. Seaborn, 68.
Covenant, The Half-Way, *see* Half-Way Covenant.
Crafts, Rev. Thomas, 365.
Crocker, Rev. Zebulon, *cited*, 401.
Cromwell, Oliver, 182.
Cromwell, Richard, 182.
Cushman, Robert, 25.
Cutler, Rector Timothy, 226.

D

Danforth, Rev. Samuel, 143.
Danforth, Rev. Samuel, Jr., 166, 168.
Davenport, Rev. Addington, 289.
Davenport, Rev. James, 281, 285.
Davenport, Rev. John, conceals Cotton, 67 ; settlement at New Haven, 79 ; at Boston, 132, 133 ; death, 170 ; *mentioned*, 91, 107.
Derby, 54.
Dexter, Prof. Franklin B., 228 ; *cited*, 220, 222, 226, 249, 260, 322.
Dexter, Rev. Dr. Henry M., 3, 39 ; *quoted*, 55 ; *cited*, 17, 22, 23, 38, 92, 130, 151, 162.
Disinterested Benevolence, *see* Benevolence.
Doddridge, Rev. Dr. Philip, 252, 298, 369.
Dorchester, settled, 53 ; origin of its churches, 109, 110 ; Richard Mather settled at, 110-112 ; Increase Mather born at, 176 ; attitude toward Half-Way Covenant, 131-134 ; Eliot's missionary efforts in, 155.

Dorset, The earl of, 66.
Drake, Sir Francis, 7.
Druillettes, Gabriel, 41, 148.
Dudley, Gov. Joseph, 196, 208.
Dudley, Justice Paul, 292.
Dudley, Gov. Thomas, 53, 66, 112.
Dummer, Jeremiah, 222.
Dunster, Pres. Henry, 154, 178.
Dwight, Rev. Dr. Sereno E., *cited*, 219-223, 226, 228, 239, 244, 246-252, 254, 255, 261, 262, 278, 280.
Dwight, Pres. Timothy, 362, 367, 368, 386, 399.

E

Echard, Laurence, *cited*, 58.
Education Society, The (Congregational), 389.
Edwardeanism, 361-363, 370, 372, 377, 385, 391, 399-402, 434, 437 (*see also* Edwards and Hopkins).
Edwards, Esther, Mrs. Burr, 260.
Edwards, Jerusha, 243.
Edwards, Pres. Jonathan, home and early life, 217-219, 269 ; precocity, 219, 220 ; student at Yale, 220-222 ; conversion, 222-224 ; ministry at New York, 226 ; call to Bolton, 226 ; his *Resolutions*, 226 ; a tutor at Yale, 226 ; settled at Northampton, 227 ; marriage, 227, 228 ; characteristics, 143, 228, 247, 248, 262 ; a slaveholder, 349 ; quality of his ministry, 229, 232 ; his great work, 232 ; his preaching, 232, 235, 236 ; physical demonstrations under it, 280 ; majority of mankind to be lost, 307; the revival at Northampton, 232-237; the *Narrative of Surprising Conversions*, 236 ; meets Whitefield, 237 ; protests against certain traits of Whitefield, 278-280 ; criticises Chauncy, 283 ; his *Thoughts*, 238, 286 ; Mrs. Edwards's religious experiences,

INDEX

Edwards—*Continued*.
238–240; his opinion on "Willingness to be Damned," 239, 347; his *Religious Affections*, 240–242; the *Life of Brainerd*, 242, 243; efforts for union in prayer, 243, 244; his difficulties at Northampton, 244; his change of view on terms of communion, 244–246; the *Humble Inquiry*, 247; dismissed from Northampton, 248; Hopkins's studies under and friendship for him, 320–324; called to Stockbridge, 249, 323; missionary labors and scholastic studies, 250; his writings, 251; the *Freedom of Will*, 251–254, 304; the *End for which God Created the World*, 251, 254; treatise on *True Virtue*, 251, 255, 257, 344, 400; volume on *Original Sin*, 251, 257–259; his influence, 259–263; removal to Princeton and death, 261; *mentioned*, 267, 268, 282, 284, 297, 298, 302, 329, 331, 335, 345, 352, 354, 379, 385.

Edwards, Mrs. Jonathan, *see* Sarah Pierpont.

Edwards, Rev. Dr. Jonathan, Jr., 225, 252, 254, 256, 306, 307.

Edwards, Richard, 218.

Edwards, Rev. Timothy, 218, 219.

Edwards, William, 218.

Eliot, Bennett, 138, 139.

Eliot, Dr. Ellsworth, *cited*, 138, 139.

Eliot, Rev. John, his title of "Apostle," 138; early life, 138; education, 139; assists Thomas Hooker, 139–141; conversion, 141; settles at Roxbury, 142; marriage, 142, 143; pastoral labors, 143–145; personal characteristics, 145–148; the *Bay Psalm Book*, 121, 148; his *Christian Commonwealth*, 148–150; his *Communion of Churches*, 150, 151; his missionary labors, 151–171; preaches to Waauban, 155–158; education for the Indians, 158, 160, 161; founds Natick, 161; his translations, 162–164; results of his work, 166–170; his last days, 170, 171; *mentioned*, 175, 250.

Elizabeth, of England, 7, 10, 12, 13, 50, 56, 107.

Ellis, A. B., *cited*, 56, 60, 269–272.

Emerson, Rev. William, *cited*, 269–272, 299.

Emlyn, Rev. Thomas, 298.

Emmons, Rev. Dr. Nathaniel, 143, 314, 335, 374, 376, 379, 385.

Endicott, Gov. John, 36, 53, 106.

Episcopacy, controversy over, 289–297.

Erskine, Rev. Dr. John, 248–250.

F

Farrar, Samuel, 381.

Felt, Rev. Joseph B., *cited*, 288.

Finney, Pres. Charles G., 146, 402.

Fisher, Prof. George P., *cited*, 220, 258.

Fiske, John, *cited*, 167.

Flavel, Rev. John, 72, 200, 281.

Fletcher, Rev. Henry, curate at Austerfield, 11, 16.

Foster, Rev. Isaac, 146.

Foster, Capt. William, 146.

Fowler, Prof. W. C., *cited*, 268, 269.

Foxcroft, Rev. Thomas, 270, 271, 277.

Francis, Saint, 240.

Franklin, Benjamin, 367.

Freeman, Rev. James, 377.

French, Rev. Jonathan, 380.

Froude, James Anthony, *cited*, 9, 10.

Fuller, Deacon Samuel, 25, 36, 37.

G

Gainsborough, Separatist congregation at, 18–20.

INDEX

463

Gardiner, Prof. H. Norman, *cited*, 220.
Gardner, Newport, 356.
Garrison, William Lloyd, 446, 447.
Gay, Rev. Ebenezer, 299.
George I., of England, 209.
Gill, Lieut.-Gov. Moses, 364.
Gillespie, Rev. Thomas, 248.
Glas, John, 302.
Goodwin, J. A., *cited*, 25, 27, 32, 40, 42, 43.
Goodwin, Rev. Thomas, 91.
Gookin, Daniel, 154, 166, 168.
Gott, Charles, *cited*, 36.
Graham, Rev. John, 280, 317.
"Great Awakening," The, *see* Awakening.
Great Barrington, Hopkins's pastorate at, 322-324, 329, 338, 339.
Grosart, Rev. Alexander B., 250.
Guyse, Rev. Dr. John, 236.

H

Half-Way Covenant, The, 126-134, 184, 244-247, 249, 329, 374.
Hall, Rev. Gordon, 137, 388, 389.
Hall, John, of Roxbury, 85.
Hamilton College, 424.
Hamilton Theological Seminary, 387.
Hankridge, Sarah, wife of John Cotton, 60, 67, 69; of Richard Mather, 60.
Harrison, Rev. John, 102.
Hart, Rev. William, 341, 344, 361.
Hartford, *mentioned*, 110, 277, 410, 411, 413, 416, 418, 424.
Hartford Theological Seminary, 386, 400, 436.
Harvard, Rev. John, 57, 178.
Harvard University, early conditions of entrance, 101; Chauncy's presidency, 268, 269; in Increase Mather's student days, 177-179; Mather's presidency, 194, 195, 203, 207, 208; gives Mather a doctorate, 202; efforts for a charter, 202, 203; the Hollis professorship, 367, 370, 371, 378, 380; the Dudleian lectureship, 292, 293; Whitefield's criticism, 279; in Woods's time, 365-368, 370, 373; passes to anti-Trinitarians, 378; *mentioned*, 269, 452.
Hawes, Rev. Dr. Joel, 416.
Hawksley, John, *cited*, 225.
Hawley, Joseph, 248, 252.
Haynes, Gov. John, 68, 74, 82.
Heads of Agreement, The, 200.
Hemmenway, Rev. Moses, 340, 345, 361.
Henry VIII., of England, 8, 9.
Herle, Rev. Charles, 119.
Hiacoomes, Indian chief, 165.
Higginson, Rev. Francis, 36, 53.
Hill, H. A., *cited*, 133.
Hillhouse, Senator James, 417.
Hobart, Rev. L. Smith, 430.
Hobbes, Thomas, the philosopher, 253.
Hollis, Thomas, 195, 212.
Hollis, Thomas, the younger, 292.
Holt, Katherine, marries Richard Mather, 105, 106.
Hooker, Rev. Thomas, at Emmanuel College, 57; English ministry, 139-141; Eliot influenced by, 139, 141; as a preacher, 71; flight from England, 67, 68; founder of Hartford, 74, 110; advice to Mather, 108, 109; moderator in 1643, 119; death, 170; services to Congregationalism, 86; on conversion, 181, 225, 234; on "Willingness to be Damned," 347; *mentioned*, 91, 94, 105, 107, 134, 151, 227.
Hooper, Bishop John, 10.
Hopkinsianism, 362-365, 369, 370, 374-377, 381-385, 399, 405.
Hopkins, John, Version of the Psalms, 120.
Hopkins, Rev. Dr. Samuel, significance as a theologian, 314, 315, 352-355, 361; his autobiography, 315; early life, 316; a student at Yale, 317; his religious experience, 317-322; discipleship

Hopkins—*Continued.*
and friendship toward Edwards, 249, 320-324; called to Simsbury, 322; settled at Great Barrington, 322, 323; marriages, 323, 328, 329; personal traits, 324-329; confidence in his doctrines, 327, 328; trials at Great Barrington, 329, 330; treatise on *Sin*, 330, 331; controversy over "unregenerate doings," 333-338; his *Enquiry*, 333; his *Two Discourses*, 335; views on divine sovereignty, 337, 338; dismission from Great Barrington, 338, 339; criticism of Chauncy, 341; on Arianism in Boston, 299; his reply to Mills, 340; attacked by Hart, 341, 342; his settlement at Newport, 342-344; his reply to Hart, 344; his *True Holiness* 345; view of the nature of virtue, 345, 400; his *Dialogue*, 346; view on "Willingness to be Damned," 346, 347, 370, 371; his hopefulness, 347; confident of infant salvation, 348; defends divinity of Christ, 299, 348; views on future punishment, 348, 349; expectation of a millennium, 349; opposition to slavery, 256, 349-351; his doctorate, 352; his *System*, 328, 338, 351, 352, 355, 371; his influence, 353-355, 362; old age and death, 355-357; *mentioned*, 372; his writings cited elsewhere than in the lecture on him, 222, 223, 228, 247, 250, 262, 362.
Horrocks, Elizabeth, marries John Cotton, 59, 60.
Hort, Rev. F. J. A., *cited*, 57.
Hough, Atherton, 68.
Howard, Rev. Dr. Bezaleel, 272, 273, 287.
Howe, Rev. John, 182, 200.
Hubbard, Rev. William, the historian, 38, 75.
Hunter, Rev. Joseph, *cited*, 9, 11.
Hutchinson, Mrs. Anne, 75, 81.

Hutchinson, Gov. Thomas, 38, 197; *cited*, 75, 291.

I

Immersion of Infants, 268.
Independent, The, 443, 449.
Ingersoll, Joanna, wife of Samuel Hopkins, 323, 328.

J

James I., of England, 50, 52, 57, 106.
James II., of England, 196, 197.
Jefferson, President Thomas, 367.
Johnson, "Mr.," Cotton's teacher, 55.
Johnson, Isaac, 53.
Johnson, Lucy, Mrs. Leonard Bacon, 418.
Judson, Rev. Adoniram, 137, 388, 389.

L

Lacy, John, the "prophet," 286.
Landaff, the Bishop of (John Ewer), 293.
Lamb, Charles, 138.
Lane Theological Seminary, 387.
Laud, Archbishop William, 51, 57, 63, 67, 106, 107, 140, 141, 268.
Law, Rev. William, 57.
Lawrence, Prof. E. A., *cited*, 364, 365, 367-370, 373, 374, 386, 388-390, 396, 404.
Leavitt, Rev. Dr. Joshua, 421, 449.
Lebanon, Conn., excitement at, during the "Great Awakening," 280.
Lechford, Thomas, *cited*, 154.
Lecky, William E. H., the historian, quoted, 259.
L'Ecluse, Jean de, 22.
Leicester Academy, 365.
Leverett, John, emigrant, 68.
Leverett, Pres. John, tutor at Harvard, 195, 202; in "Liberal" movement, 204-207; president of Harvard, 208.

Leverett, Ruling Elder Thomas, 68, 69.
Leyden, The Separatists in, 21-24, 45.
Liberal Theology in eastern Massachusetts, 267, 297-310, 339, 361, 363, 375, 377, 378, 380, 395-398.
Liberator, The, 446.
Lincoln, President Abraham, 447, 450, 451.
Lincoln, The earl of, 66.
Lindsey, Rev. Theophilus, 310.
Locke, John, the philosopher, 220, 253, 254, 258, 300.
London, The Bishop of (Edmund Gibson), 291.
Ludlow, Roger, 53.
Luther, Martin, 222.
Lyford, Rev. John, 31, 32, 35.

M

Mahan, Pres. Asa, 395, 402, 403.
Malebranche, Nicolas, the philosopher, 220.
Marshpee, Indian mission at, 165, 167.
Martha's Vineyard, Indian mission on, 164-169.
Mary II., of England, 197.
Mary, Queen of Scots, 7.
Massachusetts Missionary Magazine, The, 374, 377, 384, 387.
Massasoit, Indian chief, 29.
Mather, Rev. Dr. Cotton, graduation from Harvard, 100; colleague pastor with his father, 194, 195; in Salem witchcraft, 201; desires the presidency of Harvard, 208; his voluminous writings, 114, 209, 210; his wig, 148; on the religious state of Austerfield, 11; on Bradford's business ventures, 22; his description of Cotton, 72, 73; his description of Eliot, 139, 144, 170, 171; *mentioned*, 38; his *Magnalia* quoted, 55, 114, 144; *cited*, 16, 17, 21, 22, 25, 42, 43, 54, 55, 58-60, 65, 68, 70, 72, 74, 90, 93, 94, 98, 104, 105, 112, 121, 141, 143, 144, 146-148, 161, 162, 165, 170, 171, 190, 194, 268; his *Parentator* quoted, 177, 180, 186, 212; *cited*, 182, 183, 185, 187, 194, 199, 202, 209.
Mather, Rev. Eleazer, 131.
Mather, Horace E., *cited*, 98, 99.
Mather, Rev. Dr. Increase, early life, 177; education, 177-182: conversion, 180, 181; in Ireland, England, and Guernsey, 182; settled at Boston, 183; at the Synod of 1662, 131, 184; change of view on Half-Way Covenant, 131, 184; marriages, 184; early trials, 185; personal traits, 186-188; leader in the Reforming Synod, 188-194; his *Necessity of Reformation*, 191, 192; the "Confession of 1680," 194; president of Harvard, 194, 195; his son Cotton his colleague, 194, 195; successful political mission to England, 196-199; the Massachusetts charter, 198; efforts to unite English Congregationalists and Presbyterians, 199, 200; attitude toward Salem witchcraft, 201, 202; his growing unpopularity, 202, 203; his opposition to the Brattle Church movement, 203-207; his *Order of the Gospel*, 206, 207; loses the Harvard presidency, 207, 208; disappointments, 208, 209; proposed mission to George I., 209; his writings, 114, 209-211; his growing tolerance, 211; his books burned, 281; his last days, 212; his tomb, 213; *mentioned*, 115, 365; his *Life and Death of Richard Mather*, quoted, 98, 104, 106, 128, 133; *cited*, 100, 102-108; other works cited, 90, 171.
Mather, Rev. Moses, 345, 361.
Mather, Rev. Nathanael, 115-117, 182.

INDEX

Mather, Rev. Richard, early life and education, 98–103; teacher at Toxteth Park, 101; conversion, 102; at Oxford, 103; his ministry at Toxteth Park, 103–107; his Puritanism, 104, 107; his marriages, 60, 105, 106, 184; flight from England, 107–109; settlement at Dorchester, 109–112; spiritual struggles, 113, 114; his services to Congregationalism, 86, 97, 115–125; his *Church Government*, 115, 116; his *Apologie*, 116–118; his *Answer*, to Herle, 119; his *Reply to Rutherford*, 119; the *Bay Psalm Book*, 120–122; the Cambridge Synod and its *Platform*, 123–126; opinion regarding the Half-Way Covenant, 126–134; ordination of his son Increase, 183; his death, 133, 134, 170; *mentioned*, 176.
Mather, Rev. Samuel, 182.
Mather, Thomas, 98.
Maverick, Rev. John, 53, 109.
May, Dorothy, Bradford's wife, 22, 27.
May, Bishop John, 22.
Mayhew, Rev. Experience, 332.
Mayhew, Rev. Dr. Jonathan, 291–293, 298, 333, 339.
Mayhew, Thomas, Sr. and Jr., 164, 165, 168.
Mayo, Rev. John, 183.
McCulloch, Rev. William, 251.
McNamee, Theodore, 449.
Mildmay, Sir Walter, 56.
Mills, Rev. Jedidiah, 339, 340, 361.
Mills, Samuel J., Jr., 137, 387, 388.
Ministerial education, 378, 379.
Missions, wide interest in, 138; Eliot's labors, 151–171; legislative encouragement, 158; foreign missionary society formed in England, 159, 160; Indian churches, 161, 165, 167, 168; Eliot's translations, 162–164; the work of the Mayhews, 164, 165; results of early Indian missions, 166–170; Brainerd's missionary zeal, 243; Edwards's work at Stockbridge, 250; Hopkins's efforts, 350, 351; the American Board formed, 387–389.
Mitchell, Rev. Jonathan, 181.
Monthly Anthology, The, 375, 377.
Morse, Rev. Dr. Jedidiah, 374, 375, 380–382, 396.
Morton, Nathaniel, 17. 36, 38, 44.
Morton, Thomas, adventurer, 30.
Morton, Bishop Thomas, 104.
Mumford, Hanna, marries John Eliot, 142.

N

Nantucket, Indian mission on, 165, 167.
Natick, Indian settlement at, 161, 167–169.
Neile, Archbishop Richard, 107.
Newell, Rev. Samuel, 137, 388, 389.
New Englander, The, 442.
New Haven, settled, 79; the First Church, 398, 399, 415–418, 423, 443, 451, 453.
New Haven Theology, The, 434–436, 451.
Newman, Prof. A. H., *cited*, 19.
Newport, Hopkins's ministry at, 342, 343, 355, 356.
Newton Theological Seminary, 387.
New York, Edwards at, 226.
Norris, John, 581.
Northampton, Edwards's settlement at, 227; revival at, 232–237, 280, 321; Whitefield at, 237, 277; Edwards's dismission, 244–249; Hopkins's life at, 320–322.
Norton, Rev. John, 114, 180, 181.
Nott, Rev. Samuel, 388, 389.
Nye, Rev. Philip, 91.

O

Oakes, Pres. Urian, 194.
Oberlin College, 402, 403, 430, 432.

INDEX   467

Oberlin Theological Seminary, 386.
Oldham, John, 32.

P

Paine, Thomas, 367.
Palfrey, John G., the historian, *cited*, 26, 41, 44, 75, 148, 154, 155, 160, 161, 166-168, 291, 292.
Palin, Rev. Mr., 102.
Panoplist, The, 375, 377, 384.
Park, Prof. Edwards A., 315, 344; *cited*, 324-326, 328-330, 335, 341, 343, 348-351, 356, 385.
Parker, Rev. Dr. E. P., *cited*, 438.
Parks, Alice, marries David Bacon, 410.
Parris, Rev. Samuel, 201.
Parsons, Rev. Jonathan, 238, 280, 281.
Partridge, Rev. Ralph, 124.
Patten, Rev. Dr. William, 324, 348.
Patteson, Bishop John C., 138.
Pearson, Prof. Eliphalet, 375, 380-383, 385, 386.
Pemberton, Rev. Ebenezer, 205.
Penn, William, 412.
Perkins, Rev. William, Puritan leader, 102.
Perry, Bishop W. S., *cited*, 291.
Philip's War, 167, 169, 190.
Phillips Academy, 380, 381, 383.
Phillips, Rev. George, 53.
Phillips, John, 380.
Phillips, John, Jr., 381.
Phillips, Mrs. Phœbe, 381.
Phillips, Rev. Samuel, 231, 232, 332.
Phillips, Samuel, 380.
Phips, Sir William, 203.
Pierce, William, 68.
Pierpont, Rev. James, 227.
Pierpont, Sarah, marries Jonathan Edwards, 227, 228; character, 228, 229; spiritual experiences, 238-240, 257, 321; welcomes Hopkins, 320.
Pierson, Rev. Abraham, 166.

Plan of Union, The, 429, 430.
Plymouth, settled, 24; growth of, 26; famine at, 27, 28; divisions in, 30-33; socialistic experiment at, 33-35; life a struggle, 42; Ainsworth's version of the Psalms used at, 121; Indian mission at, 165; Pres. Chauncy at, 268; the Mayflower Church divided, 377; Burial Hill in, 43, 44.
Pomeroy, Rev. Benjamin, 280.
Porter, Prof. Ebenezer, 414.
Prayer Book, The English, 9, 64, 65, 120, 183.
Presbyterian Church, Discussions in, 433-435.
Preston, Rev. Dr. John, Puritan leader, 58.
Priestley, Rev. Joseph, 310, 368.
Prince, Rev. Thomas, 38, 40, 279, 364.
Princeton, Mass., Woods's early home, 364, 365, 368, 370, 371.
Princeton Theological Seminary, 386.
Princeton University, 260, 261, 351.
Puritans, The, their aims and scruples, 11-13, 50-52, 63-65; the lectureships, 140.

Q

Quincy, Edmund, 68.
Quincy, Pres. Josiah, *cited*, 178, 365, 367.
Quint, Rev. Dr. A. H., 427.

R

Raine, Rev. John, *cited*, 8, 10.
Raleigh, Sir Walter, 7.
Randolph, Edward, 196, 197.
Rasières, Isaac de, 44.
Rathband, Rev. William, 128.
Rawson, Rev. Grindall, 166, 168.
Reforming Synod, *see* Synod.
Revivals, under Stoddard, 232; under Edwards at Northampton, 232-237; the "Great Awaken-

Revivals—*Continued*.
  ing," 237, 240, 241, 270, 275–287; later revivals, 355, 370, 387, 418.
Reynor, Rev. John, 42.
Rice, Rev. Luther, 388, 389.
Richards, Rev. James, 388.
Robbins, Rev. Chandler, *cited*, 180, 183.
Robinson, Rev. John, the Pilgrim leader, 17–29, 23, 24, 42, 49, 55, 117.
Ross, Rev. A. Hastings, 3.
Russel, Rev. Joseph, 368–370.
Russel, Rev. Noadiah, 368.
Rutherford, Prof. Samuel, 88, 90, 93, 119.
Rylands, J. P., 98.

S

Salem, 35–37, 53, 54, 106, 201, 381.
Saltonstall, Sir Richard, 53.
Sancroft, Archbishop William, 57.
Sandeman, Robert, 302.
Savage, James, *cited*, 109.
Savoy Confession, *see* Confession.
Saybrook Platform, The, 200.
Saye and Sele, Lord, 74.
Scrooby, The Separatists at, 15–20, 45, 49, 56.
Separatists, The, 14, 18–20, 49.
Sewall, Rev. Joseph, 281.
Sewall, Judge Samuel, 38, 103, 104, 197, 350.
Seward, William H., 449.
Shakespeare, William, 7.
Shepard, Rev. Thomas, of Cambridge, at Emmanuel College, 57; on conversion, 225, 234; on "Willingness to be Damned," 347; mentioned, 71, 76, 155, 158, 164.
Shrewsbury, The earl of, 159.
Shute, Rev. Daniel, 299.
Sibbes, Rev. Richard, 58.
Sibley, John Langdon, *cited*, 101, 113, 165, 166, 179, 184, 195, 202–205, 209, 269.

Simpson, Rev. Sidrach, 91.
Skelton, Rev. Samuel, 36, 53.
Slavery, opposed by Jonathan Edwards the younger, 256; Hopkins's efforts against, 256, 349–351, 358; declaration at Albany Convention, 431; Bacon's opposition to, 445–451.
Smalley, Rev. John, 379.
Smith, Rev. Ralph, 42.
Smith, Rev. Samuel, 221.
Smyth, Prof. Egbert, C., *cited*, 220.
Smyth, John, the Separatist, 17–19.
Society for Propagating Christian Knowledge among the Indians, The, 291.
Society for the Propagation of the Gospel in Foreign Parts, The, 291, 293.
Society for the Propagation of the Gospel in New England, The, 159, 160, 249.
Some (Soame), Rev. Dr. Robert, 58.
South Windsor, 217, 218, 226.
Southworth, Mrs. Alice, 27.
Sparks, Pres. Jared, 397.
Spenser, Edmund, 7.
Sprague, Rev. Dr. William B., *cited*, 269, 272, 287, 296, 355–357, 364, 368–371, 373, 374.
Spring, Rev. Dr. Samuel, friendship for Woods, 374, 376; founding of Andover Seminary, 381–384, 386, 388.
Squanto, Indian, 28, 44.
Standish, Capt. Myles, 29, 43, 44.
Sternhold, Thomas, 120.
Stiles, Pres. Ezra, anti-slavery efforts, 350; letters to, quoted and *cited*, 286, 287, 289, 295, 296, 300, 302, 304, 306, 309, 341.
Stiles, Dr. Henry R., *cited*, 218.
Stockbridge, 249, 250, 260, 261, 316, 323, 324.
Stoddard, Rev. Solomon, 219, 227, 232, 245–247.

INDEX 469

Stoddardeanism, 245–247, 249, 304, 305.
Stone, Rev. Samuel, 57, 68, 74.
Storrs, Rev. Dr. H. M., 427.
Storrs, Rev. Dr. Richard S., 420, 449.
Story, William, 60.
Stoughton, Judge John A., *cited*, 218, 219.
Stoughton, Lieut.-Gov. William, 54, 113, 189.
Stuart, Prof. Moses, 372, 388, 398, 415–417.
Synods,—of 1637, 77, 80; at Cambridge, 1646–48, 93, 123–126, 159, 193; of 1662, 131, 184; the Reforming, of 1679–80, 146, 147, 188–194, 211; attempted in 1725, 290.

T

Tackawompbait, Indian pastor, 168.
Tallmadge, Ohio, 412, 413.
Tappan, Prof. David, 370, 371, 373, 375, 378.
Taylor, Rev. John, 257, 258, 298, 300.
Taylor, Prof. Nathaniel W., 395, 398–402, 416, 417, 435, 436.
Taylor and Tyler Controversy, The, 398–402, 435–437.
Temperance reform, 443–445; *see also* Am. Temperance Society.
Tennent, Rev. Gilbert, 238, 318, 319.
Tenney, Rev. Caleb J., 356.
Terry, Catherine Elizabeth, Mrs. Leonard Bacon, 418.
Thompson, Rev. Dr. A. C., *cited*, 154, 165.
Thompson, Rev. Dr. J. P., 430, 449.
Thompson, Pishey, *cited*, 59, 60.
Thorowgood, Thomas, 138.
Toleration Act, The, 199.
Tompson, Rev. William, 114, 119.
Townshend, C. H., *cited*, 22.
Toxteth Park, Richard Mather at, 101–107.

Tracy, Rev. Joseph, *cited*, 276, 279–281, 388.
Treat, Rev. Samuel, 165.
Trumbull, Dr. J. Hammond, *quoted*, 163; *cited*, 149, 150, 153, 155.
Tuckney, Rev. Dr. Anthony, 61, 87.
Tuthill, Elisabeth, wife of Richard Edwards, 218.
Twisse, Rev. Dr. William, 62.
Tyler, Pres. Bennet, 400, 436.
Tyler, Prof. Moses Coit, *cited*, 122, 269.

U

Union Theological Seminary, 387.
Unitarianism, *see* Liberal Theology.

V

Vane, Gov. Henry, 77, 78.

W

Waaubon, Indian chief, 155–158.
Walker, Rev. Dr. George Leon, *cited*, 140, 276, 347, 433, 452.
Walter, Rev. Nehemiah, 143.
Ward, Rev. Nathaniel, 74.
Ware, Prof. Henry, 378, 395, 398.
Warham, Rev. John, 53, 109, 114, 219.
Waterbury, Hopkins's life in, 316, 317, 320.
Watts, Rev. Dr. Isaac, 236, 252, 298.
Webster, Rev. Samuel, 257.
Welde, Rev. Thomas, 121, 142, 143.
Wendell, Prof. Barrett, *cited*, 176.
Wesley, Rev. John, 57, 222, 225, 229.
West, Elizabeth, wife of Samuel Hopkins, 328, 329.
West, Rev. Stephen, 250, 316.
Western Theological Seminary, The, 61, 62.

Westminster Assembly, The, Congregationalists in, 91, 92 ; *mentioned*, 61, 62, 81, 85, 116, 118, 119, 123.
Westminster Catechism, The, 87, 383, 384.
Westminster Confession, *see* Confession.
West Newbury, Woods's relations to, 371-375, 382-385, 394.
Weston, Thomas, 29, 30.
Wethersfield, 221, 222.
Wheeler, Abigail, Mrs. Leonard Woods, 372.
Wheeler, Joseph, 372.
Wheelock, Rev. Dr. Eleazer, 280, 281.
Wheelwright, Rev. John, 76, 77.
Whiston, Prof. William, 298.
Whitaker, Rev. Dr. Nathanial, 341.
Whitby, Rev. Daniel, 252, 298, 300.
Whitefield, Rev. George, the "Great Awakening," 237, 276-282 ; his preaching, 276-278 ; his censoriousness, 278,279; estimate of Harvard and Yale, 279 ; at New Haven, 278, 318 ; views on conversion, 225 ; emphasis on bodily effects,279; commendation of Edwards, 237 ; characterization of Boston, 275 ; estimate of Davenport, 281 ; mentioned. 286.
Whitgift, Archbishop John, 51.
Whiting, Rev. Samuel, quoted, 58, 59, 61-63 ; *cited*, 55, 56, 60, 64.
Whitmore, W. H., *cited*, 197.
Willard, Rev. Samuel, 203, 207, 208.
William III., of England, 197, 198, 200.
Williams College, 387, 388.
Williams, Col. Elisha, 221.
Williams, Bishop John, 64, 66, 68.
Williams, Roger, his banishment, 81, 82; his controversy with Cotton, 81-86 ; his efforts to Christianize the Indians, 153, 162 *mentioned*, 110.
Williams, Rev. Solomon, 280, 281.
"Willingness to be Damned," Doctrine of, 239, 240, 257, 321, 346, 347, 371.
Wilson, Rev. John, of Boston, 53, 69, 70, 77, 79, 81, 109, 142, 155.
Wilson, Rev. John, Jr., 113.
Winslow, Gov. Edward, 25, 29, 39.
Winthrop, Gov. John, arrival, 53; in the Antinomian dispute, 77, 79 ; at the organization of the Dorchester church, 111 ; at a Dorchester council, 112, 113 ; his *Journal* quoted, 69,70, 111-113 ; *cited*, 68, 73-75, 78-80, 83, 119, 142, 159, 268.
Winwick, The grammar school, 99.
Witchcraft, at Salem, 201.
Wituwamat, Indian chief, 29.
Wood, Anthony, *cited*, 101-103.
Woods, Prof. Leonard, early life, 364 ; at Harvard, 365-368 ; religious experience, 368, 369 ; theological training, 370, 372 ; marriage, 372 ; pastorate at West Newbury, 371-373 ; creed revision, 372 ; his master's oration, 373 ; friendship for Spring, Morse and Pearson, 374, 375 ; deemed a moderate Hopkinsian, 374, 375 ; his irenic spirit, 375, 376, 384, 385 ; two theological schools planned, 379-382 ; united in Andover Seminary, 382-385 ; is appointed Professor of Theology, 383, 385 ; his inauguration, 385, 386 ; interest in missions and reforms, 387-389 ; as a teacher, 389-394 ; his writings, 394-404 ; their courtesy, 396 ; his *Letters to Unitarians*, 395, 397, 398 ; his *Letters to Taylor*, 395, 398-402 ; his controversy with Mahan, 395, 402, 403 ; his *History of Andover*, 404 ; his lectures, 404 ; last days, 403-405 ; *mentioned*, 409.

Woolsey, Pres. Theodore D., *cited*, 414, 417, 432.
Worcester, Rev. Dr. Samuel, 388, 389.

X

Xavier, Francis, 138.

Y

Yale University, in Edwards's student days, 220–222, 226, 227; Hopkins's student life at, 317–320; Whitefield's criticism of, 279; comes under Edwardean influences, 362; religious state at the close of the eighteenth century, 367; Bacon's connection with, 413, 414, 421, 452, 453; instruction in theology at, 378, 380; the Divinity School of, 386, 399, 416, 452, 453; *see also* New Haven Theology, and Taylor and Tyler Controversy.
Young, Alexander, Collections of sources edited by, *cited*, 25, 39, 55, 56, 58, 59, 60, 63, 67, 68, 98, 108, 147.
Youngs, Rev. David, 318.

www.ingramcontent.com/pod-product-compliance
Lightning Source LLC
Chambersburg PA
CBHW070057020526
44112CB00034B/1410